LONE STAR
LEGACY QUILTS

12 Modern Projects

LINDLEE SMITH

stashBOOKS®
an imprint of C&T Publishing

Publisher: Amy Barrett-Daffin

Creative Director: Gailen Runge

Senior Editor: Roxane Cerda

Editor: Madison Moore

Technical Editor: Debbie Rodgers

Cover/Book Designer: April Mostek

Production Coordinator: Tim Manibusan

Illustrator: Kirstie Pettersen

Photography Coordinator: Rachel Ackley

Front cover and lifestyle photography by Hayley Heser Photography

Instructional photography by Lindlee Smith, unless otherwise noted

Published by Stash Books, an imprint of C&T Publishing, Inc., P.O. Box 1456, Lafayette, CA 94549

Library of Congress Control Number: 2025010189

Printed in China

10 9 8 7 6 5 4 3 2 1

DEDICATION

To Margot and Wilson. I can call myself an author now, but *Mom* will always be my favorite title.

ACKNOWLEDGMENTS

To Ashlee Doyle, the talented longarm quilter: ***Thank you*** for quilting all of the quilts and projects in this book (and so many before this!). I am grateful I found a local quilter who has also become a friend.

To Hayley Heser, the amazing photographer: ***Thank you*** for agreeing to be the photographer for this book without hesitation. You are a treasure and I'm so thankful for your years of friendship and talent. You've captured all of my big life moments so it is only fitting you would also be involved with this. This book wouldn't be the same without you!

To my husband, Brandon: ***Thank you*** for your support and encouragement especially while I was working on this book. Thank you for tolerating the endless piles of quilts all over our house. This won't be changing anytime soon.

To my mom, Carma Bartel: ***Thank you*** for passing down your love of fabric and quilts. I didn't appreciate the trips to the fabric store when I was young, but now I would gladly spend hours browsing with you!

To The Log House in Lewistown, MT: Thank you for creating the cabin of my dreams and for allowing us to take the photos for this book there. It was the perfect location!

CONTENTS

Introduction

People quilt and have quilted over time for so many different reasons—necessity, hobby, tradition, as a form of therapy, meditation, art, or personal expression. Some people learn from the generations before them and others are self-taught. One thing I love most about quilting is how we each bring our own uniqueness to the craft. One hundred people will take the same quilt pattern and you will see one hundred distinct quilts. My hope is that you use this as a guidebook to make projects and quilts that are your own.

This book requires some intermediate and advanced skills. *However*, if you don't consider yourself an intermediate or advanced quilter please keep reading. I made a Lone Star quilt when I was still very much a beginner quilter and, while that quilt is full of "mistakes" and I didn't really understand what I was doing, it is still a quilt my husband and I use regularly over 10 years later. A quilt doesn't have to be (and maybe shouldn't be) perfect to be loved and treasured. The best way to improve your skills and confidence is to challenge yourself and practice and just go for it. So *welcome*! I am so glad you are here reading this book. I see an amazing star quilt in your future. Let's get started.

My first Lone Star Quilt

Before Getting Started

At minimum, to make the projects in this book, you need to know how to use a sewing machine, accurately cut fabric, and sew with a precise ¼″ seam allowance.

Precision is key to making these blocks and patterns. I am not a perfectionist, but I do strive for precision when I'm sewing because it lends itself to a more enjoyable experience overall. The last thing you want is to spend hours cutting and sewing only to face headaches during quilt top assembly because pieces aren't lining up like they should. Taking the time *up front* to be precise with cutting, piecing diamonds, and sewing those Y-seams will pay off—trust me!

QUILTING TERMS

RST (Right Sides Together): While piecing, place 2 pieces of fabric together with their *right* (front) sides touching.

WST (Wrong Sides Together): While piecing, place 2 pieces of fabric together with their *wrong* (back) sides touching.

On The Bias / Bias Grain: The *bias* of quilting cotton runs 45° to the selvage. Cutting on the bias means cutting the fabric 45° to the selvage.

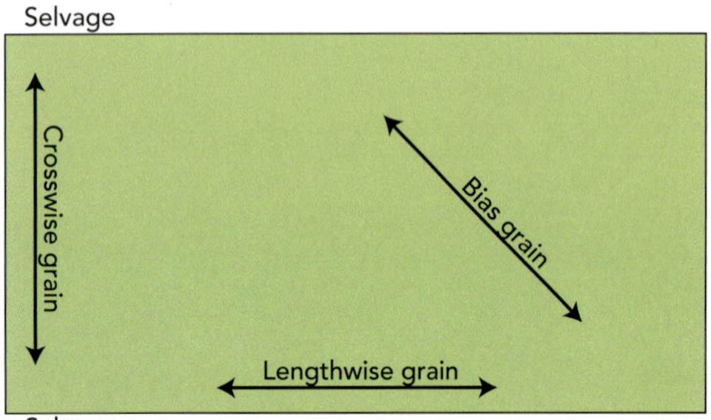

Quarter Inch Seam Allowance: I sew with a standard ¼″ seam allowance. But sometimes quilters recommend using a scant ¼″ seam allowance, which is just barely smaller. This is to compensate for the tiny amount of fabric lost to the seam after pressing. If you prefer to use a scant ¼″ seam allowance, you are welcome to, but I stick with the true ¼″.

Selvage (also spelled selvedge): Selvage is the finished, non-fraying edge of the fabric that runs the entire length.

WOF (Width of Fabric): WOF is the distance between the 2 selvage edges of a piece of fabric. Width of Fabric in this book is assumed to be 42″ (which is common with quilting cottons). WOF varies by manufacturer and bolt, so your WOF may be shorter or longer.

Slow Down and Embrace the Process

When I was thinking about this book, I wanted to name it, *These Are Not Quick Quilt Patterns*. Quick is sometimes assumed to be superior to slow. We don't like to wait for things. Instant gratification is so much easier than having patience or working towards something. Who wants to slow down or wait when we can immediately get what we want?

But I am here to challenge the idea that slowness should be avoided. While there is nothing wrong with a quick quilt pattern that can be put together in a day or weekend, there is a huge feeling of accomplishment when you slow down to spend time on a challenging or intricate quilt pattern and then *finish it*! While I am proud of all of my quilts, my most treasured quilts and the quilts I am most proud of are the ones that took me the most time to piece.

About the Lone Star & Broken Star

The patterns in this book are all based on Lone Star and Broken Star quilt designs. A Lone Star quilt has a single star in the center, often made with diamonds. A Lone Star quilt usually has 6 or 8 points.

Steppe Star (page 82), a classic Lone Star

A Broken Star quilt has a Lone Star center, but also includes diamonds encircling the star.

Broken Trail Star (page 142), a broken star

It is not known when or where the first Lone Star or Broken Star quilt designs originated. Broken Star quilt designs started to appear after 1880. Until quilting cotton became readily available, most quilts were made with what people had available (clothes, feed sacks, etc.). Diamonds were cut out individually from these materials using a template and then pieced together by hand.

Today, star-quilting blends many different cultural traditions. I grew up on the Northern Plains of Montana, which is home to the Assiniboine and Sioux tribes. In the late 1800s and early 1900s, missionaries from Dakota Presbytery introduced star quilt-making to the tribes on the Fort Peck Indian Reservation. Native women eventually made star quilts their own by using colors and designs that were traditional to them. According to tribal historians, star quilts were used as a cultural replacement of buffalo robes, which were quickly disappearing due to over-hunting of buffalo. Today, star quilts remain one of the most honorable items a family can give or receive in many Native American communities. Giveaways of star quilts are held at pow-wows, basketball tournaments, memorials, and other events.

About the Patterns in this Book

The patterns in this book are arranged from easiest to most challenging. I recommend starting with the block patterns to gain familiarity with the concepts in this book. The blocks can then be made into one of Single Block Projects (page 67) or can be incorporated into one of the quilt patterns. The first seven projects are all crib or throw size quilts, and the last two projects are bed-size quilts.

Supplies

In addition to a sewing machine and thread, there are a few supplies you will need to make the projects and quilts in this book. Below are two lists: the first contains what you *need* to be successful with these projects, and the second has supplies that I use and recommend, but that are not required.

Required Supplies

Rotary Cutter: A rotary cutter is a requirement for precise cutting. My favorite rotary cutter is the Olfa 45mm Ergonomic Rotary Cutter.

Large Cutting Mat: If you have the space, I recommend a 24″ × 36″ cutting mat. A large mat allows for easier cutting and trimming when working with large cuts of fabric or quilt tops. I use the Christopher Thompson 24″ × 36″ Cutting Mat from Riley Blake.

Quilting Ruler with 45° line: I recommend a ruler at least 24½″ long because when cutting fabric off of a bolt, you will not have to move the ruler when the fabric is folded in half. A 45° line is a *must* since each quilt in this book requires cutting diamonds on a 45° angle. My go-to ruler is the Creative Grids 8½″ × 24½″ ruler.

Iron: A trusty iron is a quilter's best friend! It does not have to be fancy, but I love my Oliso TG1600 ProPlus Iron. It heats up wonderfully and has a safety shut-off if I forget to unplug it.

Marking Tool: There are lots of fabric marking tools out there. Use whatever feels most comfortable and useful to you. I have been using the Sewline Fabric Mechanical Pencils for years because I love the variety of leads available. The lines are thin, but still visible when marking on fabric.

Pins: You probably already have your preference in pins if you have been quilting any amount of time. That's great! Use what you have and love. I like Dritz Flower Head Pins because the pin is slightly thicker than other glass head pins. When I pull out the pin I can see exactly where I need to stop my needle when sewing a Y-seam. If I want a thinner pin, I use fine Magic Pins.

Fabric: When I was choosing fabric for my first quilt, I remember my mom explaining that not all quilting cottons are created equal. While some options are more budget friendly than others, a higher quality quilting cotton will lend to a more enjoyable piecing experience and a longer-lasting quilt. My favorite solids for sewing are Robert Kaufman Kona Cotton Solids. I like both the feel of the fabric as well as all of the color options—there are so many color options. If you are drawn to solids more than prints, I highly recommend getting a color card from your favorite line of solid fabrics. It is much easier to compare colors from a color card than it is to see the variations on your computer or phone screen.

If I'm not using Kona solids, I am probably sewing with a yarn-dyed woven fabric. I love the feel of a fabric with texture. My favorite lines of woven fabric are from Fableism Supply Co and Ruby Star Society, specifically fabrics designed by Alexia Abegg.

oliso

Batting: Although it is not a visible part of the quilt after a quilt is finished, the batting you use for your quilt is an important choice for both look and feel. Batting comes in a variety of materials, and the most common are listed below. I used The Warm Company 100% cotton batting in either Warm & Natural or Warm & White for all quilts in this book.

- **100% Cotton**: This is generally a lightweight batting that washes and ages well through use. Cotton shrinks slightly, which is not necessarily a bad thing, because it gives the quilt a nice, crinkly appearance after a wash, which many people prefer.
- **Cotton/Poly Blend**: Polyester provides extra warmth and does not shrink as much as 100% Cotton. Polyester is also less expensive so a Cotton/Poly blend is a more cost effective option.
- **Polyester**: Polyester is a synthetic material, so it is less expensive than natural fiber battings. You might choose polyester if you are looking for a high loft batting that makes a puffier quilt.
- **Wool**: If you are looking for a lightweight and also warm batting, wool is a great choice. Be sure to check if the batting is pre-shrunk because otherwise it will shrink after a wash.
- **Bamboo**: Bamboo batting is a good choice if you are looking for a durable and sustainable material. Bamboo is also breathable and lightweight.

Optional, But Helpful Supplies

Stripology Ruler: I *highly* recommend a Creative Grids Stripology Ruler if you are cutting a lot of strips (like in these projects). It speeds up the process so much. I have used the XL Ruler for years and have never regretted investing in this tool.

Small Ruler for Making ¼″ Seam Marks: Sometimes it's nice to have a smaller ruler handy when you aren't cutting large pieces of fabric. I use a 2½″ × 12½″ Creative Grids ruler for making the ¼″ seam marks on my diamond strips.

Tailor's Clapper: I learned about tailor's clappers for quilting a couple years ago. I don't use this for every seam but I especially like it when sewing and pressing smaller pieces (like the interchangeable quilt blocks in this book!). Applying pressure to the seam with the tailor's clapper after it is pressed really does give much flatter, crisper seams. I use a 12″ hardwood tailor's clapper from Hard Rock Wood Works.

Smoothing Spray: Flatter smoothing spray is a great alternative to starch if you don't want to spray starch in your sewing space. And it comes in many great scents!

Starch: If you have stubborn wrinkles in your fabric or quilt top that you want to flatten, Best Press Spray Starch is the way to go. I also recommend using starch when sewing with fabrics with a looser weave than traditional quilting cotton. It helps the fabric stay where it needs to and not move around as you are cutting and sewing.

flatter
EARTH AND PEOPLE FRIE
Mary Ellen's
Best Press
The Clear Starch and Sizing Alternative
Lavender Fields
KONA

Color Inspiration

I'm just not good at putting colors and fabrics together. I'm afraid the fabrics I pick will look ugly. My color palettes never turn out the way I hope. Have these things crossed your mind? I get it—I've been there, and sometimes I still get stuck when trying to choose fabric for my next quilt. While I don't have a foolproof method or formula for choosing the fabrics for my quilts, I do have some suggestions that I hope will help inspire you and get you unstuck. Instead of relying on color theory, I like to build palettes based on color combinations I'm already enjoying in my life.

My Color Picking Philosophy

There are no rules. Really! Use the fabrics and colors *you* love and that make *you* happy to look at. Don't be afraid to break a "rule" you might have heard at some point in your life about which colors do or don't look good together. If you like it, go for it.

What are you drawn to? Bright, bold prints? Subtle textures and colors? Just like in anything, becoming confident in choosing fabrics takes practice. It takes time to find your style. For many years, I would buy prints that were so pretty I couldn't resist. And while these fabrics really were beautiful, I wasn't drawn to them when gathering fabrics for a quilt. I came to realize I was much happier mixing solids with textured wovens or subtle prints than most of the bold prints I had in my stash. Notice what color patterns you've used in past work.

SOMETHING TO THINK ABOUT

If you are using prints, think about how the scale of the print will look in the quilt. Are you using a large scale print for a 2½″ strip? If so, you might lose the overall look of the print when it's cut into strips and then diamonds.

Sources of Inspiration

Nature: Notice the colors around you when you are outside—the different colors of the plants and flowers can all be inspiration, especially through different seasons. Take in the different colors of sunrises and sunsets. Take pictures of what you are drawn to and save them to a folder in your phone. Then, pull out the colors that strike you. There are even some apps and websites that can generate a palette of colors based on an image.

The Everyday: Don't let it stop with the natural world. Your home, your neighborhood, your favorite restaurants, and frequented coffee shops all contain color inspiration. Your camera is a tool for recording things to pull from later.

Labels and Brands: One day, I looked at a shirt that I wear all the time and realized how cool the colors on that shirt would look in a quilt. Look in unusual places. You might see a label on a product in a store that has colors that you never thought of putting together.

Pinterest: Search for anything + *color palette* and you will be sure to get some interesting and inspiring results: *retro color palette, soft color palette, happy color palette, moody color palette*... you get the idea. After I do a search like this and find a palette I want to use, I look at my Kona fabric swatches to see what colors most closely match the search results. If you are feeling stuck or overwhelmed, there are also websites and apps that can help you choose colors for a quilt pattern by generating random palettes.

I would generally describe the palettes I gravitate towards as warm. I prefer them over cool colors, though blue makes a great contrast background with warm colors.

Color Value

Although there are no "rules" for picking your fabrics, once you have found inspiration and color palettes you are drawn to, I suggest being very intentional with color placement. In the three examples to the right, you can see how I strategically place the fabrics based on color value. *Value* refers to the darkness or lightness of a color (how close it is to black or white).

I arrange the fabrics so the value goes from light to dark (or vice versa) within the star, and sometimes back to light (or dark) again. When arranging fabrics by color value in this way, it gives a radiating appearance, like there is movement in the star.

I also place colors that are similar hues and values next to each other to build gradients. For example, in the Broken Trail Star (bottom row), I placed Kona Natural (off white) and Kona Sky (light blue) next to each other in the center of the star. I have Warp and Weft Stitch in Cayenne (red), Fableism Everyday Chambray in Cinnabar (dark red), and Kona Earth (brown) arranged together in the center of the star which gives the radiating effect of light to dark.

Backwoods Star (page 118)

Majestic Star (page 126)

Broken Trail Star (page 142)

Cutting and Sewing Diamonds

Have you ever looked at a Lone Star quilt and admired all the amazing diamonds that made up the star? Me too. *All the time.* There is something mesmerizing about diamonds and star quilts that drew me in immediately. If you've also looked at a Lone Star quilt and thought, "I could never do that," then I am here to tell you that *you definitely can do that*!

Each block and quilt pattern in this book has diamonds. But have no fear—I am here to share all the tips I have learned while making countless star quilts, walking you through the process step-by-step. It may seem daunting at first, but before you know it you will be admiring your own amazing star quilt (made of diamonds!).

NOTE

If cutting and sewing on the bias is a new concept to you, make sure to read this chapter before diving into a block or quilt pattern.

Tips for Cutting and Sewing on a Bias

1. Starch and press fabric before cutting on the bias. This is especially important when using a fabric with a looser weave than typical quilting cotton.

2. Use a new blade in your rotary cutter. Using a dull blade will result in snags, frustration, and possibly inaccurate cutting.

3. Decrease the stitch length on your sewing machine to under 2mm. I usually sew with a 1.7–1.8mm stitch length.

How to Cut Diamonds

1. Cut a WOF strip the width of the required diamond. If the pattern calls for a 2½″ diamond, cut a 2½″ × WOF strip. If the pattern calls for a 6½″ diamond, cut a 6½″ × WOF strip.

2. Line up the top or bottom of each strip with a 45° line on the ruler and cut off the selvage on the left side of the strip. *fig. A*

3. Line up the top or bottom of the strip with the 45° line on the ruler. Line up the left side of the strip (cut in Step 2) with the correct measurement on your ruler (2½″ for a 2½″ diamond, 6½″ for a 6½″ diamond). Cut. *fig. B*

A

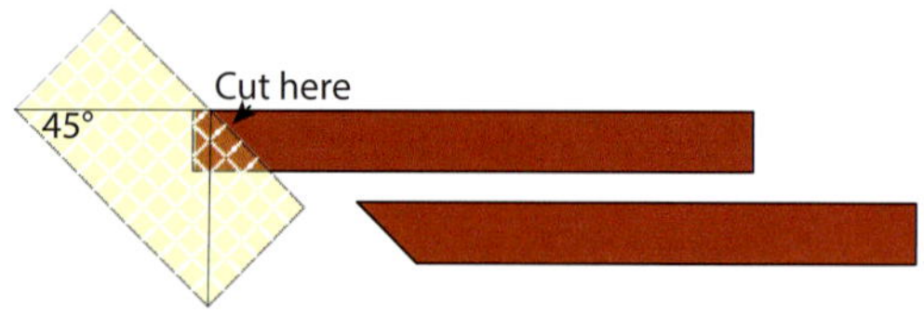

B

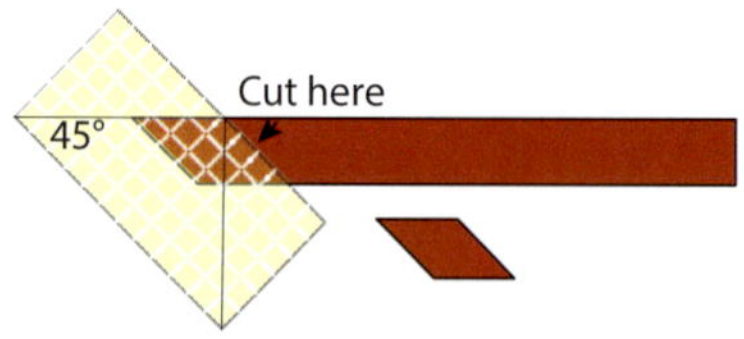

CHECK YOUR WORK

Not sure you cut your diamond to the correct size? There is an easy way to check.

Lay the diamond on the ruler vertically with the right edge of the diamond along the right edge of the ruler (as shown). The left edge of the diamond should be lined up with the correct measurement. *fig. C*

Now, rotate the diamond. No matter which edge of the diamond is aligned with the side of the ruler, the measurement should be the same. *fig. D*

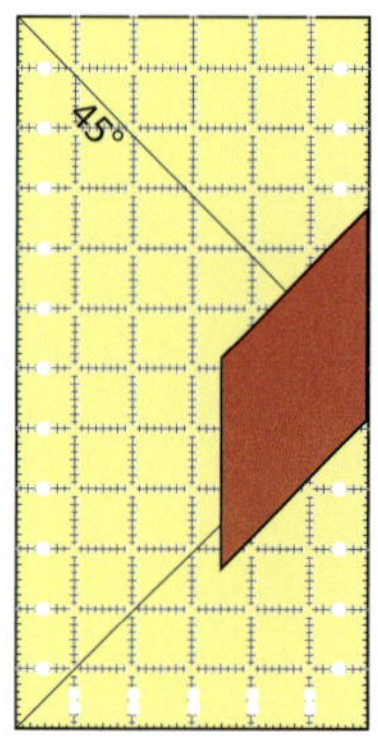

C

This example shows a 2½″ diamond.

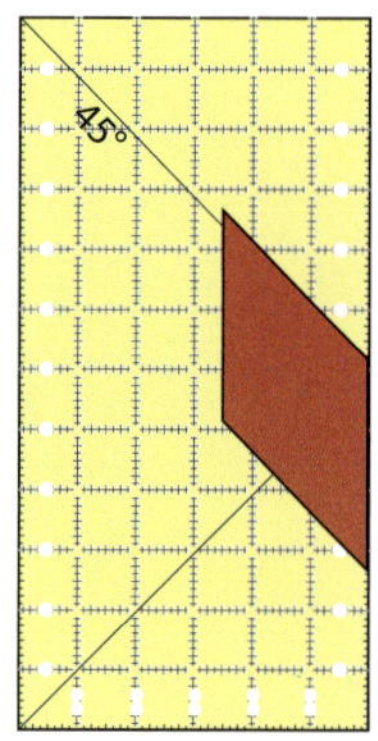

D

NOT LINING UP CORRECTLY?

Are the 45° line and desired measurement on the ruler not lining up correctly? Sometimes as you are cutting diamonds, the strip or strip set sometimes becomes wonky. If the correct measurement on the ruler is not perfectly lined up with the edge of the strip when the 45° line is correctly lined up, then you will need to trim the 45° angle before continuing.

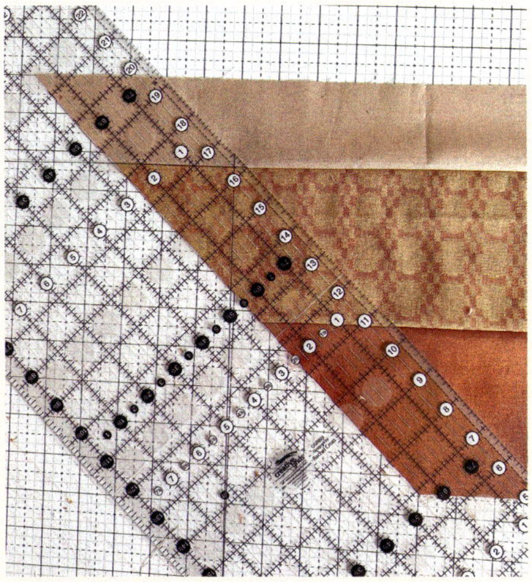

Correct for 2½″ diamonds; continue cutting.

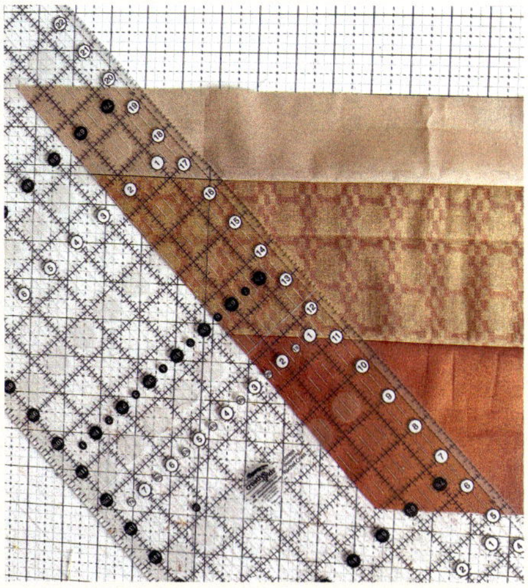

The 2½″ measurement is off; the 45° angle needs to be trimmed before continuing.

1. *Rotate the strip set so the 45° angle is on the right side. Line up the 45° line on the ruler with a seam of the strip set. If cutting a single strip, line up the 45° line on the ruler with either the top or bottom of the strip.* fig. A

2. *Trim the uneven excess.* fig. B

3. *Rotate the strip set so the 45° angle is on the left side again and continue cutting diamonds.* fig. C

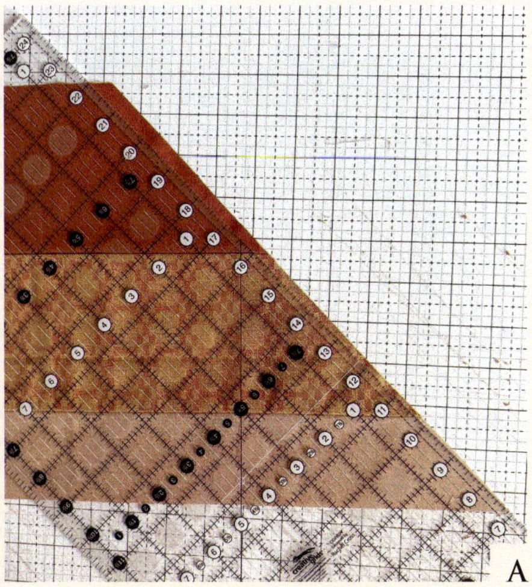

A

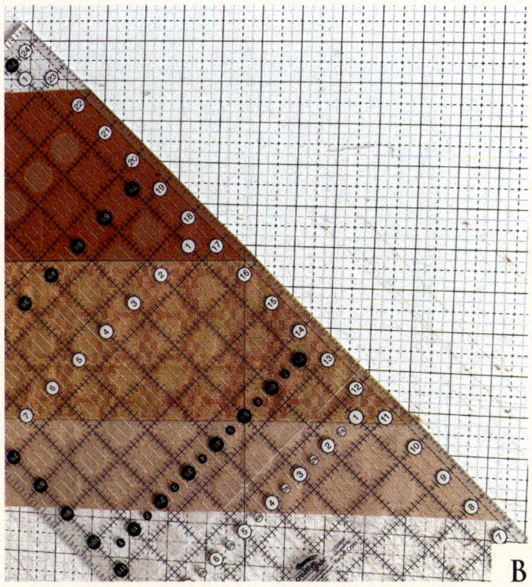

B

C

How to Sew Diamonds

1. Arrange the diamonds as desired for the design. Place 2 diamonds RST as shown, offset by ¼″ (circled area). *fig. E*

E

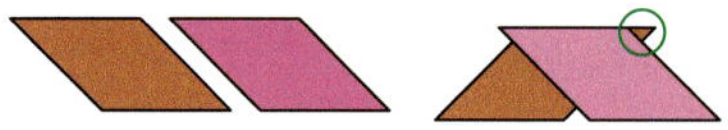

2. Sew the diamonds together. Measure the overhang on each side of the seam to ensure you have correctly offset the diamonds by ¼″. *fig. F*

F

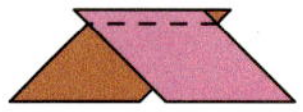

3. Press the seam open. *fig. G*

G

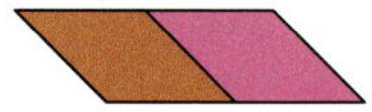

PERFECT STRIP DIAMOND POINTS

Most of the quilts in this book are composed of diamond strips, rather than individual diamonds. The diamond strips are cut from strip sets, then sewn together to form larger diamond units. Often, the most frustrating part of sewing strip sets together is when the diamond points do not line up correctly. My goal is to achieve perfect (or near perfect) diamond points the first time so my seam ripper gets dusty from disuse!

1. Arrange the diamond strips as desired. Prepare to piece together 2 strips. *fig. H*

H

2. Flip over one of the strips to the wrong side. Start with the first diamond strip. Using the ruler and a marking tool, mark ¼″ from the edge of the fabric at each seam on the right side of the fabric. Repeat at each seam of the second diamond strip on the wrong side of the fabric. *fig. I*

I

3. Place the 2 strips RST. Insert pins directly through the seams on the ¼″ marks on both strips. There should be a ¼″ overhang on each strip (green circle). *fig. J*

J

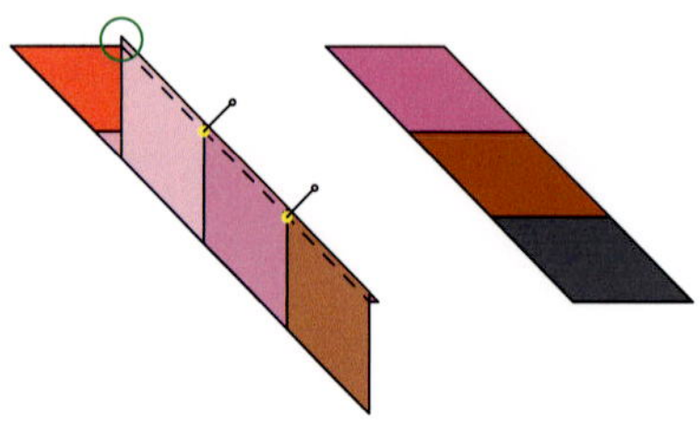

4. Sew diamond strips together and press the seam open. *fig. K*

5. Repeat Steps 2–4 to sew the third strip onto the unit from Step 4. *figs. L–N*

K

L

M

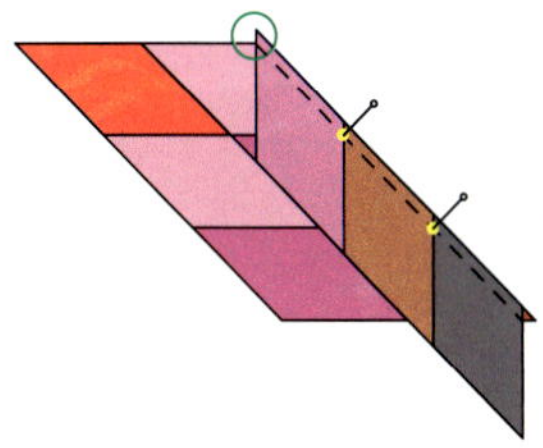

N

NOTE

If you aren't happy with how the points are (or aren't) lining up, try sewing with a scant ¼″ seam. Making that small adjustment to your seam allowance may be just the thing to make your points perfect.

Keep practicing. *It takes time and work to learn something new. You've got this!*

PERFECT CENTER STAR POINTS

When you sew two halves of a star block or star quilt together, you want all of the diamonds to come together in a perfect point at the center.

Before beginning, make sure there is ¼″ from the edge of each unit half to where the diamond points will come together. If there is more than ¼″, trim the excess. If there is less than ¼″, you may have to sew with a scant ¼″ seam for the points to line up. *figs. O–P*

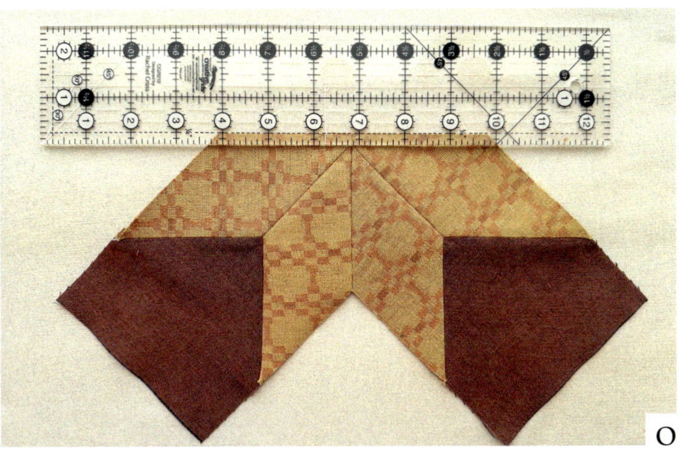

O

P

Q

R

S

T

1. Prepare to sew the two halves of the block by placing them RST.

2. Insert a pin through the top block's center seam, where the points come together, from wrong side to right side. *figs. Q–R*

3. Insert the same pin through the bottom block's seam in the same spot, from right side to wrong side. Keep the pin vertical. *fig. S*

4. Insert 2 more pins horizontally through the halves, one on each side of the vertical pin in the center, then remove the vertical pin. Insert 2 more pins, one at the beginning and one at end of the seam. *figs. T–V*

U

V

W

X

Y

5. Sew the two halves together, and press the seam open. *figs. W–Y*

Embracing the Y-Seam

Does seeing the term *Y-seam* in a quilt pattern give you instant anxiety? Is it an automatic disqualifier when you are looking at a quilt pattern? If your hands are getting sweaty right now just thinking about it, and you're tempted to shut this book without giving it another glance, I am asking you to take a deep breath and reconsider your preconceived fears and past frustrations with the "dreaded" Y-seam. Believe me—I used to feel those very same fears and frustrations.

If you have absolutely no idea what a Y-seam is, then I am so glad you are here! A *Y-seam* is also called an *inset seam* or *set-in seam*. In this kind of seam, 3 edges of fabric are sewn together to form a Y shape.

Before I even understood what a ¼″ seam allowance was (let alone consistently sewed with one), I made a queen size Lone Star quilt with Y-seams. Long story short, I finished it, and I still use it today, but making that quilt without really understanding what I was doing turned me off of Y-seams for *years*. Even when I started designing and writing my own quilt patterns, I took great care to write my patterns without Y-seams. I think that making many of my patterns without Y-seams has benefited people who might not have attempted the quilt otherwise.

But, I have come to embrace and even *enjoy* sewing with Y-seams. My goal with this book is to help you gain confidence in learning a new skill, help you overcome that fear of Y-seams, and give you new quilt designs to try out once you've got it down.

Why Use a Y-Seam?

Sometimes a Y-seam is absolutely necessary in a quilt pattern. Other times, it makes more sense to use a Y-seam instead of cutting a square shape into 2 triangles, only to sew them back together in the exact place the square was cut apart. You'll find that if you want to place a star block in the background of a quilt, using a Y-seam avoids having to cut the star block in half to piece it without one. Y-seams really open up the number of options for a quilt's design!

Sewing a Y-Seam

Begin with 3 pieces of fabric (this will be specified in each project). In this practice example, use 2 diamonds 2½″ and 1 square 3½″ × 3½″.

1. Place the 2 diamonds RST. On the wrong side of the top diamond, measure lines ¼″ from the right and bottom edges of the diamond, and mark where they intersect. *figs. A–B*

2. Pin the diamonds together through the mark from Step 1. *fig. C*

3. Sew the diamonds together, starting at the top of the diamonds and ending at the mark from Step 1. Keep the needle in the fabric at the end of the seam, then backstitch 2–3 stitches. Press the seam open. *figs. D–E*

4. On the wrong side of the square, measure lines ¼″ from the two edges of the square. Make a mark where they intersect. *fig. F*

5. Place the square RST with one side of the diamond unit from Step 3. Align and then insert a pin through the mark on the square and the last stitch in the seam from Step 3. *fig. G*

A

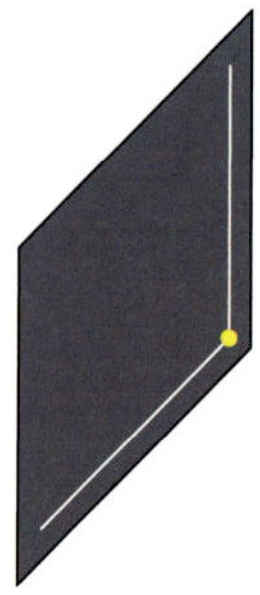
B

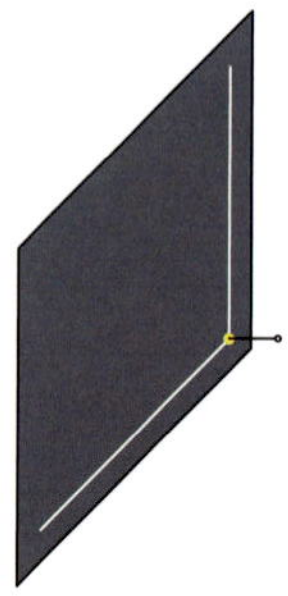
C

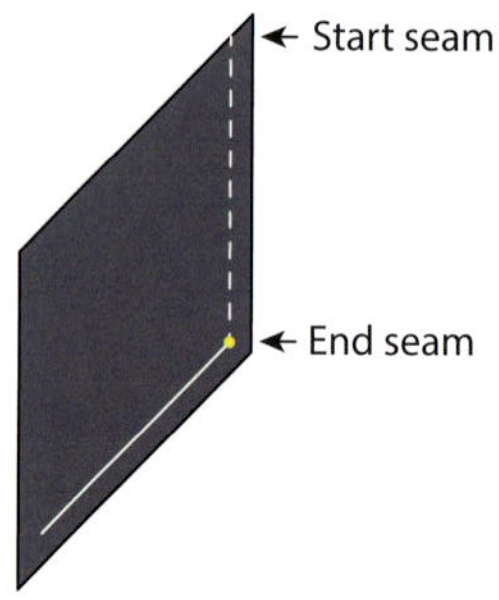

D

E

F

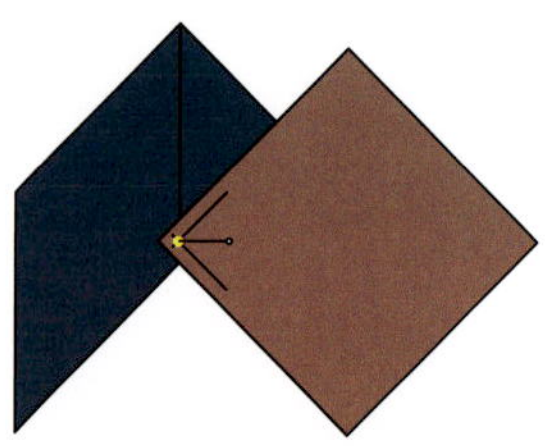
G

6. Sew the square to the diamond, starting at the outer edge of the block and ending at the mark from Step 4. Keep the needle in the fabric at the end of the seam, then backstitch 2–3 stitches. *fig. H*

7. Flip the background square so it is RST with the adjacent side of the Y-seam (the bottom edge of the other diamond). Pin through the point where the marks made in Step 4 intersect, then through the last stitch in the seam from Step 6. *fig. I*

8. Sew the square to the other diamond, starting at the outer edge of the block and ending at the point where the seam from Step 6 ends. Backstitch 2–3 stitches. *fig. J*

9. Press the seams open. *fig. K*

VIOLA!

That's it! I hope that felt easier than you thought it would be. But please don't get frustrated if it's not perfect. Anything new takes practice! Keep at it.

The quilt patterns in this book have more than just one Y-seam, but every Y-seam is no more complicated than these steps were. So, take one seam at a time, one step at a time, and before you know it you will be so proud of the quilt (probably, quilts) you made.

H

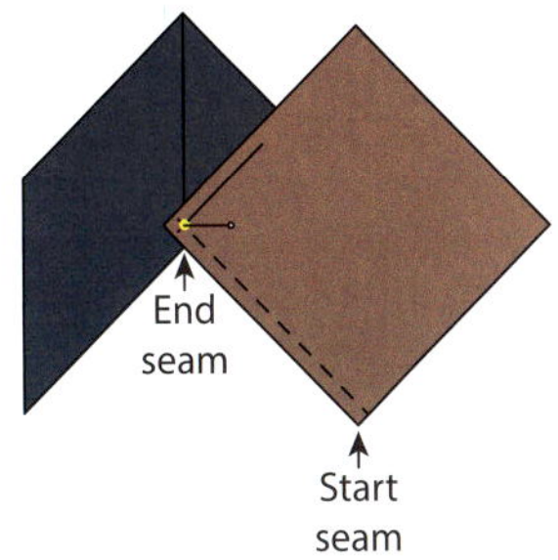

I

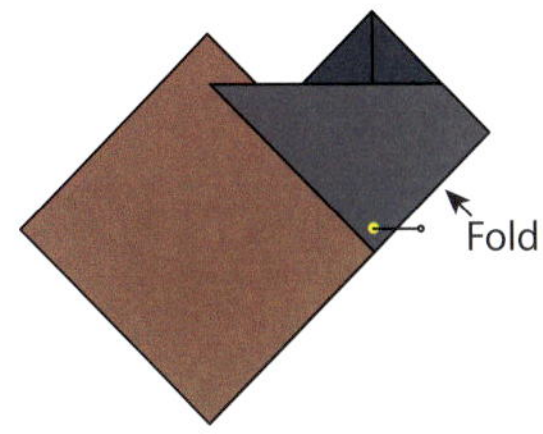

J

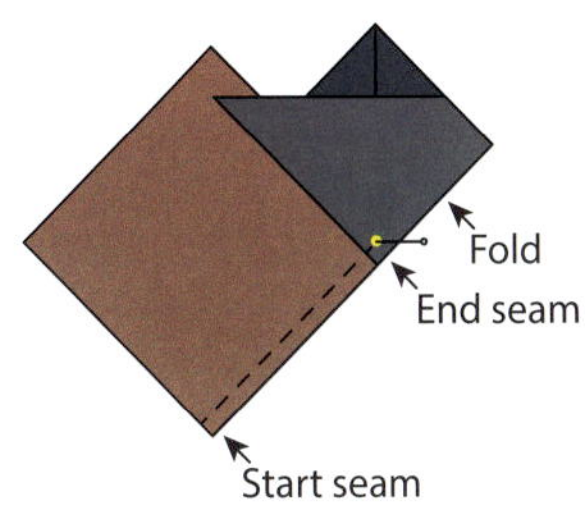

K

Broken Star Quilt Assembly

Every Broken Star quilt pattern in this book will be assembled the same way. Although the design will differ between patterns, and you should start by choosing one of the specific patterns, the steps for assembly are found in this chapter. Refer back here as directed. After you have assembled the Broken Star, you will refer back to the specific pattern instructions for any final steps, like adding additional borders.

PIECED DIAMONDS

The assembly instructions in this chapter are shown with whole (not strip-pieced) diamonds all using the same fabric. Keep the design of the quilt you are working on in mind as you assemble your version because, while it won't appear so here, the orientation of the diamonds does matter in most of the patterns. Each pattern will also provide quilt-specific illustrations for assembly.

SUCCESSFUL STITCHING

Each time you stop sewing, finish with the needle down through the fabric. If possible, set your machine to this setting. Set your stitch length under 2mm. I sew with a 1.7–1.8mm stitch length. Use a ¼″ seam allowance for all assembly.

Background Square Units

You can always swap an interchangeable block (page 50) for a background square.

Unit 1

MAKE 16.

Required

2 diamonds

1. Arrange the 2 Unit 1 diamonds as shown. *fig. A*

2. Place the 2 diamonds RST. On the wrong side of the top diamond, measure lines ¼″ from two edges of the diamond as shown. Make a mark where the lines intersect on the bottom right corner. Pin through the mark. *fig. B*

3. Start sewing at the top right corner and stop sewing at the mark from Step 2. Backstitch 2–3 stitches. Press the seam open. *fig. C*

4. Repeat Steps 1–3 to create 16 Unit 1s. *fig. D*

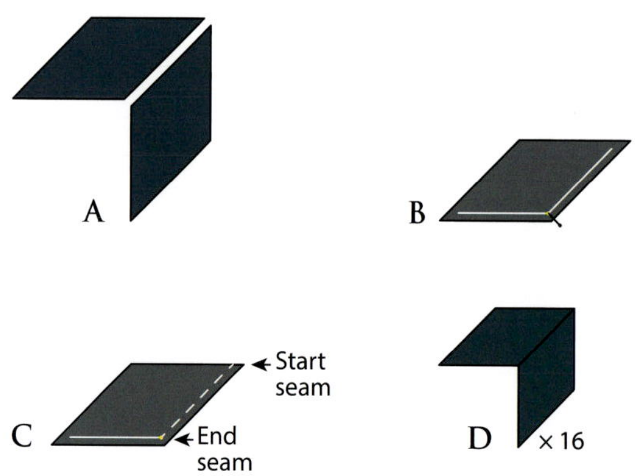

Unit 2

MAKE 4.

Required

2 Unit 1s

2 background triangles

1 background square (or interchangeable block)

1. On the wrong side of 1 background triangle, measure lines ¼″ from two edges that meet at the 90° corner. Make a mark where the lines intersect in the corner. *fig. A*

2. Put the background triangle and left side of a Unit 1 RST. Align the mark from Step 1 with the mark on the Unit 1 where the seam ended. Pin through that point. *fig. B*

3. Start sewing at the outer left edge of the unit and stop sewing (with the needle down) at the mark intersection from Step 2. Backstitch 2–3 stitches. *fig. C*

4. Flip the background triangle so it is RST with the other side of Unit 1. Pin through the mark on the background triangle (from Step 1) and through the point of Unit 1 where the seam ended in Step 3. *fig. D*

5. Start sewing at the outer edge of the unit and stop sewing (with the needle down) at the mark intersection from Step 4. Backstitch 2–3 stitches. Press the seams open. *fig. E*

6. Repeat Steps 1–5 to create 8 units. *fig. F*

A

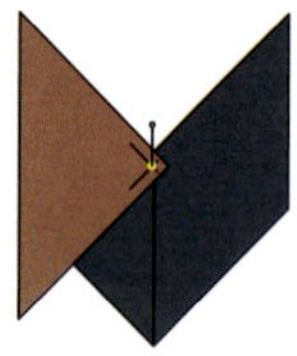

B

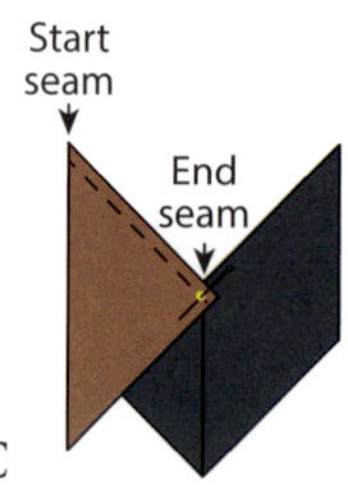

C

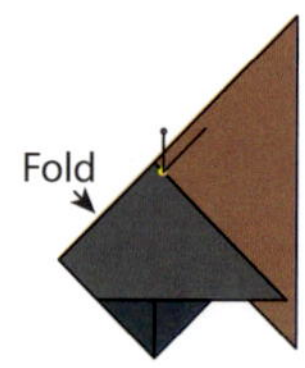

D

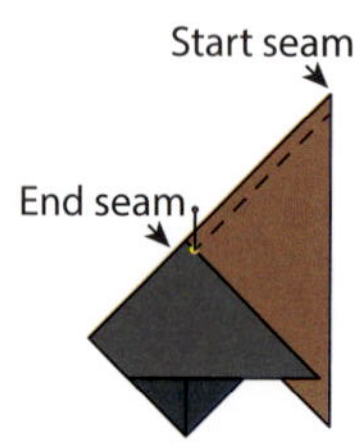

E

F

7. Place 2 of the units from Step 6 RST. On the wrong side of the top unit, measure lines ¼″ from the two edges that meet at the right side corner (as shown). Make a mark where the lines intersect. Pin through the mark. *fig. G*

8. Sew together, starting in the top right corner and stopping (with the needle down) at the mark from Step 7. Backstitch 2–3 stitches. Press the seam open. Repeat Steps 7–8 to make 4 units. *figs. H–I*

9. On the wrong side of the background square (or interchangeable block), measure lines ¼″ from two edges that meet at one corner. Make a mark where the lines intersect. *fig. J*

10. Place the background square and a Step 8 unit RST, aligning the mark from Step 9 and the end of the seam from Step 8 as shown. Pin through the marks. *fig. K*

11. Start sewing at the bottom point of the square and stop sewing (with the needle down) at the mark intersection from Step 10. Backstitch 2–3 stitches. *fig. L*

12. Flip the background square so it is RST with the bottom point of the unit on the other side. Align the mark on the background square from Step 9 with the end of the seam from Step 11. Pin through the marks. *fig. M*

13. Start sewing at the bottom point of the square and stop sewing (with the needle down) at the mark intersection from Step 12. Backstitch 2–3 stitches. Press the seams open. *fig. N*

14. Repeat Steps 9–13 to make 4 Unit 2s. *fig. O*

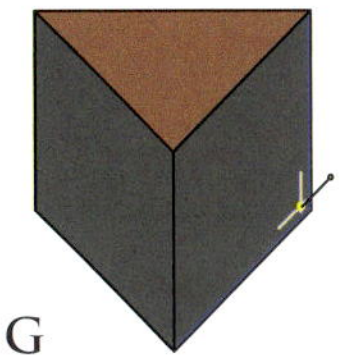

G

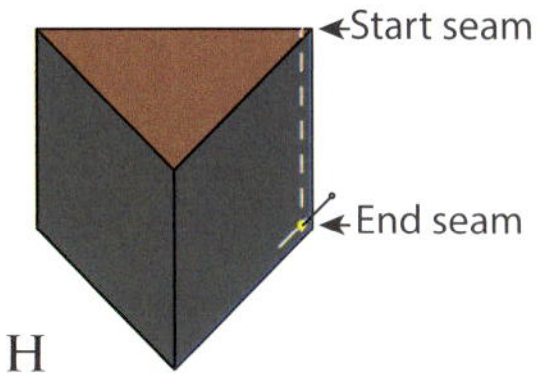

H

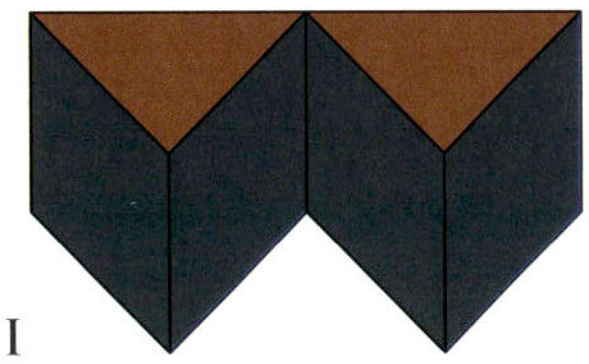

I

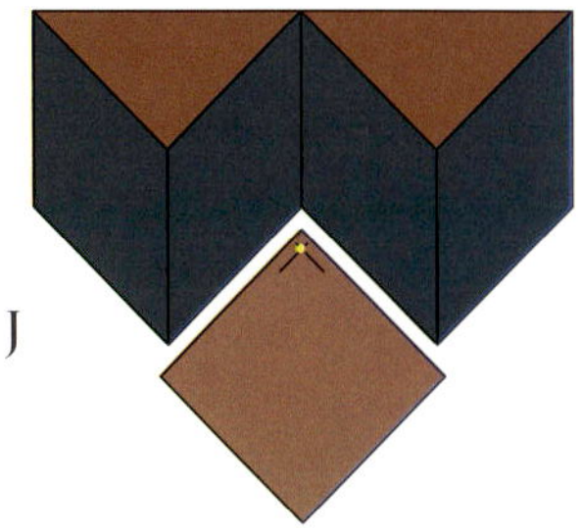

J

K

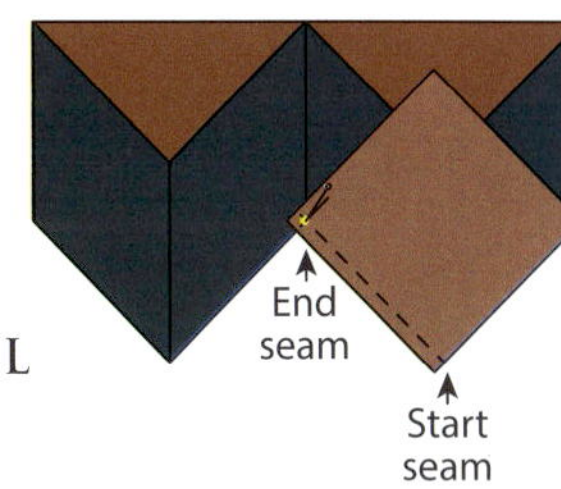

L

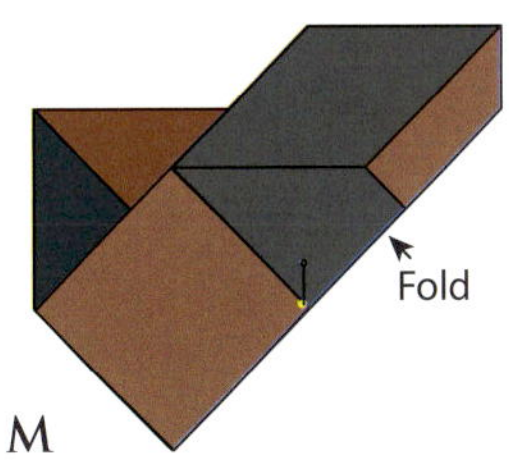

M

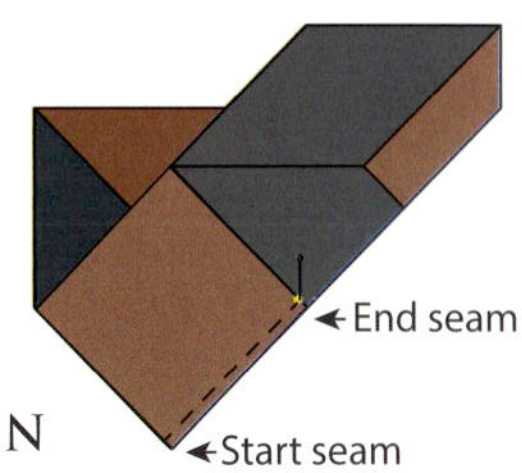

N

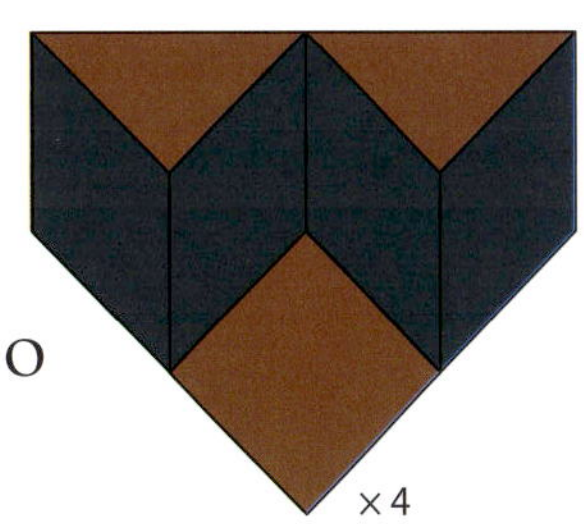

O

Unit 3

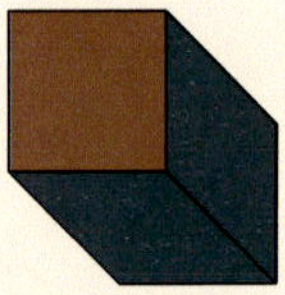

MAKE 4.

Required

1 Unit 1

1 Background square (or interchangeable block)

A

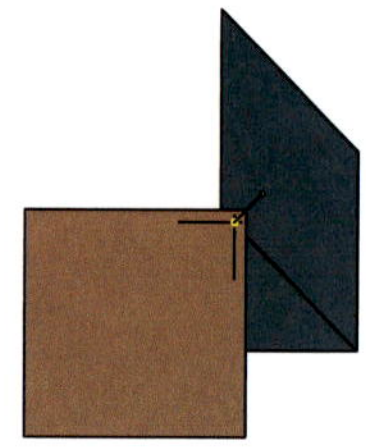

B

1. On the wrong side of the background square (or interchangeable block), measure lines ¼″ from two edges that meet at one corner. Make a mark where the lines intersect. *fig. A*

2. Place the background square and Unit 1 RST, aligning the mark from Step 1 with where the seam ended on the Unit 1. Pin through this intersection. *fig. B*

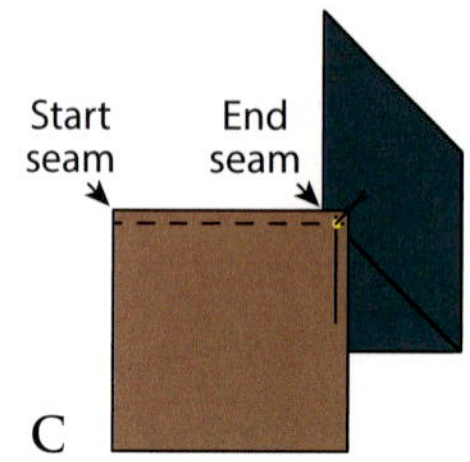

C

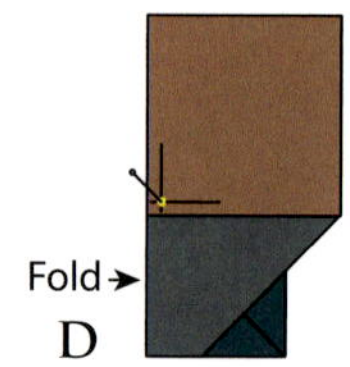

D

3. Start sewing from the left outer edge, and and stop sewing at the marked intersection from Step 2. Backstitch 2–3 stitches. *fig. C*

4. Flip the background square so it is RST with the other half of the Unit 1. Align the mark from Step 1 and the spot the seam ended in Step 3, and pin through the intersection. *fig. D*

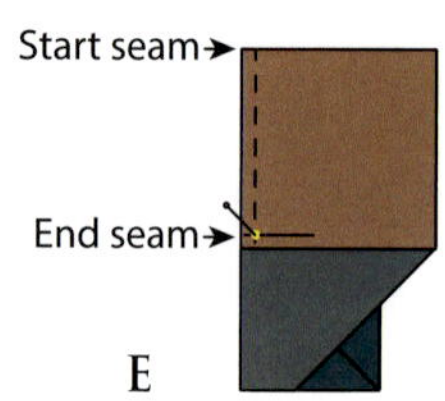

E

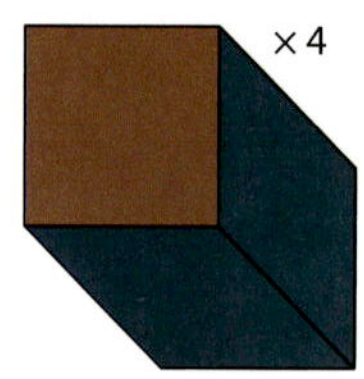

F

5. Start sewing at the upper edge of the unit and stop at the mark intersection from Step 4. Backstitch 2–3 stitches. Press the seams open. *fig. E*

6. Repeat Steps 1–5 to create 4 Unit 3s. *fig. F*

Unit 4

MAKE 4.

Required

1 Unit 3

1 Unit 1

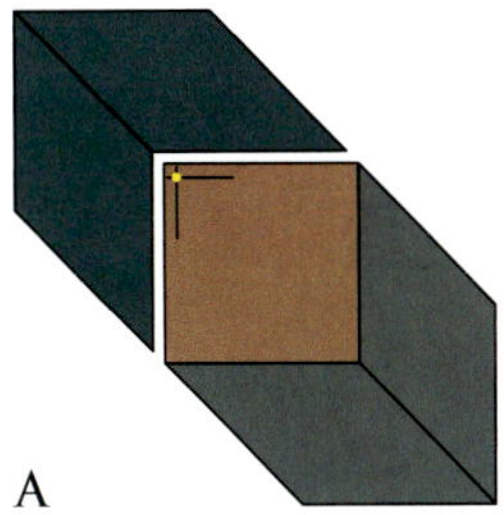

A

B

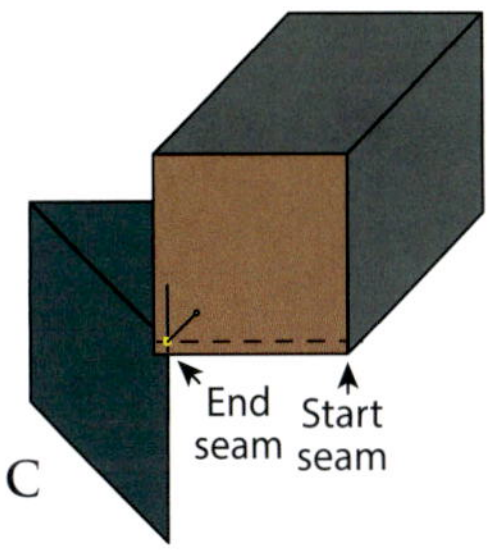

C

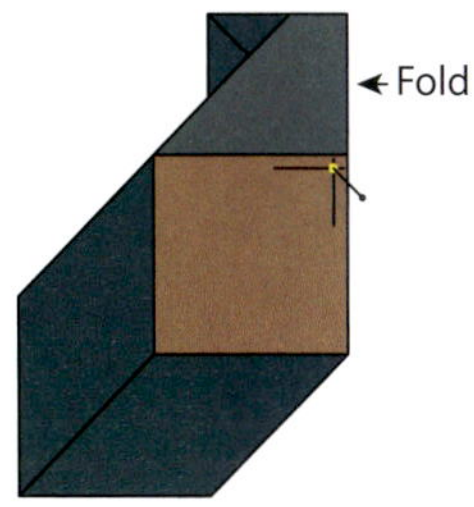

D

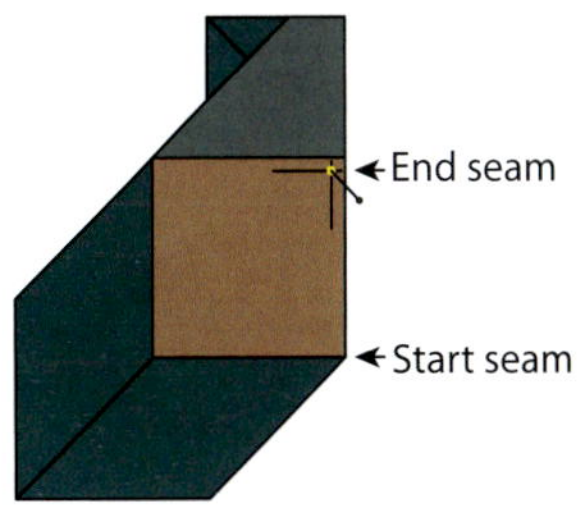

E

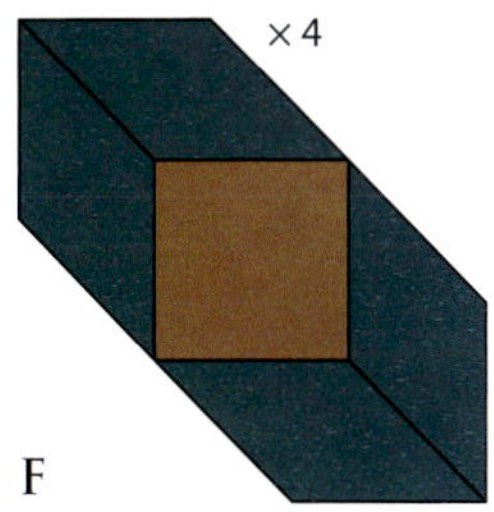

F

1. Arrange Unit 1 and Unit 3 so the square sewn to Unit 3 is between the diamonds. On the wrong side of the square (opposite where it is already sewn to Unit 3), measure lines ¼″ from two edges that meet at one corner. Make a mark where the lines intersect. *fig. A*

2. Place the Unit 3 and the Unit 1 RST, aligning the mark from Step 1 with the place where the seam ended on the Unit 1. Pin through this intersection. *fig. B*

3. Start sewing from the bottom right edge of the unit and stop sewing at the mark intersection from Step 3. Backstitch 2–3 stitches. *fig. C*

4. Flip the background square so it is RST with the other side of Unit 1. Align the mark from Step 1 and the spot the seam ended in Step 3, and pin through the intersection. *fig. D*

5. Start sewing at the bottom right corner of the square and stop sewing at the marked intersection from Step 4. Backstitch 2–3 stitches. Press the seams open. *fig. E*

9. Repeat Steps 1–5 to create 4 Unit 4s. *fig. F*

UNIT 5

MAKE 4.

Required

1 Unit 4

1 background square (or interchangeable block)

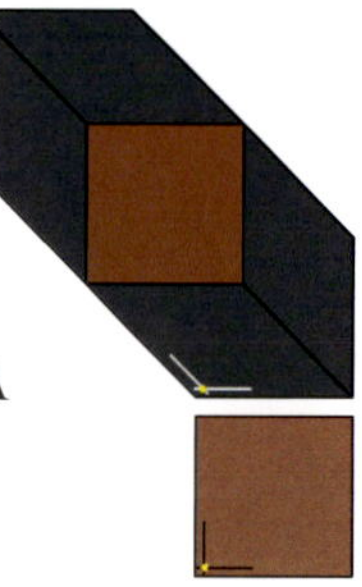

A

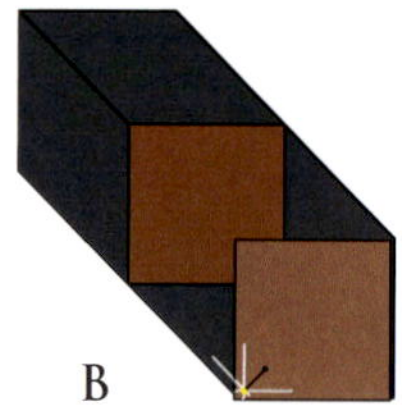

B

1. Arrange the Unit 4 and the background square (or interchangeable block) as shown. On the wrong side of the square, measure lines ¼″ from two edges that meet at the bottom left corner. Make a mark where the lines intersect. Repeat on the wrong side of the bottom left Unit 4 corner. *fig. A*

2. Align the marks from Step 1, placing the units RST. Pin through the intersection. *fig. B*

3. Start sewing at the bottom right corner and stop sewing at the mark intersection from Step 2. Backstitch 2–3 stitches. Press the seam open. *fig. C*

4. Repeat Steps 1–3 to create 4 Unit 5s. *fig. D*

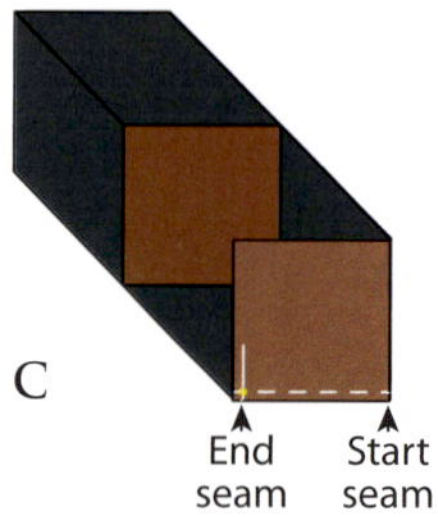

C

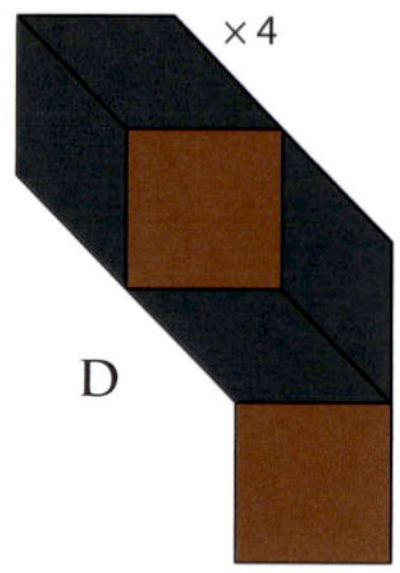

D

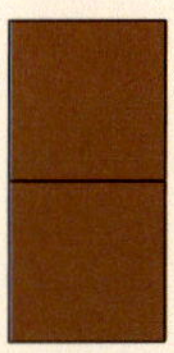

MAKE 4.

Required

2 background squares (or interchangeable blocks)

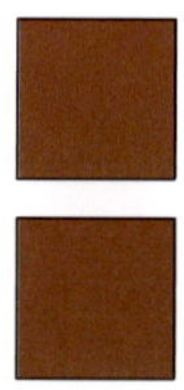

E

1. Pair 2 background squares or interchangeable blocks together. *fig. E*

2. Align the squares RST. Sew the pair together along one side and press the seam open. Repeat to make 4 Background Square Units.

Unit 6

MAKE 4.

Required

1 Unit 5

1 Background Square Unit

A
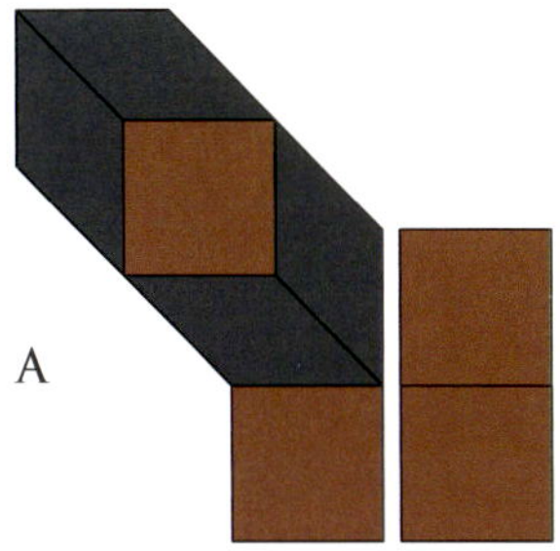

B
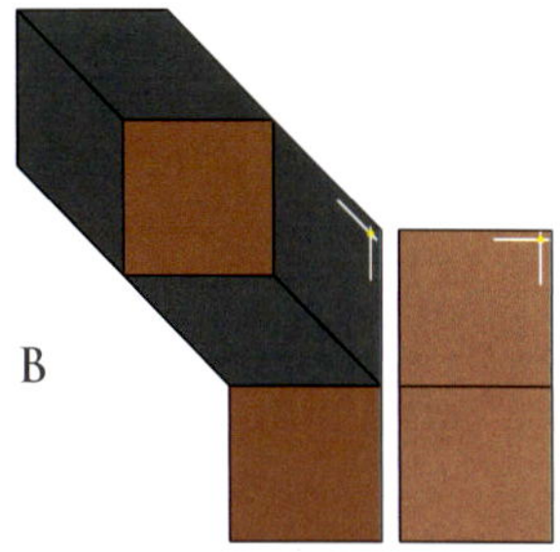

1. Arrange the Unit 5 and the Background Square Unit as shown. *fig. A*

2. On the wrong side of the Background Square Unit, measure lines ¼″ from two edges that meet at the upper right corner. Make a mark where the lines intersect. Repeat on the corner of Unit 5 as shown. *fig. B*

3. Place the background pair and Unit 5 RST. Align the two marks from Step 2, then pin through the mark intersection. *fig. C*

4. Start sewing at the mark intersection. After sewing 2–3 stitches, backstitch 2–3 stitches, then continue sewing the rest of the seam to the edge of the unit. Backstitch again. Press the seam open. *fig. D*

5. Repeat Steps 1–4 to make 4 Unit 6s. *fig. E*

C
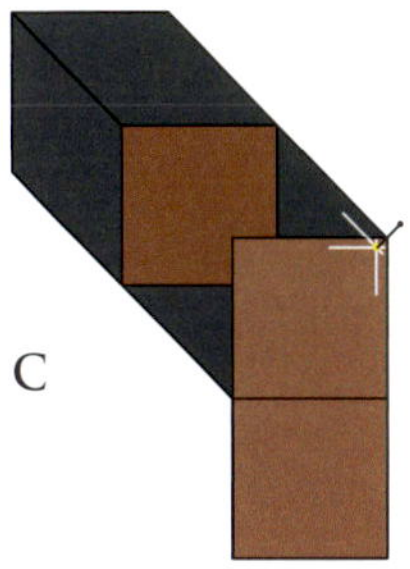

D
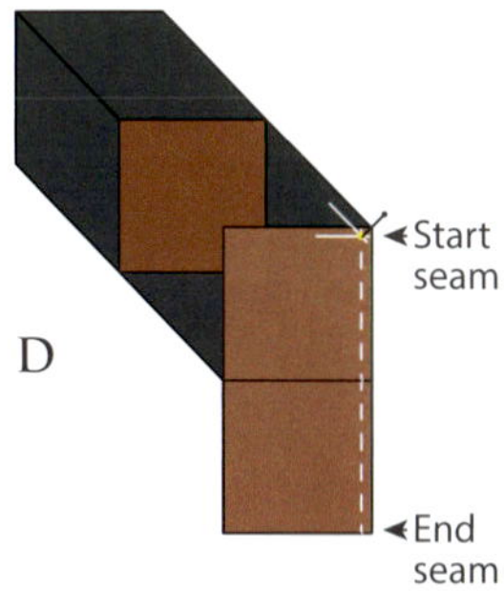

E
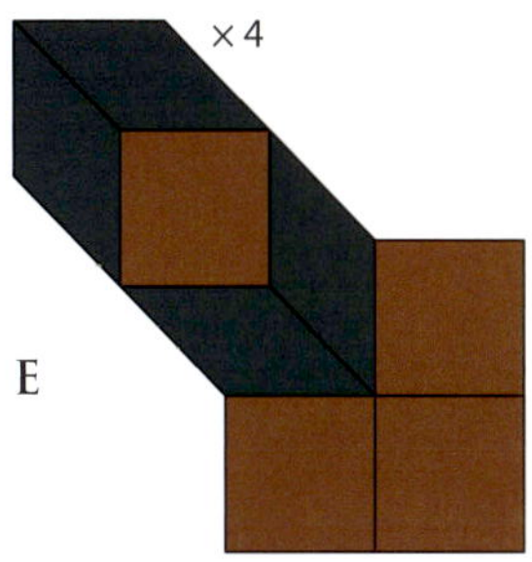

UNIT 7

MAKE 2.

Required

2 Unit 6s

1. Place 2 Unit 6s RST. On the wrong side of the top unit, measure lines ¼″ from two edges that meet at the corner as shown. Make a mark where the lines intersect. Pin through the mark. *fig. A*

2. Start sewing at the upper diamond point and stop sewing at the mark from Step 1. Backstitch 2–3 stitches. Press the seam open. *fig. B*

3. Repeat Steps 1–2 to create a second Unit 7. *fig. C*

A

B

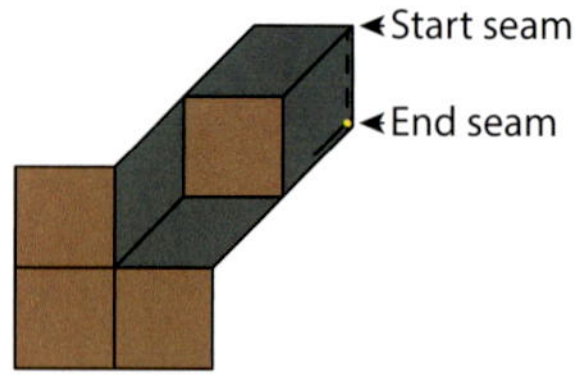

C

UNIT 8

MAKE 2.

Required

1 Unit 7

1 Unit 2

1. On the wrong side of Unit 2, measure lines ¼″ from two edges that meet at the top point. Make a mark where the lines intersect. Repeat on the 2 corners to the left and right as shown. *fig. A*

2. Place Unit 2 and Unit 7 RST as shown. Align the first mark from Step 1, and the place the seam ended in the center of Unit 7. Align the bottom mark from Step 1 as shown. Pin through both marks. *fig. B*

A

B

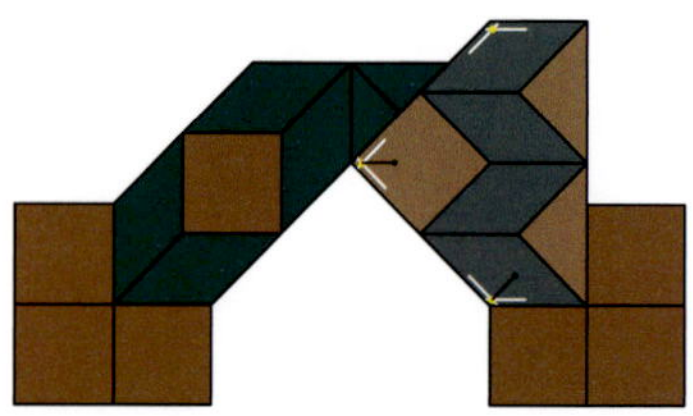

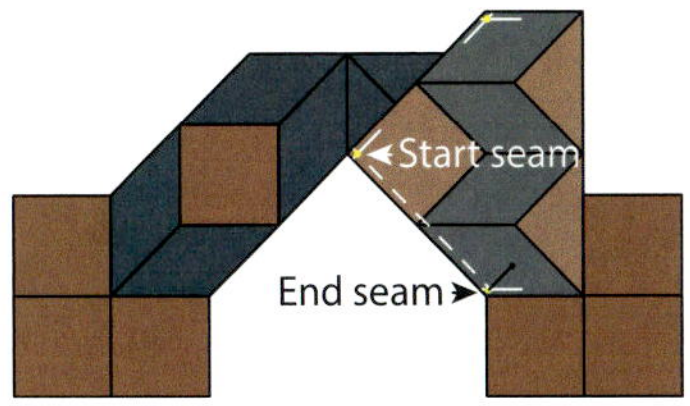

C

D

3. Start sewing at the first marked intersection. Sew 2–3 stitches, then backstitch 2–3 stitches. Stop sewing at the second mark. Backstitch 2–3 stitches. *fig. C*

4. Fold the units so the edge of Unit 2 diamond (with the remaining mark from Step 1) and a background square from Unit 7 (where the seam ended in Step 3) are aligned. Pin through intersection. *fig. D*

5. Start sewing at the intersection. Sew 2–3 stitches, then backstitch 2–3 stitches. Continue sewing to the edge of the units. *fig. E*

6. Repeat Steps 2–5 for the adjacent side as shown. *figs. F–G*

7. Press all of the seams open.

8. Repeat Steps 1–7 to create a second Unit 8. *fig. H*

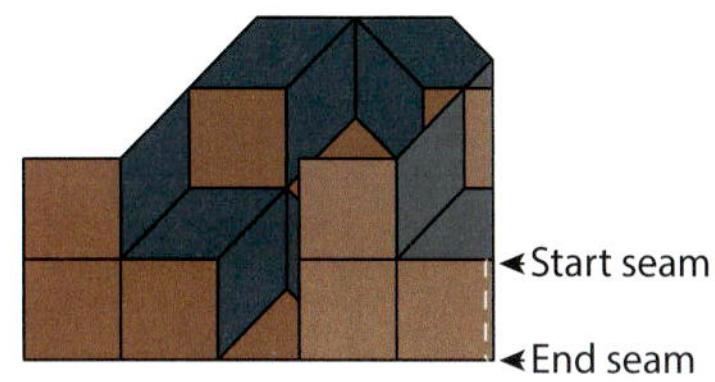

E

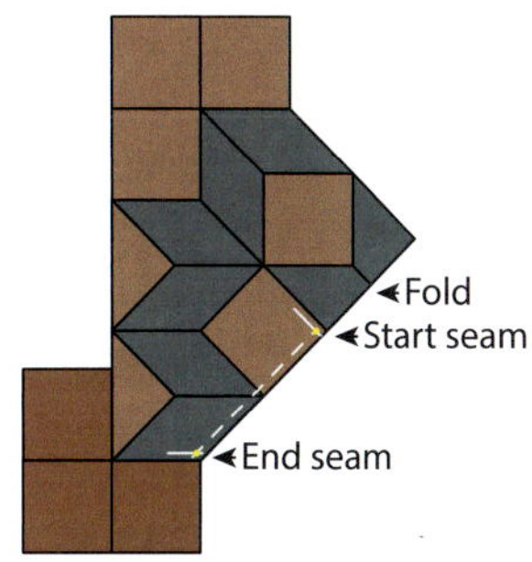

F

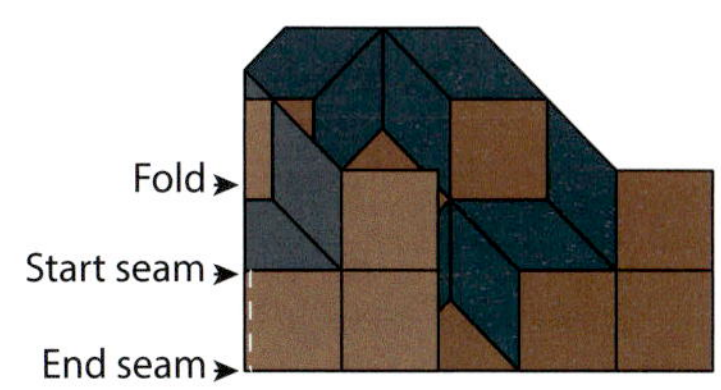

G

H

Unit 9

MAKE 1.

Required

2 Unit 8s

A

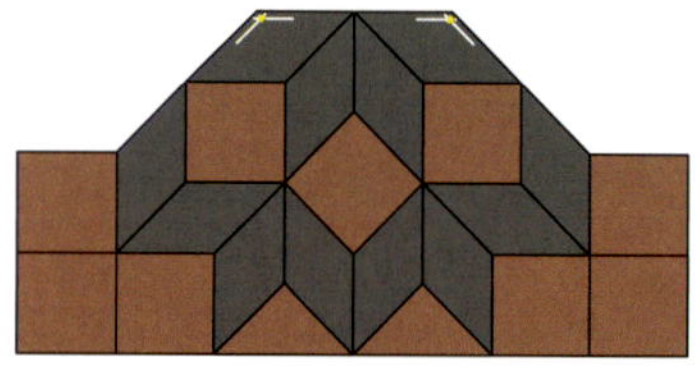

B

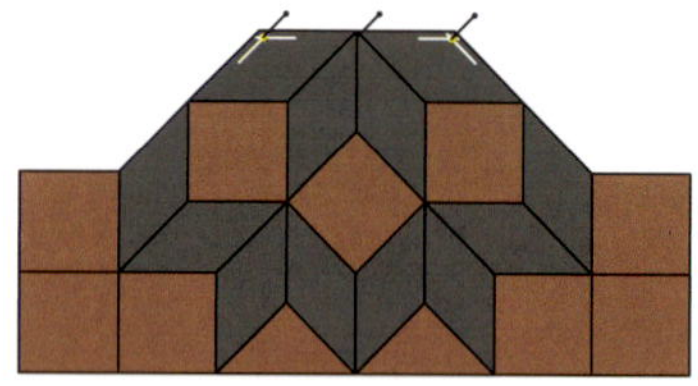

C

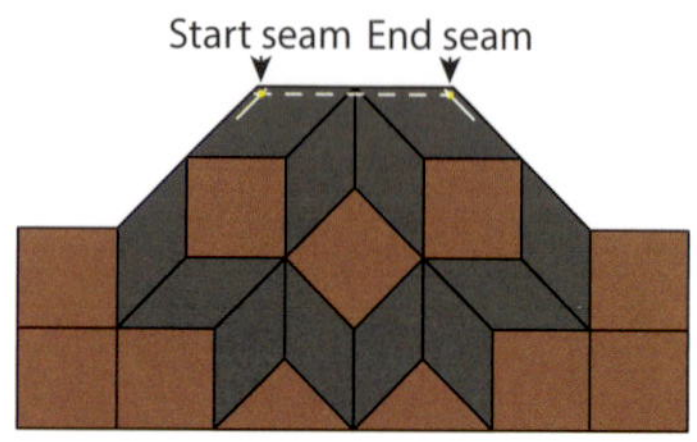

1. Place the Unit 8 pieces RST. On the wrong side of the top unit, measure lines ¼″ from two edges that meet at the top corners. Make a mark where the lines intersect. *fig. A*

2. Insert pins through each mark. Also pin through the center seam of both units to ensure the units come together at a point. *fig. B*

3. Start sewing at the first mark. After 2–3 stitches, backstitch 2–3 stitches. Continue to the second mark. Backstitch 2–3 stitches. *fig. C*

4. Press the seam open.

Unit 10: Assembled Broken Star

MAKE 1.

Required

1 Unit 9

2 Unit 2s

This unit is the final step in Broken Star quilt assembly.

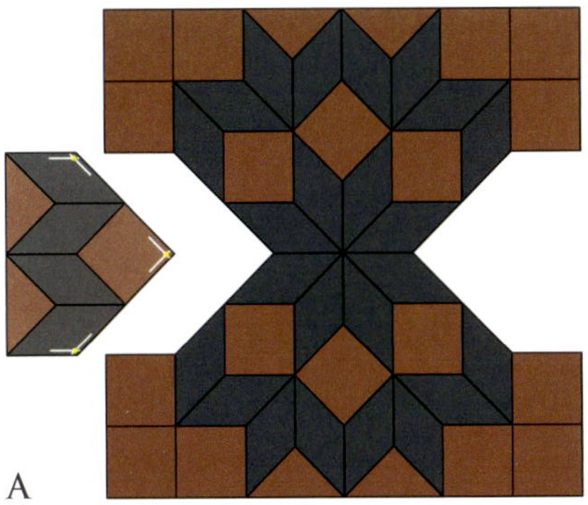

A

B

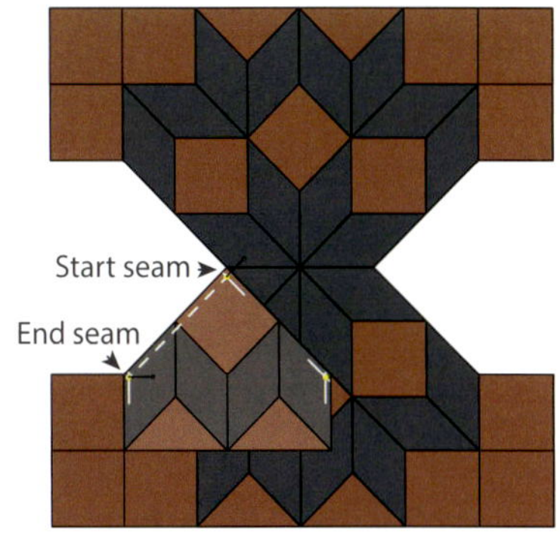

C

1. On the wrong side of a Unit 2, measure lines ¼″ from two edges that meet at the top point. Make a mark where the lines intersect. Repeat on the two adjacent corners as shown. *fig. A*

2. Place Unit 2 and Unit 9 RST. Align 2 of the marks from Step 1 with the spots where the seams ended on Unit 9 as shown. Pin through the marks. *fig. B*

3. Start sewing at the first mark. Stitch 2–3 stitches, then backstitch 2–3 stitches. Continue sewing to the next mark. Backstitch 2–3 stitches. *fig. C*

4. Arrange the units so the outer edge of the Unit 2 diamond and the background square on Unit 9 are aligned. Align the bottom mark on Unit 2 and the spot the seam ended in Step 3. Insert a pin through the mark. *fig. D*

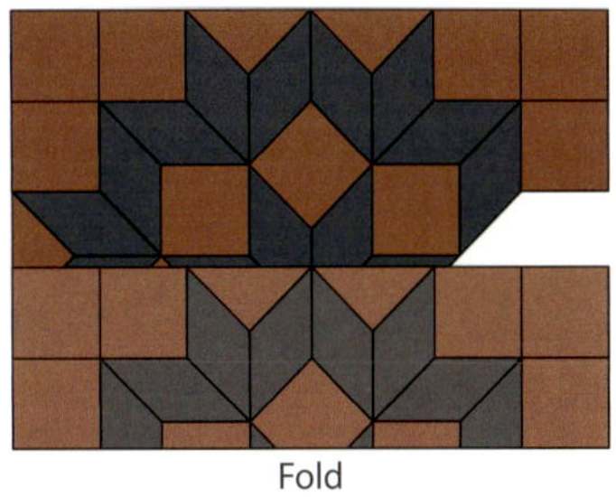

D

5. Start sewing at the mark/pin. Stitch 2–3 stitches, then backstitch 2–3 stitches. Continue sewing to the edge of the unit. *fig. E*

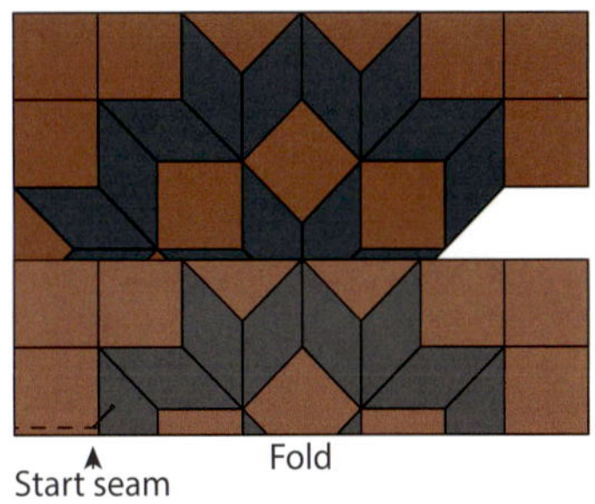

E

6. Repeat Steps 2–5 for the other side of the same Unit 2. Press the seams open. *fig. F*

F

7. Repeat Steps 1–6 to attach the second Unit 2.

Congratulations! You have assembled your Broken Star Quilt!

Finishing the Quilts

Refer back to this chapter after the quilt top is finished and the backing is prepared.

BACKING SIZE

The backing should be 8″ wider and 8″ longer than the quilt top, 4″ larger on all sides.

There are various methods for finishing a quilt. The most common are machine quilting on a home sewing machine, longarm quilting by a professional on a longarm quilting machine, and hand quilting. I have a confession. I love the cutting and piecing steps of making a quilt but I don't love the quilting. So after I finish piecing a quilt, I will most often send it to a professional longarm quilter to quilt a computerized edge to edge quilting design. A few years ago, I found a local quilter, Ashlee Doyle of Crinkly Quilts, who has quilted *many* quilts for me since then and also quilted all of the projects in this book.

Baste

NOTE

If you are having your quilt professionally longarm quilted, you can often skip the basting step. Refer to the instructions the longarm quilter sends you for how to prepare the quilt.

After the quilt top is pieced and the backing is prepared, it's time for basting. *Basting* refers to temporarily securing the three layers of the quilt (quilt top, batting, and backing) together so they can be permanently quilted.

First, make a *quilt sandwich*. Lay the backing on the floor, wrong side up. Smooth out any wrinkles and secure to the floor with masking or painters tape. Then, spread the batting on the backing and smooth out any wrinkles. Finally, lay the quilt top, right side up, on the batting. Again, smooth out the wrinkles.

Baste them together using basting spray or pins.

If using basting spray, roll back half of the quilt top and batting from the backing. Spray the backing thoroughly, then carefully smooth the batting over the backing. Spray the batting thoroughly, and carefully smooth the quilt top over the batting. Repeat with the other half of the quilt sandwich.

If using pins, pin all 3 layers together. Place pins every 4–6 inches (or a hands width) apart to keep all layers together for quilting. If possible, try to not pin where you plan on quilting.

QUILT

MACHINE QUILTING

After the quilt is basted, head right back to your machine to start quilting. For success quilting on a home sewing machine:

1. Get a pair of quilting gloves. They help give you more control when handling and maneuvering the heavy quilt sandwich through the machine.

2. Use a walking foot.

3. Increase the stitch length to 3–4mm.

4. Use a Hera marker and a ruler to mark lines where you want to quilt before you begin stitching. Alternatively, eyeball the quilting lines by quilting on either side of the seams on the quilt.

HAND QUILTING

Hand quilting is slower but more flexible than quilting on a home sewing machine. You'll need a few additional supplies. For success with hand quilting:

Hand Quilting Supplies

Hera Marker: A Hera marker is a tool to make temporary marks on the quilt sandwich to use as a guide for your hand quilting stitches.

Thimble: A thimble (or thimbles) is based on personal preference on comfort and ease of use. My favorite is a leather thimble. I use it when I'm binding my quilts also.

Quilting Hoop: A quilting hoop is used to keep a section of the quilt taut when hand quilting. Some people prefer to use a hoop while others prefer to just hold the quilt on their lap or lay it on a table when quilting. My preference is to hold the quilt without a hoop.

Needles: This is another area of personal preference among quilters. If you are new to hand quilting, I recommend starting with a pack of needles with multiple sizes. The needle eye size needs to be taken into account depending on the thread thickness you are using.

Thread: Thread comes in many colors and weights. The lower the number for thread weight the thicker the thread will be. If you are wanting more visible stitches, choose a 12wt thread. If you want a thinner thread with less visible stitches, go with a 40wt or 50wt thread.

1. Use a Hera marker and a ruler to mark the lines where you want to hand quilt. Alternatively, eyeball the lines by quilting on either side of seams on the quilt. Or, totally freehand the quilting by improvising as you go.

2. There are many ways to hold the quilt while quilting. Put the quilt in a quilting hoop or frame, lay it on a table, or hold it on your lap to quilt. I like to just lay the quilt on my lap and sit in a comfy chair—it takes lots of time, and you should be comfortable while you work.

3. Be prepared that hand quilting a quilt of any size will take *time*. Lots of it. Embracing this part of the process will help you enjoy it more than if you're just trying to get through it.

4. There are no rules. Remember, this was my motto about choosing fabrics too? Quilt with big stitches, tiny stitches, one kind of thread, multiple kinds of thread, whatever! You could even combine hand quilting and machine quilting. You are the one spending hours of your time making this heirloom. Make it how *you* want it.

LONGARM QUILTING

If you are having your quilt professionally quilted by a longarm quilter, check with them on specific requirements for preparing the quilt. Typically, they will require the following:

1. Quilt backing that is at least 4″ larger than the quilt top on all sides.

2. All seams pressed in the quilt top and backing.

3. All loose threads clipped.

4. Square quilt top and backing.

Batting can be purchased from your longarm quilter or you can provide batting if you prefer. If you are providing batting, it will also need to be 4″ larger than the quilt top on each side.

You can choose the quilting pantograph design, or work with the longarm quilter to choose the design.

Trim

After your quilt is quilted, trim off the excess batting and backing so all 3 layers line up evenly. Square up the quilt as you trim, so that all sides are the same length and the corners are 90°.

> **SQUARING QUILTS**
>
> *I never worry if my quilts are perfectly "square". My main focus is making sure I don't cut off any points from the quilt top. Ideally, the outermost star points should be at least ¼″ from the edge of the quilt.*

Bind

After the quilt is trimmed, it is ready for binding.

PREPARING & ATTACHING BINDING

1. Cut binding strips 2½″ × WOF. Join the binding strips with either a vertical or 45° seam. I typically join the binding strips with a 45° seam, but you might want to use a vertical seam if you are making a scrappy binding with different fabrics. I recommend making 16″–20″ more binding than the total quilt perimeter.

2. Press the binding strip in half, wrong sides together.

3. Leaving 8″–12″ of binding off the edge of the quilt, sew the binding onto the front of the quilt with the raw edge of the binding aligned with the raw edge of the quilt, starting at the center of one side. *fig. A*

4. Stop sewing ¼″ from the corner of the quilt, and backstitch. Cut the thread and lift the needle. *fig. B*

5. Rotate the quilt. Fold the binding at a 90-degree angle so it is laying above the quilt. Fold it back down, aligning the fold with the top edge and placing the raw edge aligned with the next raw edge of the quilt. Continue sewing at the corner of the quilt. Repeat Steps 3–5 around all four sides and corners of the quilt. *fig. C*

6. When you are 8–12″ away from where you started sewing the binding, stop and backstitch.

7. Lay the two binding tails flat along the quilt so they overlap by ½″. Trim away the excess. *fig. D*

8. With RST, sew the tails together along the 2½″ sides with a vertical seam, and finger press the seam open. *figs. E–F*

9. Fold the binding WST again, and finish sewing the binding to the front of the quilt. Press the binding away from the quilt top.

FINISHING BINDING

Now the binding can be attached to the back of the quilt by machine or hand.

Machine Binding

1. Increase the stitch length on the sewing machine to around 3mm.

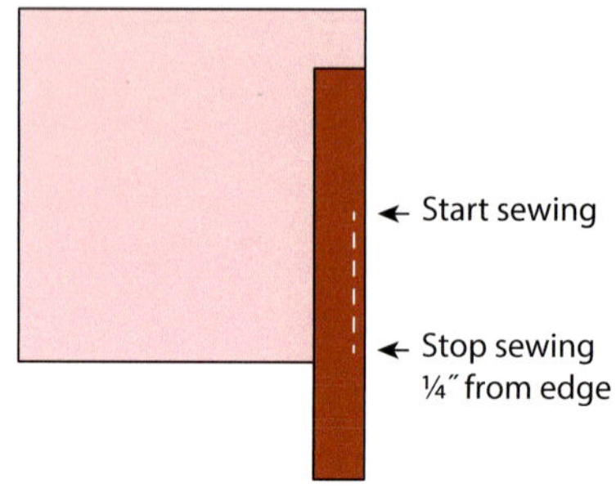

A

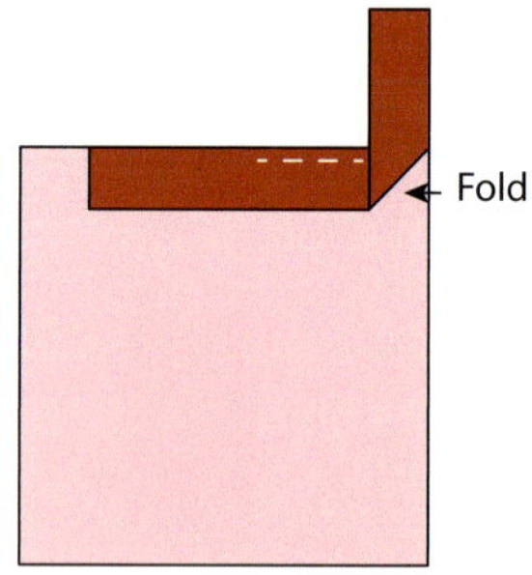

B

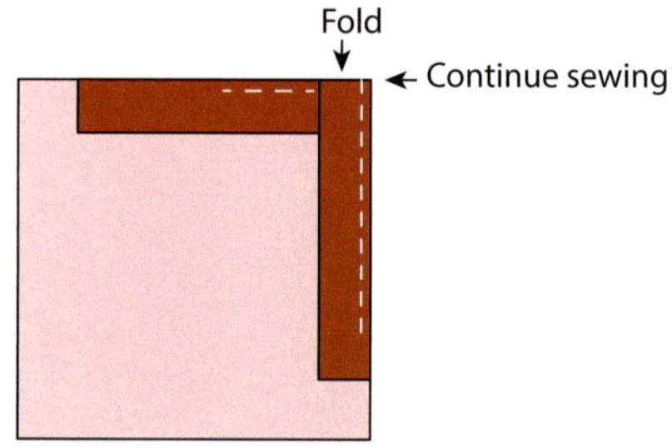

C

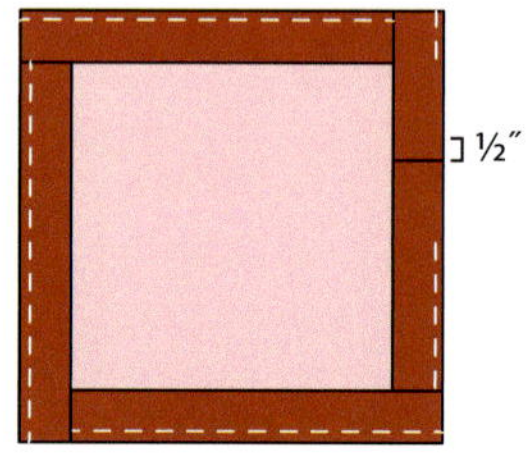

D

E

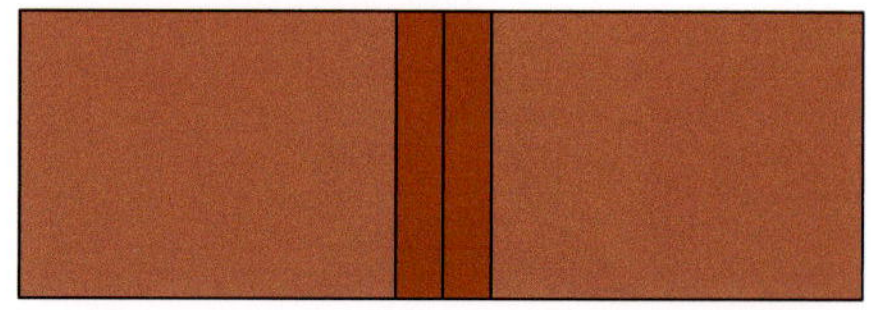

F

2. Fold the binding around the edge of the quilt, enclosing the remaining raw edge of binding and the quilt sandwich. Clip the binding in place. *figs. G–H*

3. Start sewing on one edge of the quilt. Sew as close to the edge of the binding as possible.

4. Slowly sew around the edge of the quilt, stopping with the needle down at each corner to turn the quilt before continuing. Fold the binding to form a mitered corner. *fig. I*

5. Backstitch 1–2 stitches when you overlap the starting point.

G Front

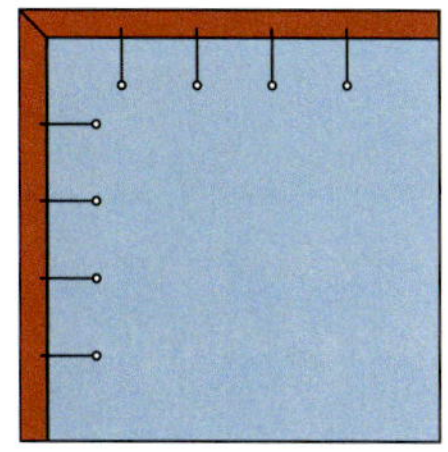

H Back

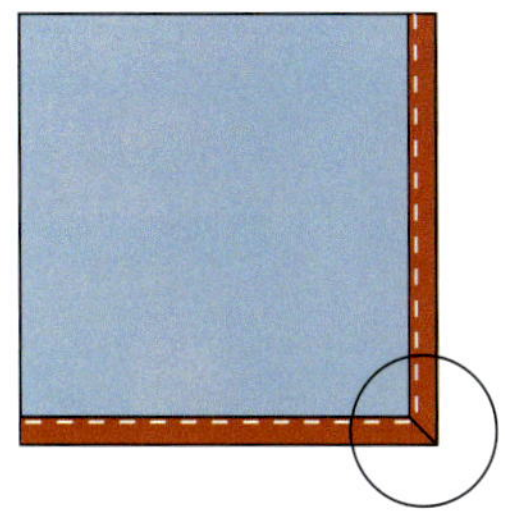

I

Hand Binding

Before beginning to stitch, follow Step 2 in Machine Binding (above) to fold the binding in place.

WHIP STITCH

My favorite finishing look is the invisible whip stitch (also called a ladder stitch). To me, it looks the cleanest because all the stitches are hidden. *fig. J*

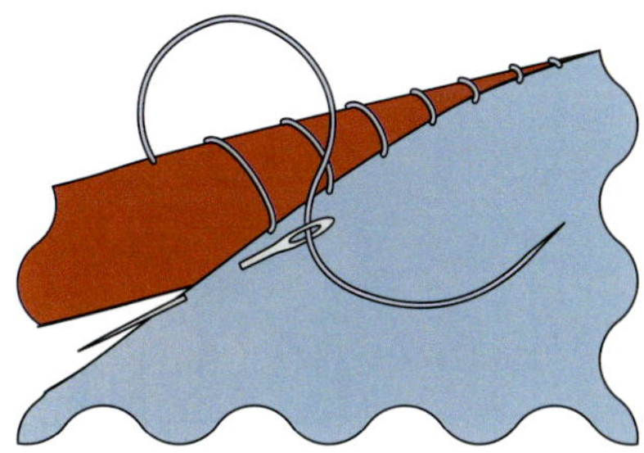

J

1. Thread a needle and tie a knot at one end of the thread. Under the binding, stitch through the backing. Then, bring the needle through the very bottom of the binding, just below the fold.

2. Insert the needle through the backing fabric behind the binding and come back through the bottom edge of the binding. Repeat. The smaller the stitches, the less puckering you will get as you sew.

3. Continue all around the quilt. Miter the corners as you go. Refer to Step 4 in Machine Binding (above) for information on stitching mitered corners.

BIG STITCH

Another fun look is big stitch binding, which doesn't show any stitches on the front of the quilt, but has a hand quilted look on the back of the binding.

1. Thread a needle and tie a knot at one end of the thread. Pull the needle through the backing fabric under the binding, then bring the needle up through the binding.

2. Insert the needle back down through the binding and backing, careful not to go through the front of the quilt top, and back up through the binding. *figs. K–M*

3. Continue in a straight line on the binding all the way around the quilt. Make an × at each corner to keep the edges sewn down. *figs. N–Q*

K

L

M

N

O

P

Q

Interchangeable Blocks

All of the quilts use background squares. If you'd like, you can replace some of the background squares with these interchangeable single quilt block designs. This can add more complexity to a quilt design and is not too complicated to incorporate. Each interchangeable block uses diamonds and Y-seams and can be made at a small size (9″ × 9″) or large size (14½″ × 14½″), unfinished sizes. The 14½″ × 14½″ blocks will work with the first and the last two quilt patterns (Steppe Star, page 82; Broken Trail Star, page 142; Broken Steppe Star, page 150). The 9″ × 9″ blocks will work with the remaining quilt patterns. These single blocks are also great for practicing the skills you need for the quilt projects.

How To

If you are replacing the background squares of a quilt with one of the interchangeable block patterns in the following pages, the background fabric requirements of the quilt pattern will be as listed in the quilt pattern chapter. The fabric requirements for the star portion of the block is listed in the Block Pattern pages.

When substituting background squares for a quilt top that uses the interchangeable blocks, refer to the chart below.

Single Block Cutting Chart

9″ BLOCK (SMALL)		14½″ BLOCK (LARGE)	
4 Blocks	8 Blocks	4 Blocks	8 Blocks
Cut 4 strips 9″ × WOF; subcut into 16 squares 9″ × 9″.	Cut 3 strips 9″ × WOF; subcut into 12 squares 9″ × 9″.	Cut 8 strips 14½″ × WOF; subcut into 16 squares 14½″ × 14½″.	Cut 6 strips 14½″ × WOF; subcut into 12 squares 14½″ × 14½″.

Lemoyne Star

SMALL BLOCK SIZE: 9″ × 9″ unfinished • LARGE BLOCK SIZE: 14½″ × 14½″ unfinished

The Lemoyne Star is a classic star block. It was first published in 1894 in Ohio Farmer, *an agricultural newspaper based in Cleveland, Ohio. I thought it was a good pattern to start with because it is so classic and is a good introduction to cutting and sewing diamonds and Y-seams.*

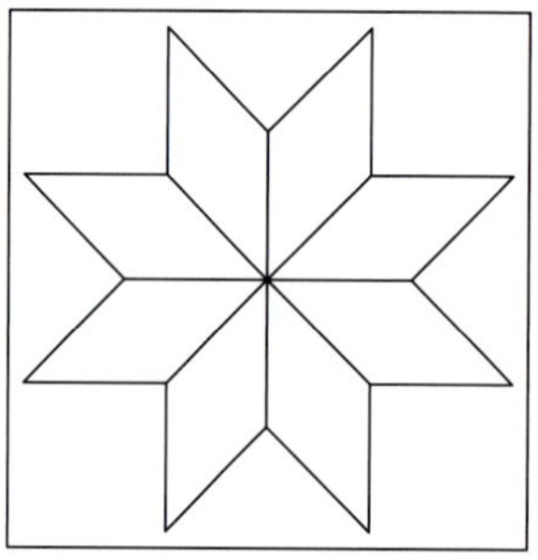

FABRIC REQUIREMENTS

Yardages are based on 42″ wide fabric. Yardage is provided based on the number of blocks you want to make.

FABRIC	9″ BLOCK (SMALL)			14½″ BLOCK (LARGE)		
	1 Block	4 Blocks	8 Blocks	1 Block	4 Blocks	8 Blocks
Fabric A	⅛ yard	¼ yard	⅜ yard	⅛ yard	¼ yard	½ yard
Background	¼ yard	⅜ yard	¾ yard	⅓ yard	¾ yard	1⅓ yards

CUTTING INSTRUCTIONS

9″ Block

FABRIC A

- Cut 1 strip 2″ × WOF; subcut into 8 diamonds 2″.

BACKGROUND

- Cut 1 square 6⅛″ × 6⅛″; subcut each square into 4 triangles by cutting along each diagonal.
- Cut 4 squares 3⅜″ × 3⅜″.

14½″ Block

FABRIC A

- Cut 1 strip 2½″ × WOF; subcut into 8 diamonds 2½″.

BACKGROUND

- Cut 1 square 9⅛″ × 9⅛″; subcut each square into 4 triangles by cutting along each diagonal.
- Cut 4 squares 5½″ × 5½″.

How to Cut Diamonds

Need a reminder on cutting diamonds? Check out these quick steps or refer to Cutting and Sewing Diamonds (page 18) as needed.

A

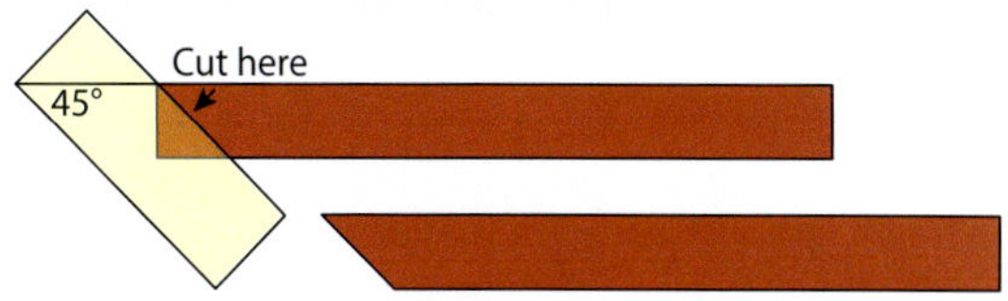

B

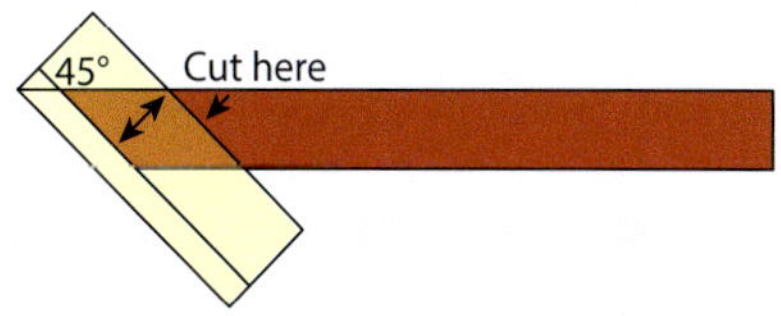

C

1. Line up the top or bottom of each strip with the 45° line on the ruler and cut off the selvage on the left side of the strip. *fig. A*

2. Line up the top or bottom of the strip with the 45° line on the ruler and line up the left side of the strip with the 2″ mark on the ruler (9″ block) or the 2½″ mark on your ruler (14½″ block) and cut. *fig. B*

3. Repeat Step 2 to cut 8 diamonds. *fig. C*

Block Assembly

DIAMOND PAIRS

1. Place 2 diamonds RST. On the wrong side of the top diamond, measure lines ¼″ from two edges that meet at one corner as shown. Make a mark where the lines intersect. Pin through the mark. *fig. A*

2. Start sewing at the top of the diamond, and stop sewing (with the needle down) at the mark from Step 1. Backstitch 2–3 stitches. Press the seam open. *fig. B*

3. Repeat Steps 1–2 to make 4 pairs of diamonds. *fig. C*

A

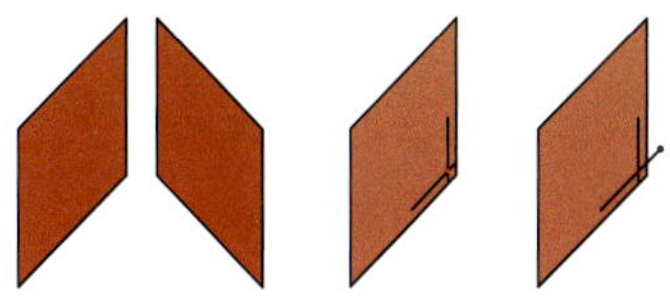

B

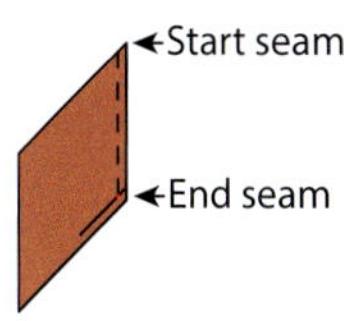

C

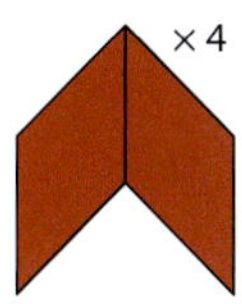

QUARTER UNIT ASSEMBLY

1. On the wrong side of each background triangle, measure lines ¼″ from two edges that meet at the top point as shown. Make a mark where the lines intersect. *fig. D*

2. Place a triangle RST with one of the diamond pairs. Align the mark from Step 1 with the place the seam ended in the diamond pair. Pin through the mark. *fig E*

D

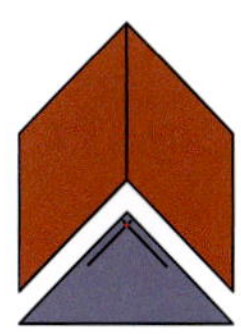

E

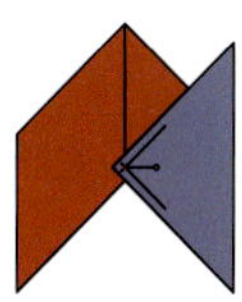

3. Start sewing at the outer edge of the block and stop sewing at the mark. Backstitch 2–3 stitches. *fig. F*

4. Flip the background triangle so it is RST with the adjacent side of the diamond pair. Align the mark from Step 1 with the place the seam ended in the diamond pair. Pin through the mark. *fig. G*

5. Start sewing at the outer edge of the block and stop sewing at the pinned mark from Step 4. Backstitch 2–3 stitches. *fig. H*

6. Press the seams open. Trim the dog ears. *fig. I*

7. Repeat Steps 2–6 to make 4 units. *fig. J*

STAR ASSEMBLY

1. Follow Steps 1–2 in Diamond Pairs (page 53) to sew the 4 quarter units into 2 halves. *figs. K–L*

2. Place the 2 halves RST. On the wrong side of the top half, measure lines ¼″ from two edges that meet at the two corners as shown. Make a mark where the lines intersect. Pin through the marks, and then through the center seam of both units. *figs.M–N*

3. Sew the halves together, starting at one mark and ending on the second mark. Backstitch 2–3 stitches at the beginning and end. Press the seam open. *figs. O–P*

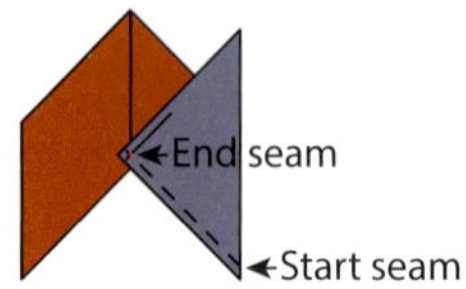

F

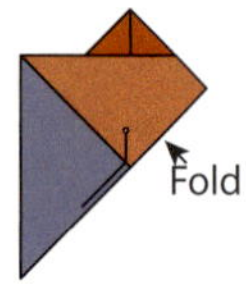

G

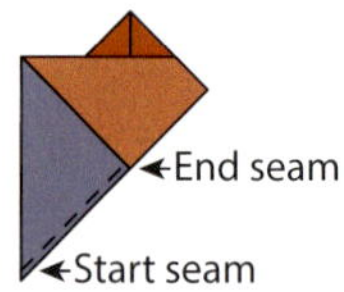

H

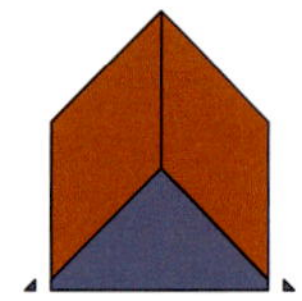
I

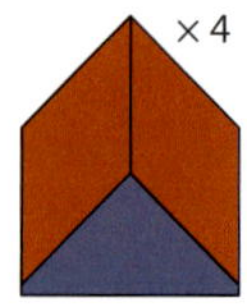

J

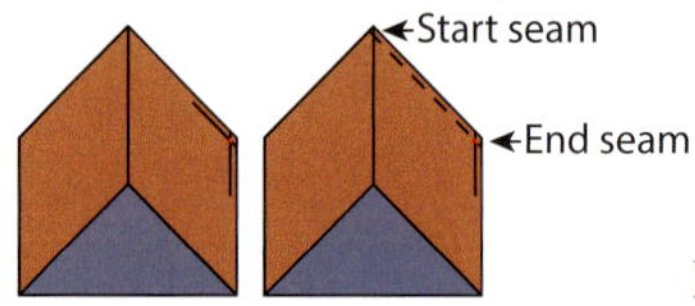

K

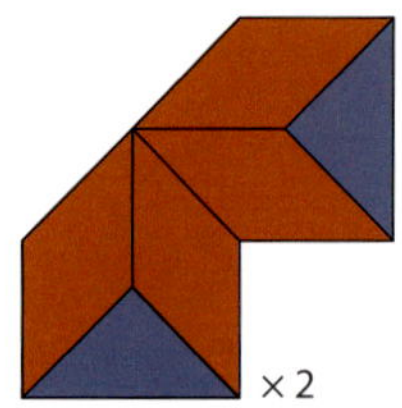

L

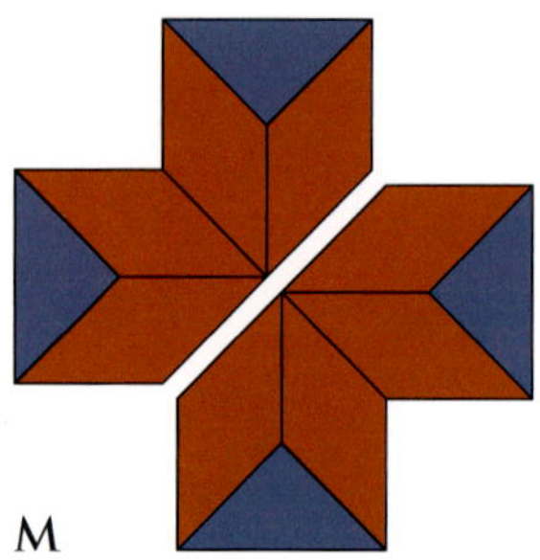
M

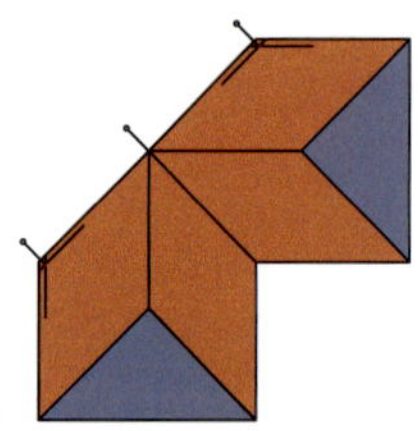
N

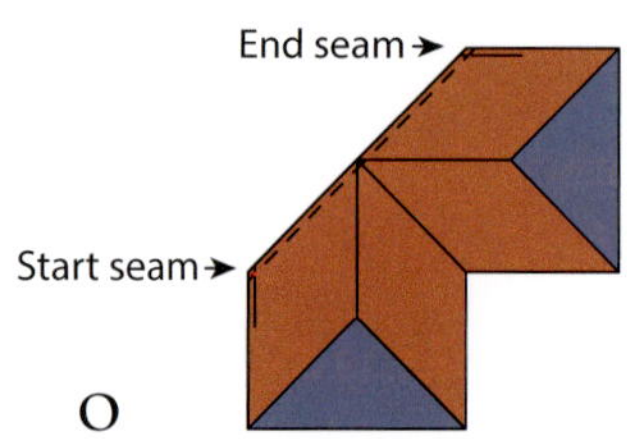

O

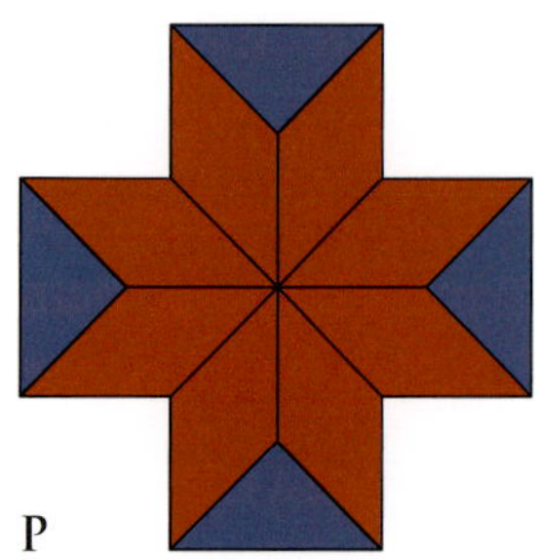
P

BACKGROUND SQUARE ASSEMBLY

1. On the wrong side of each background square, measure lines ¼″ from two edges that meet at one corner. Make a mark where the lines intersect. *fig. N*

2. Place a background square RST with the block as shown. Align the mark from Step 1 with the place where the seam ended in sewing the diamonds together. Pin through the mark. *fig. O*

3. Start sewing at the outer edge of the block and stop sewing at the pinned mark from Step 2. Backstitch 2–3 stitches. *fig. P*

4. Flip the background square so it is RST with the adjacent side of the block's corner. Align the mark from Step 1 with the place the seam ended in Step 3. Pin through the mark. *fig. Q*

5. Start sewing at the outer edge of the block and stop sewing at the pinned mark from Step 4. Backstitch 2–3 stitches. Press the seams open. *figs. R–S*

6. Repeat Steps 2–5 to attach the remaining 3 squares to the block. *fig. T*

7. Trim the block to 9″ × 9″ (small size) or 14½″ × 14½″ (large size).

FINISHED SIZE

Be sure there is at least ¼″ from each star point to the edge of the block so the points are not lost when adding the blocks to a quilt or finishing them in another project.

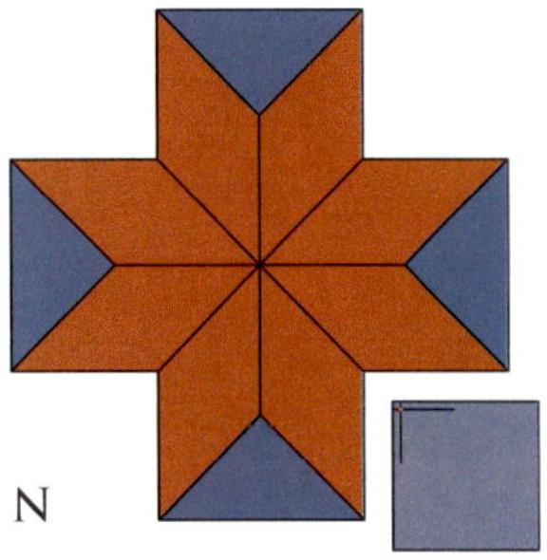

N

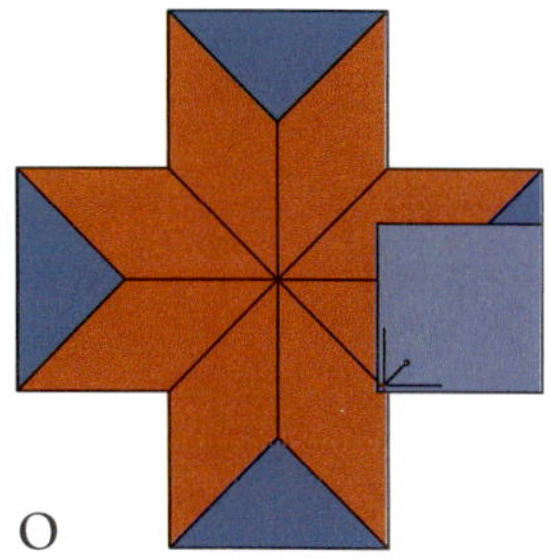

O

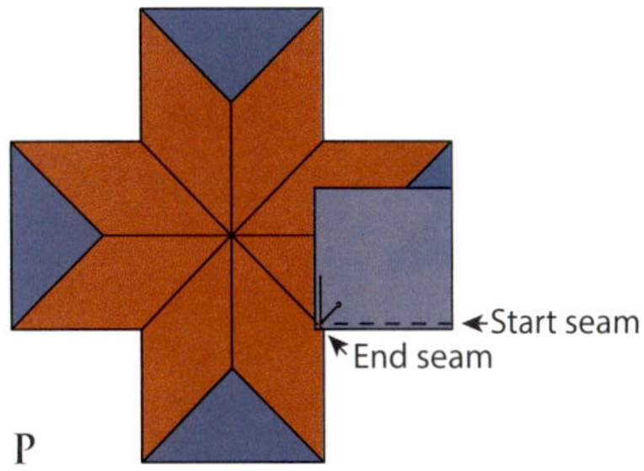

P

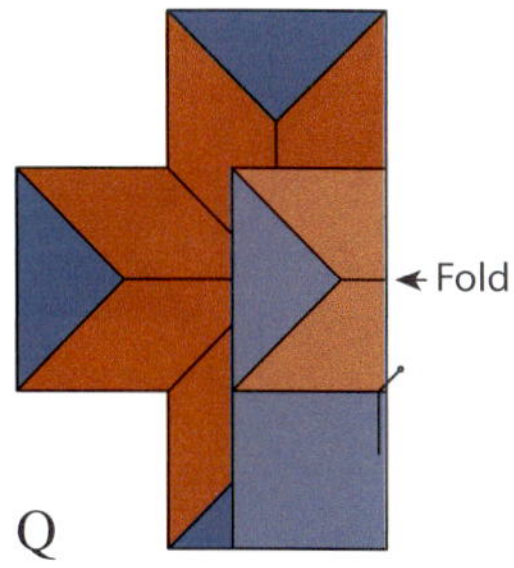

Q

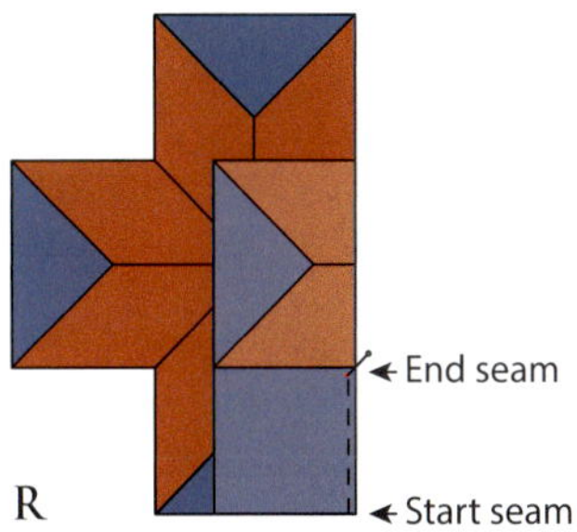

R

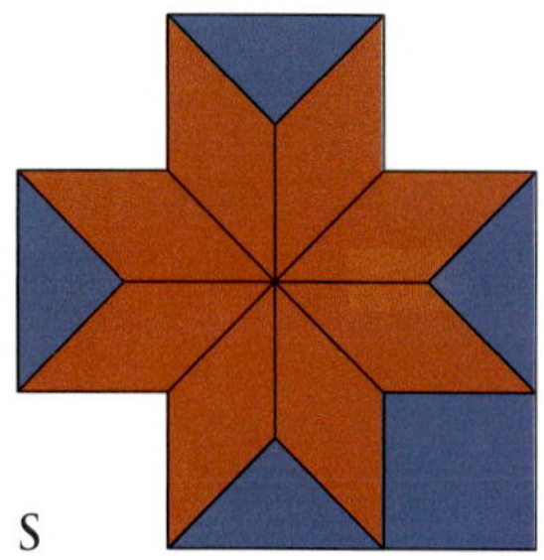

S

T

Fish Tails Star

SMALL BLOCK SIZE: 9″ × 9″ unfinished • LARGE BLOCK SIZE: 14½″ × 14½″ unfinished

Also known as the Double Star, the Fish Tails quilt block is made up of more diamonds than the Lemoyne Star, but does not require the diamond matching that the Lone Star does. This is a good block to learn how to strip piece and cut diamond strips—all skills that are used heavily in the quilt patterns.

FABRIC REQUIREMENTS

Yardages are based on 42″ wide fabric. Yardage is provided based on the number of blocks you want to make.

FABRIC	9″ BLOCK (SMALL)			14½″ BLOCK (LARGE)		
	1 Block	4 Blocks	8 Blocks	1 Block	4 Blocks	8 Blocks
Fabric A	1½″ × WOF	⅛ yard	¼ yard	2″ × WOF	¼ yard	⅜ yard
Fabric B	1½″ × WOF	⅛ yard	¼ yard	2″ × WOF	¼ yard	⅜ yard
Background	¼ yard	⅜ yard	⅝ yard	¼ yard	¾ yard	1⅜ yards

CUTTING INSTRUCTIONS

9″ Block

FABRIC A

- Cut 1 strip 1½″ × WOF; subcut into 2 strips 1½″ × 21″.

FABRIC B

- Cut 1 strip 1½″ × WOF; subcut into 2 strips 1½″ × 21″.

BACKGROUND

- Cut 1 square 5¼″ × 5¼″; subcut each square into 4 triangles by cutting along each diagonal.
- Cut 4 squares 4″ × 4″.

14½″ Block

FABRIC A

- Cut 1 strip 2″ × WOF; subcut into 2 strips 2″ × 21″.

FABRIC B

- Cut 1 strip 2″ × WOF; subcut into 2 strips 2″ × 21″.

BACKGROUND

- Cut 1 square 7″ × 7″; subcut each square into 4 triangles by cutting along each diagonal.
- Cut 4 squares 6¼″ × 6¼″.

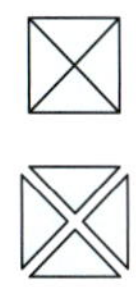

Block Assembly

DIAMOND STRIP PAIRS

1. Place an A strip and a B strip RST. Offset the strips by 2″. Sew the strips together along one long side and press the seams open. Repeat with the other 2 A and B strips, switching which strip is offset. *figs. A–B*

2. Line up the seam on each strip set with the 45° line on the ruler, and trim off the selvages and offset fabric. The cuts should be mirrored. *figs. C–D*

A

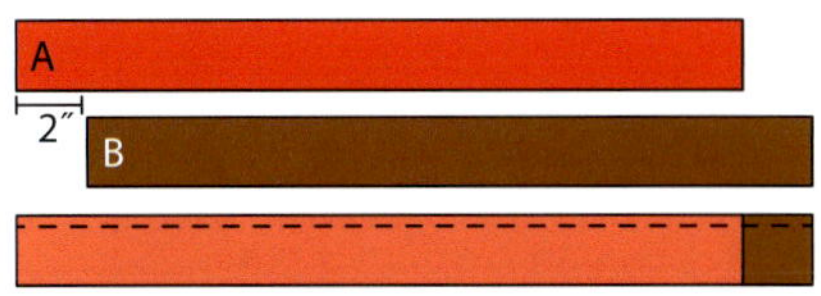

B

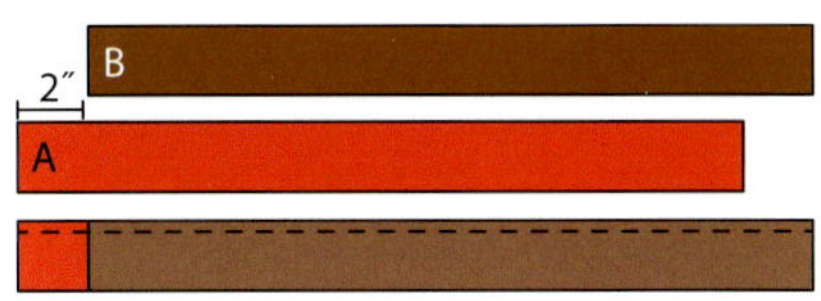

C

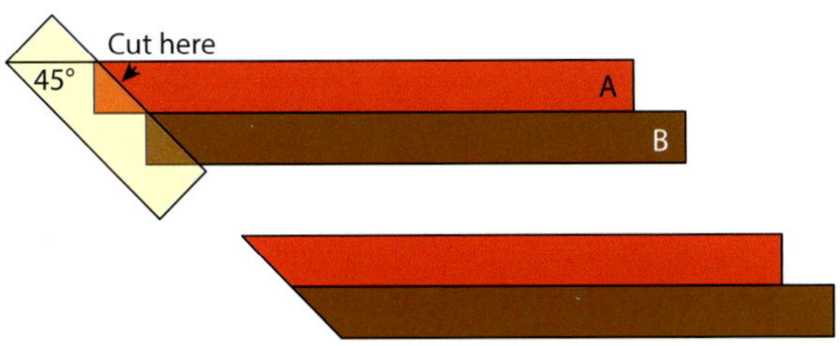

D

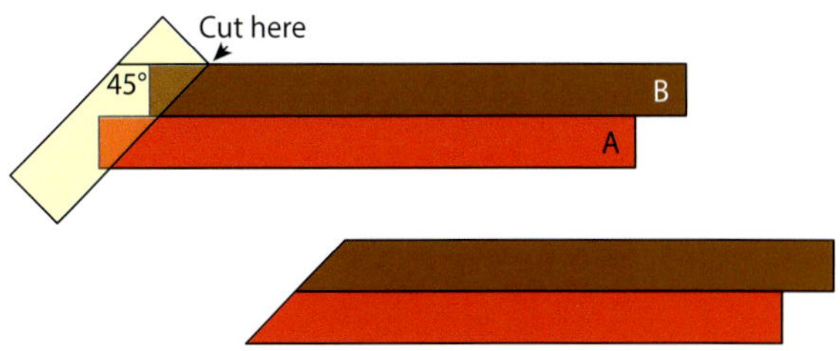

3. Line up the seam on each strip set with the 45° line on the ruler, and the left side of the strip with the 1½″ mark on the ruler (9″ block) or 2″ mark on the ruler (14½″ block). Cut 4 diamonds from each strip set. *figs. E–G*

4. Place 2 diamonds (mirrored) RST. On the wrong side of the top diamond, measure lines ¼″ from two edges that meet at one corner as shown. Make a mark where the lines intersect. Pin through the mark. *fig. H*

5. Start sewing at the top of the diamond and stop sewing (with the needle down) at the mark from Step 4. Backstitch 2–3 stitches. Press the seam open. *fig. I*

6. Repeat Steps 4–5 to make 4 pairs of diamonds. *fig. J*

QUARTER UNIT ASSEMBLY

1. On the wrong side of each background triangle, measure lines ¼″ from two edges that meet at the top point as shown. Make a mark where the lines intersect. *fig. K*

2. Place 1 triangle RST with one of the diamond pairs. Align the mark from Step 1 with the place the seam ended in the diamond pair. Pin through the mark. *fig. L*

3. Start sewing at the outer edge of the block and stop sewing at the mark. Backstitch 2–3 stitches. *fig. M*

4. Flip the background triangle so it is RST with the adjacent side of the diamond pair. Align the mark from Step 1 with the place the seam ended in the diamond pair. Pin through the mark. *fig. N*

E

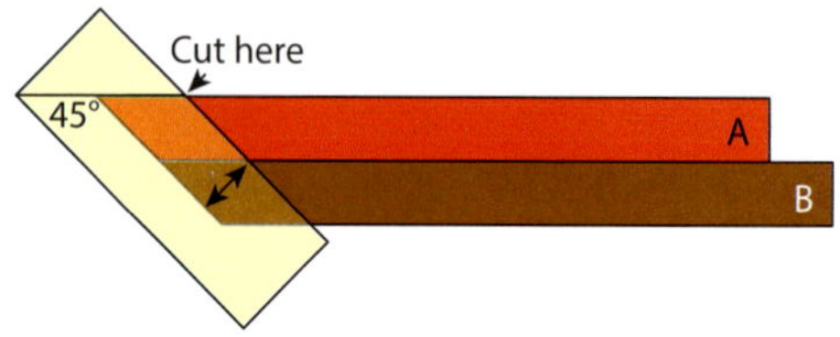

F

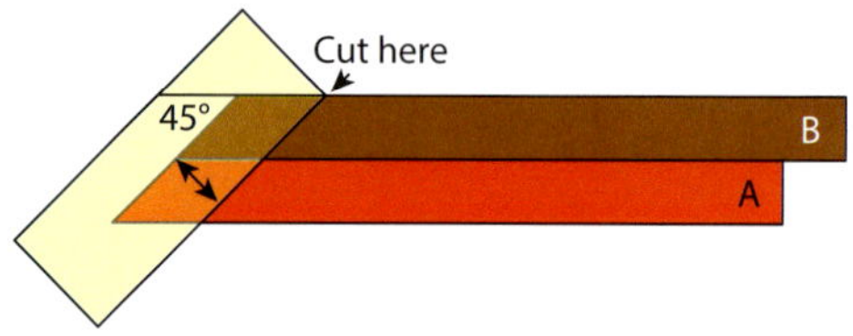

G

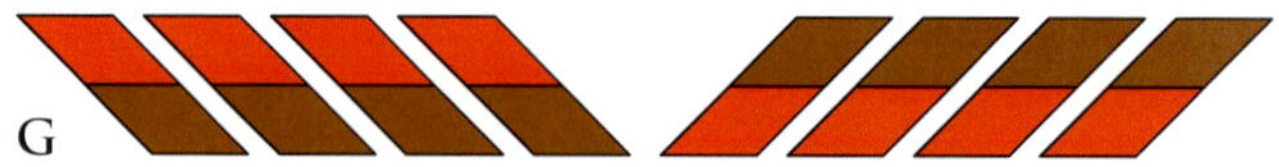

H

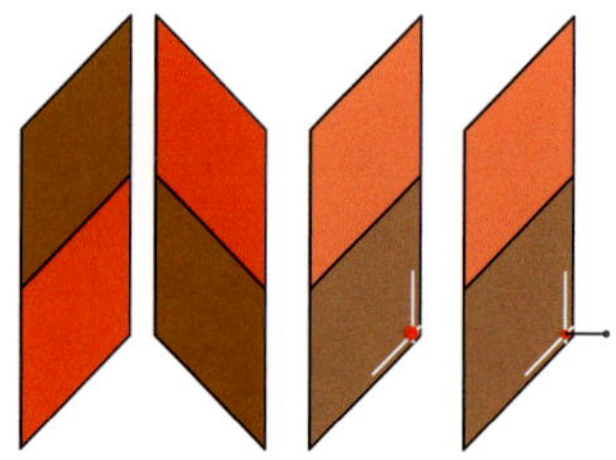

I

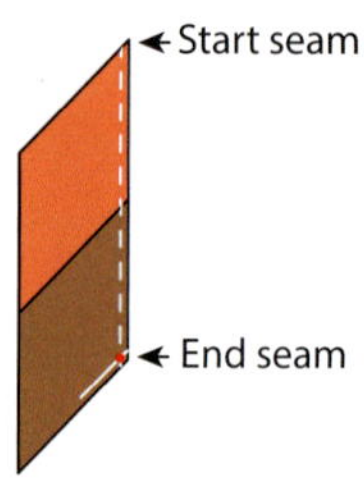

J

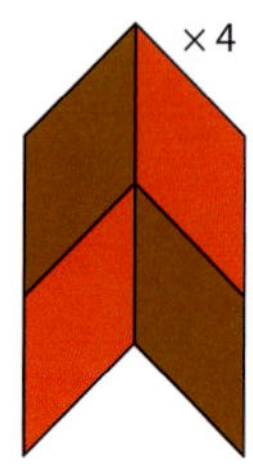

K

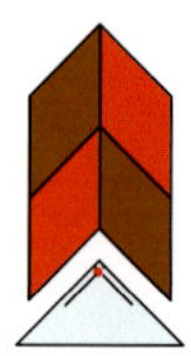

L

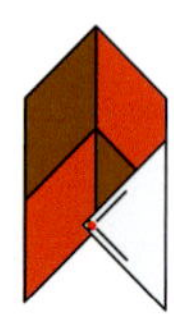

M

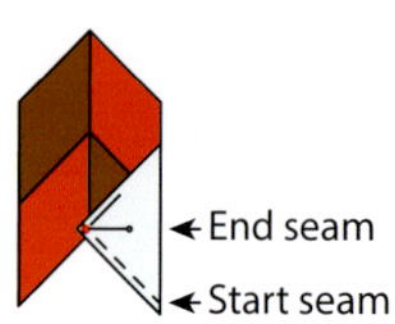

N

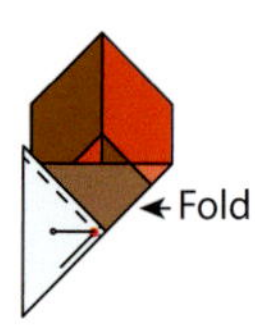

O
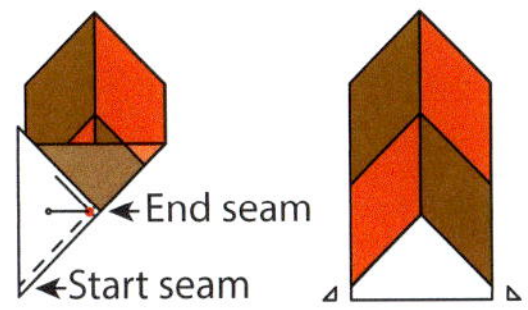

P
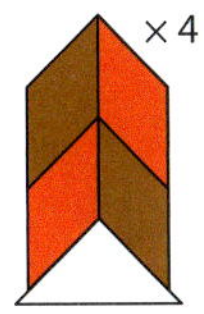

Q
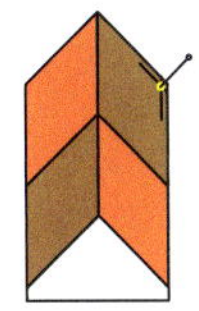

R
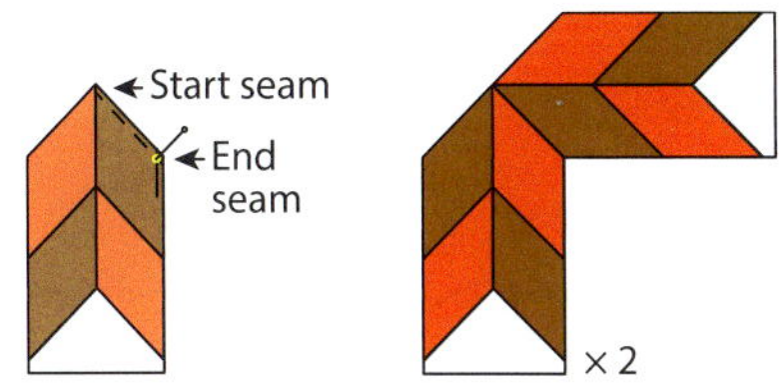

5. Start sewing at the outer edge of the block and stop sewing at the pinned mark from Step 4. Backstitch 2–3 stitches. *fig. O*

6. Press the seams open. Trim the dog ears.

7. Repeat Steps 2–6 to make 4 units. *fig. P*

FINAL ASSEMBLY

1. Place 2 quarter units RST. On the wrong side of the top right diamond, measure lines ¼″ from the two edges that meet at the once corner as shown. Make a mark where the lines intersect. Pin through the mark. *fig. Q*

2. Start sewing at the top of the diamond and stop sewing (with the needle down) at the mark from Step 1. Backstitch 2–3 stitches. Press the seam open. *fig. R*

3. Follow Steps 2–3 in Lemoyne Star, Star Assembly (page 54) to assemble the star. *fig. S*

4. Follow Steps 1–6 in Lemoyne Star, Background Square Assembly (page 55) to finish assembling the block. *figs. T–V*

5. Trim the block to 9″ × 9″ (small size) or 14½″ × 14½″ (large size). *fig. W*

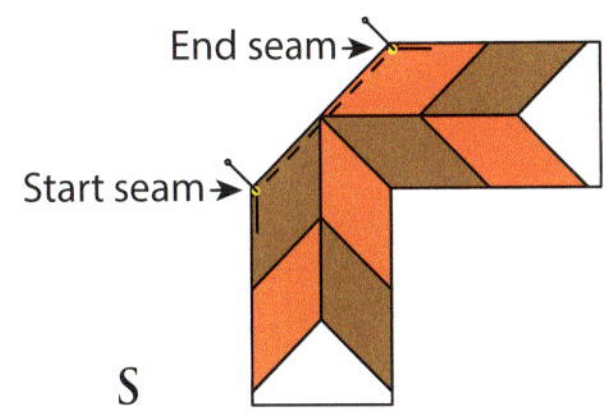

S

T

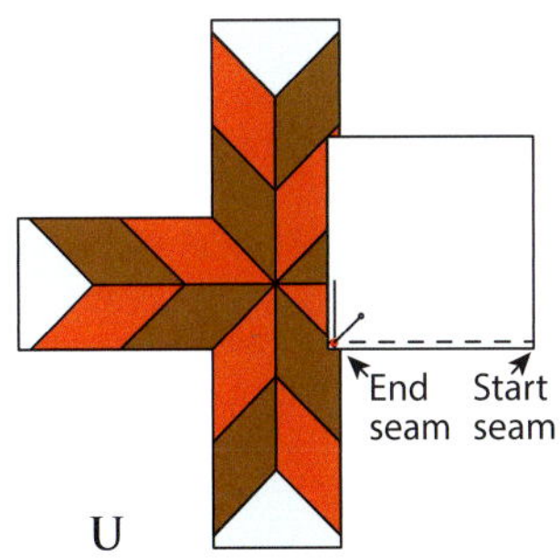

U

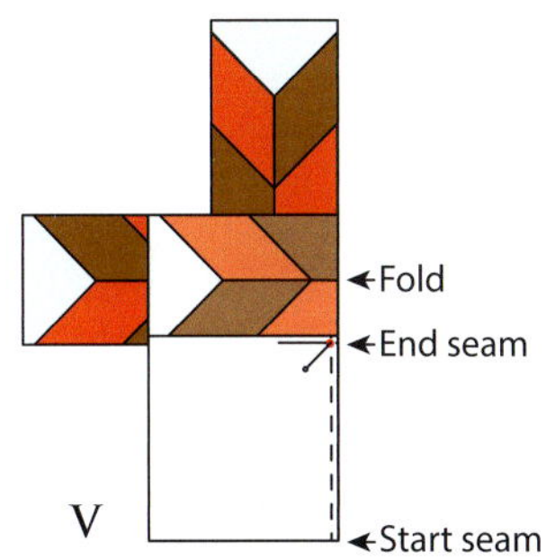

V

W

> **FINISHED SIZE**
> *Be sure there is at least ¼″ from each star point to the edge of the block so the points are not lost when adding the blocks to a quilt or finishing them in another project.*

LONE STAR

SMALL BLOCK SIZE: 9″ × 9″ unfinished • LARGE BLOCK SIZE: 14½″ × 14½″ unfinished

The Lone Star is another classic block known by many names—Blazing Star, Star of the East, Morning Star, and more. This block requires the same skills as the Lemoyne Star, and also adds the skill of matching and sewing diamond points.

FABRIC REQUIREMENTS

Yardages are based on 42″ wide fabric. Yardage is provided based on the number of blocks you want to make.

FABRIC	9″ BLOCK (SMALL)			14½″ BLOCK (LARGE)		
	1 Block	4 Blocks	8 Blocks	1 Block	4 Blocks	8 Blocks
Fabric A	1¼″ × WOF	⅛ yard	¼ yard	1½″ × WOF	⅛ yard	¼ yard
Fabric B	1¼″ × WOF	¼ yard	⅜ yard	1½ × WOF	¼ yard	⅜ yard
Fabric C	1¼″ × WOF	⅛ yard	¼ yard	1½ × WOF	⅛ yard	¼ yard
Background	¼ yard	⅜ yard	⅝ yard	⅓ yard	⅝ yard	1½ yards

CUTTING INSTRUCTIONS

9″ Block

FABRIC A

- Cut 1 strip 1¼″ × WOF.

FABRIC B

- Cut 2 strips 1¼″ × WOF.

FABRIC C

- Cut 1 strip 1¼″ × WOF.

BACKGROUND

- Cut 1 square 6⅛″ × 6⅛″; subcut each square into 4 triangles by cutting along each diagonal.

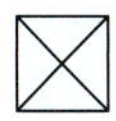

- Cut 4 squares 3⅜″ × 3⅜″.

14½″ Block

FABRIC A

- Cut 1 strip 1½″ × WOF.

FABRIC B

- Cut 2 strips 1½″ × WOF.

FABRIC C

- Cut 1 strip 1½″ × WOF.

BACKGROUND

- Cut 4 squares 5½″ × 5½″.

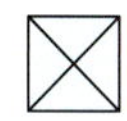

- Cut 1 square 9⅛″ × 9⅛″; subcut each square into 4 triangles by cutting along each diagonal.

Block Assembly

DIAMOND STRIPS

1. Place 1 A strip and 1 B strip RST. Offset the strips by 1½″ as shown. Place 1 B strip and 1 C strip RST. Offset the strips by 1½″ as shown. Sew the strips together along one long side, and press the seams open. *figs. A–B*

2. Line up the seam on each strip set with the 45° line on the ruler, and trim off the selvages and offset fabric. *figs. C–D*

A

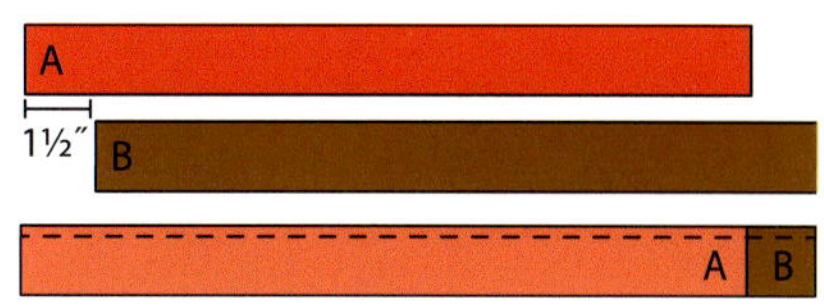

B

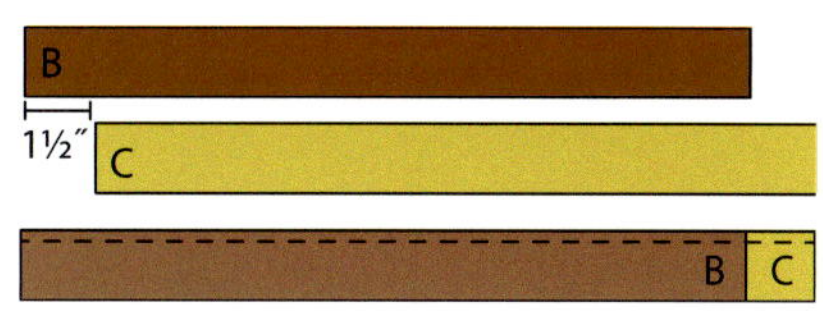

C

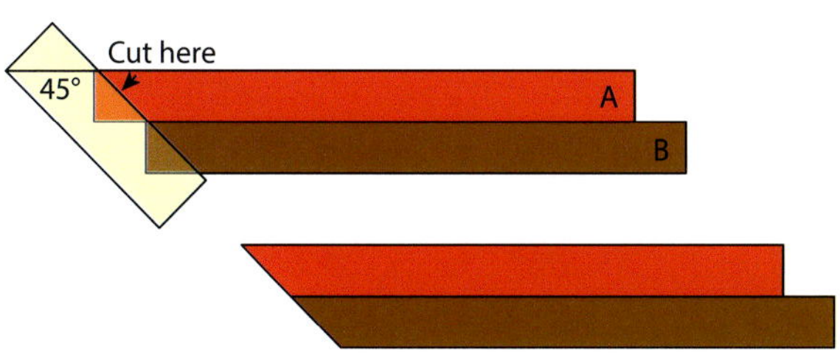

D

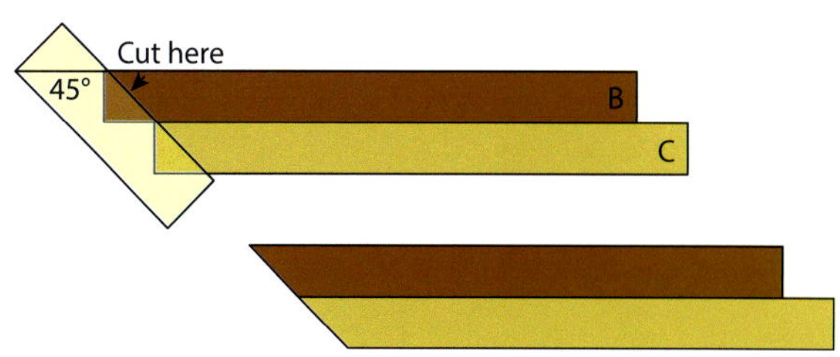

3. Line up the seam on each strip set with the 45° line on the ruler, and the left side of the strip with the 1¼″ mark on the ruler (9″ block) or 1½″ mark on the ruler (14½″ block). Cut 8 diamonds from each strip set. *figs. E–G*

DIAMOND ASSEMBLY

1. On the right side of each A/B diamond strip, measure ¼″ from the edge of the fabric on the seam. Make a mark. Repeat on the wrong side of each B/C diamond strip. *fig. H*

2. Place an A/B diamond strip and B/C diamond strip RST. Insert a pin directly through the marks from Step 1 on each strip. *fig. I*

3. Sew the diamond strips together. Press the seam open. Repeat to make 8 total diamonds. *fig. J*

DIAMOND PAIRS

Follow Steps 1–2 in Lemoyne Star, Diamond Pairs (page 53) to make 4 diamond pairs. *figs. K–M*

QUARTER UNIT ASSEMBLY

Follow Steps 1–6 in Lemoyne Star, Quarter Unit Assembly (page 53) to make 4 quarter units. *figs. N–Q*

E

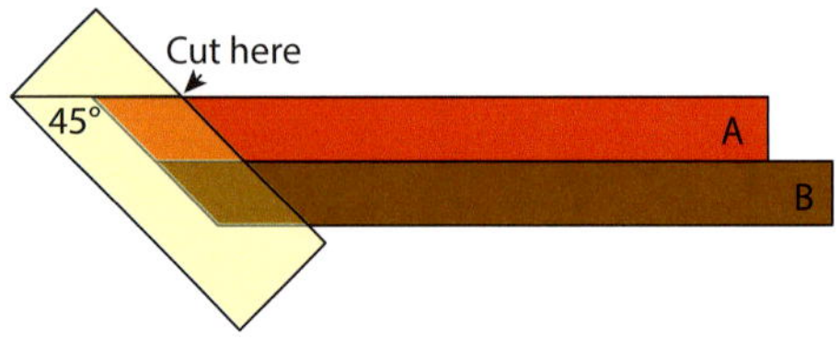

F

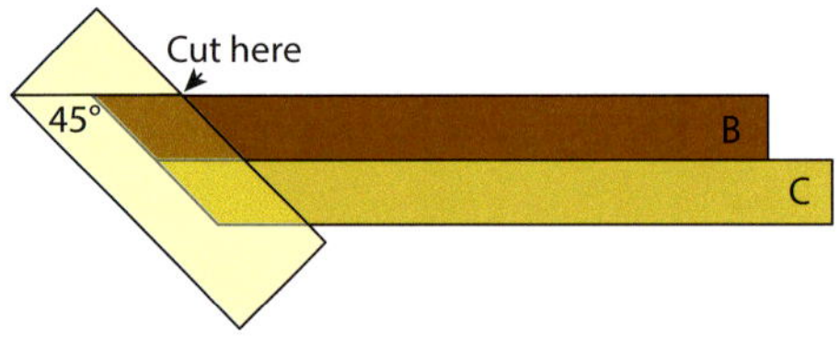

G

H

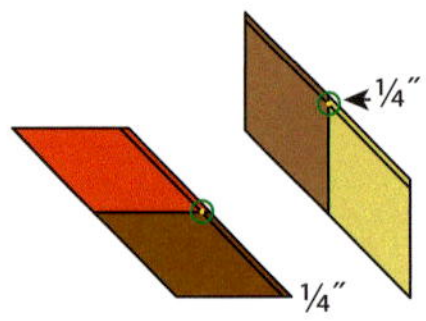

I

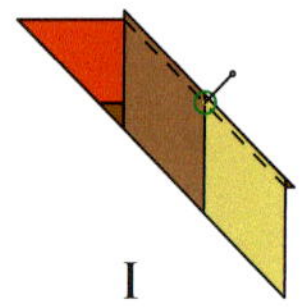

J

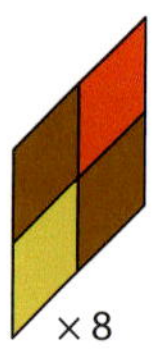

K

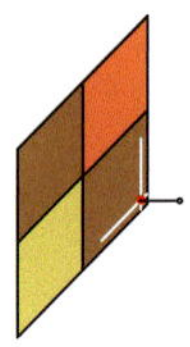

L

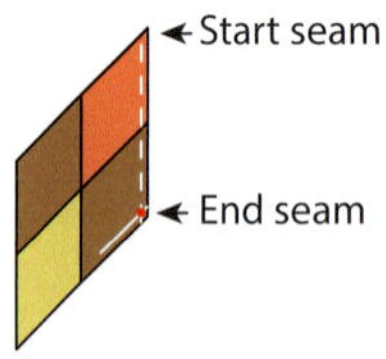

M

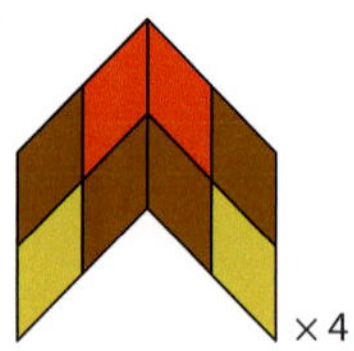

N

O

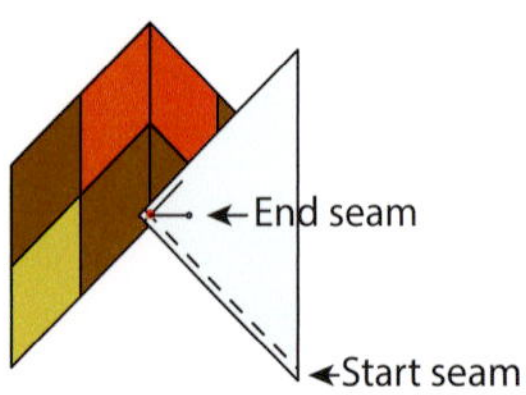

P

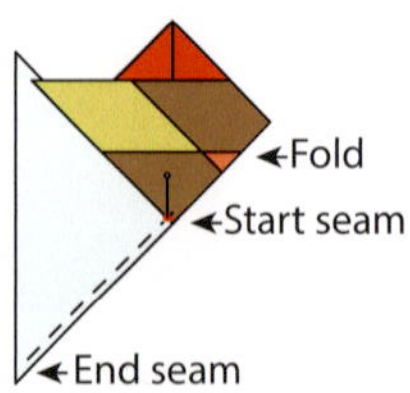

Q

FINAL ASSEMBLY

1. Follow Steps 1–3 in Lemoyne Star, Star Assembly (page 54) to assemble the star. *figs. R–V*

2. Follow Steps 1–6 in Lemoyne Star, Background Square Assembly (page 55) to finish assembling the block. *figs. W–Y*

3. Trim the block to 9″ × 9″ (small size) or 14½″ × 14½″ (large size). *fig. Z*

> **FINISHED SIZE**
> *Be sure there is at least ¼″ from each star point to the edge of the block so the points are not lost when adding the blocks to a quilt or finishing them in another project.*

R

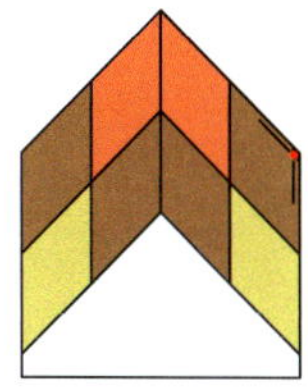
S

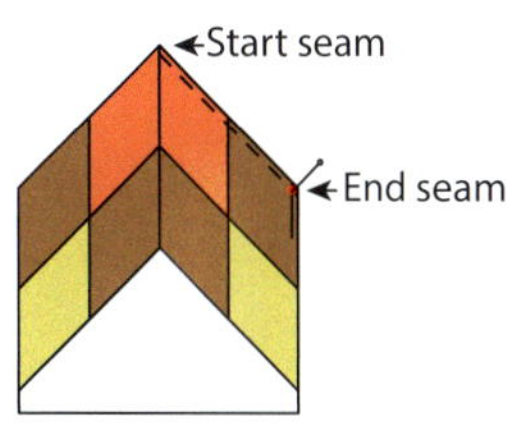

T

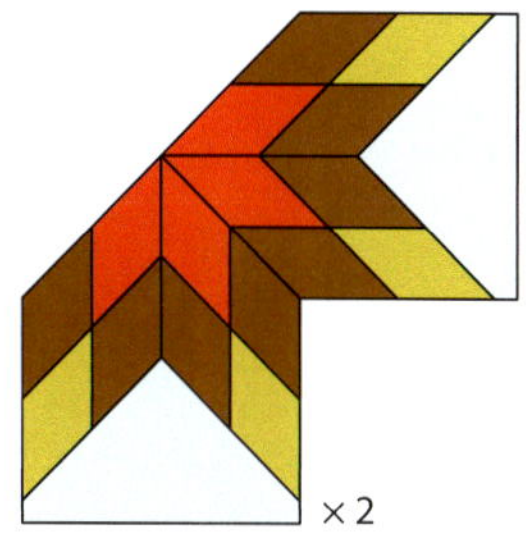

U

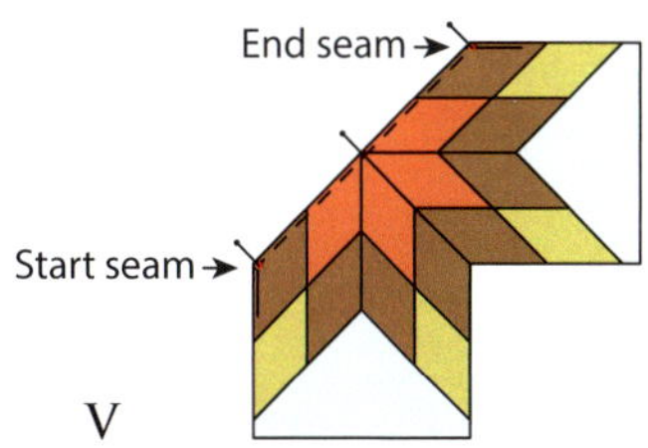

V

W

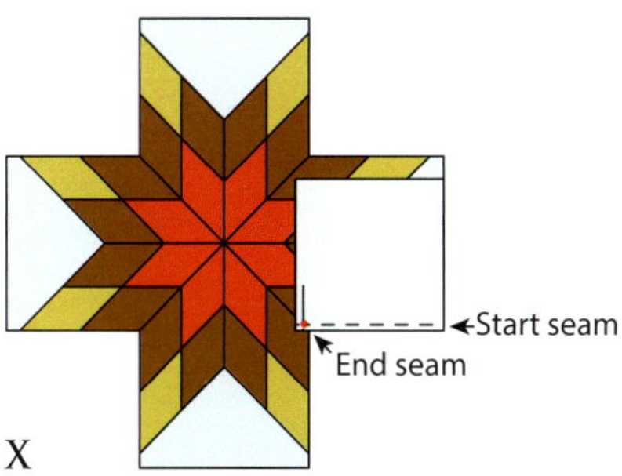

X

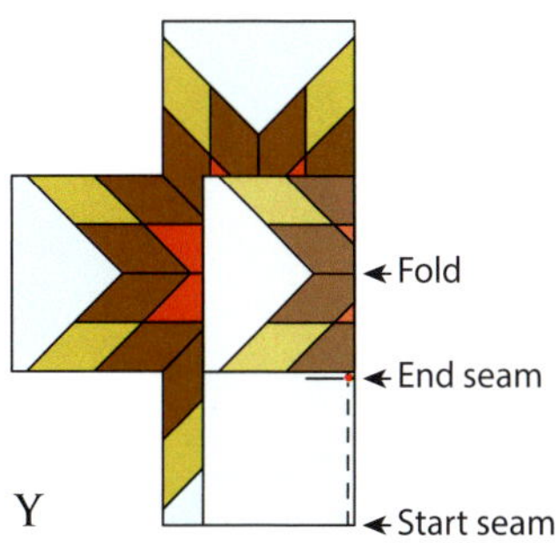

Y

Z

WINDOW STAR

SMALL BLOCK SIZE: 9″ × 9″ unfinished • LARGE BLOCK SIZE: 14½″ × 14½″ unfinished

The Window Star block is a close relative of the Lone Star block. The construction looks potentially complicated but comes together quickly because it does not require matching diamond points.

FABRIC REQUIREMENTS

Yardages are based on 42″ wide fabric. Yardage is provided based on the number of blocks you want to make.

FABRIC	9″ BLOCK (SMALL)			14½″ BLOCK (LARGE)		
	1 Block	4 Blocks	8 Blocks	1 Block	4 Blocks	8 Blocks
Fabric A	1¼″ × WOF	⅛ yard	¼ yard	1½″ × WOF	⅛ yard	¼ yard
Fabric B	⅛ yard	¼ yard	½ yard	⅛ yard	⅓ yard	⅝ yard
Background	¼ yard	⅜ yard	⅝ yard	⅓ yard	⅝ yard	1½ yards

CUTTING INSTRUCTIONS

9″ Block

FABRIC A

- Cut 1 strip 1¼″ × WOF.

FABRIC B

- Cut 1 strip 2″ × WOF.
- Cut 1 strip 1¼″ × WOF.

BACKGROUND

- Cut 1 square 6⅛″ × 6⅛″; subcut each square into 4 triangles by cutting along each diagonal.

- Cut 4 squares 3⅜″ × 3⅜″.

14½″ Block

FABRIC A

- Cut 1 strip 1½″ × WOF.

FABRIC B

- Cut 1 strip 1½″ × WOF.
- Cut 1 strip 2½″ × WOF.

BACKGROUND

- Cut 1 square 9⅛″ × 9⅛″; subcut each square into 4 triangles by cutting along each diagonal.

- Cut 4 squares 5½″ × 5½″.

Block Assembly

DIAMOND STRIP PAIRS

1. Place the A strip and the same width B strip RST. Offset the strips by 1½″. Sew the strips together along one long side and press the seams open. *fig. A*

2. Line up the seam on the strip set with the 45° line on the ruler, and trim off the selvages and offset fabric. *fig. B*

3. Line up the seam on each strip set with the 45° line on the ruler, and the left side of the strip with the 1¼″ mark on the ruler (9″ block) or 1½″ mark on the ruler (14½″ block). Cut 8 diamonds from the strip set. *fig. C*

4. Line up the top or bottom of the remaining B strip with the 45° line on the ruler, and trim off the selvages. *fig. D*

5. Line up the top or bottom of the B strip with the 45° line on the ruler and the left side of the strip with the 1¼″ mark on the ruler (9″ block) or 1½″ mark on the ruler (14½″ block). Cut 8 diamonds from the strip. *fig. E*

DIAMOND UNITS

1. Place an A/B diamond strip and B strip RST, offset by ¼″. *fig. F*

2. Sew the diamonds together. Press the seam open.

3. Repeat Steps 1–2 to make 8 total diamonds. *fig. G*

DIAMOND PAIRS

Follow Steps 1–2 in Lemoyne Star, Diamond Pairs (page 53) to make 4 diamond pairs with the 8 diamonds from Diamond Units (above). *figs. H–J*

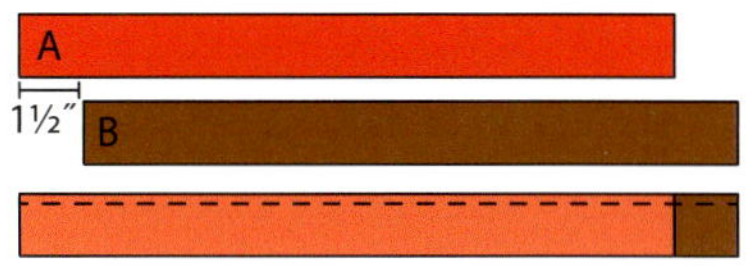

A

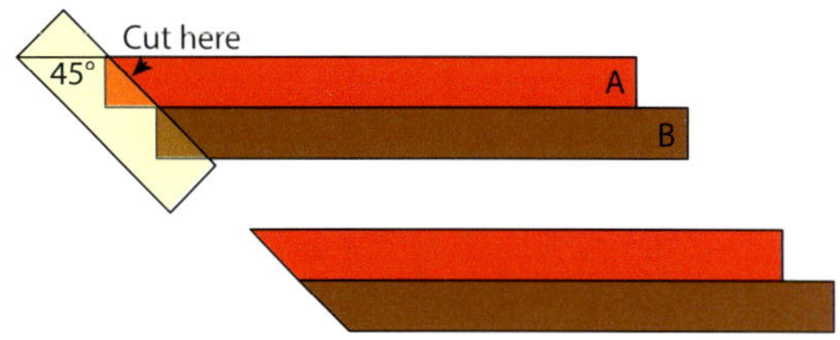

B

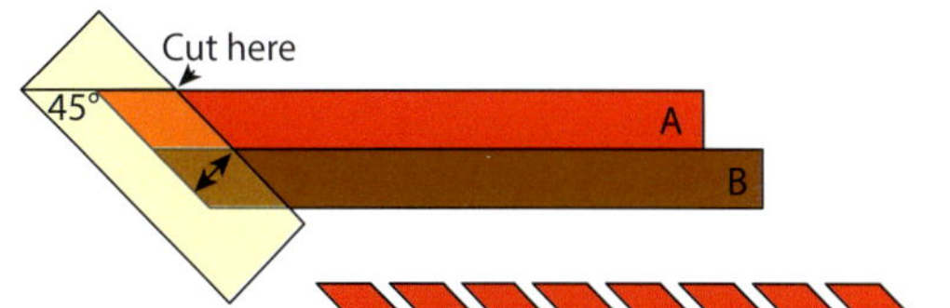

C

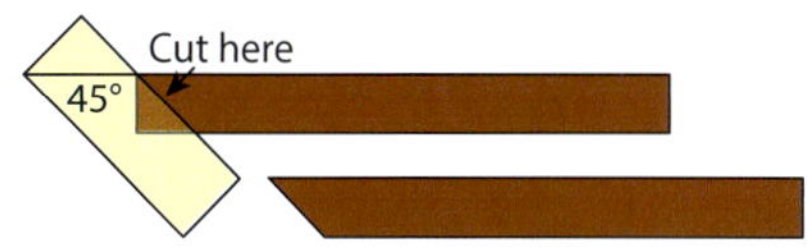

D

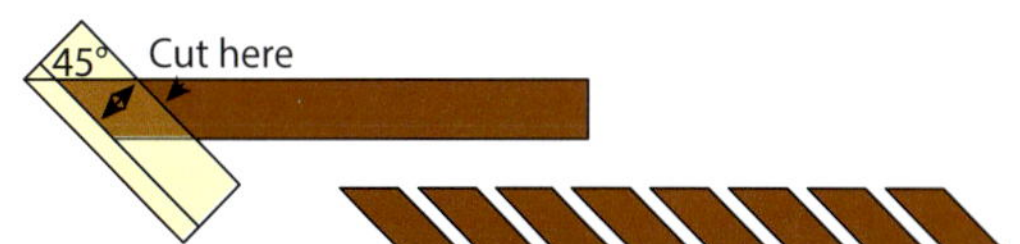

E

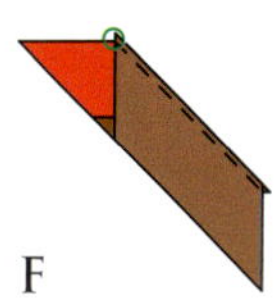
F

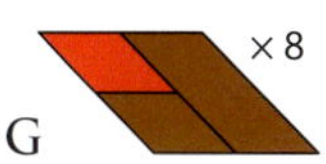

G

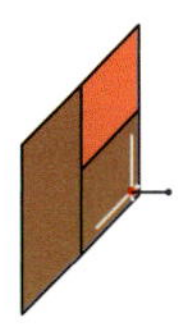
H

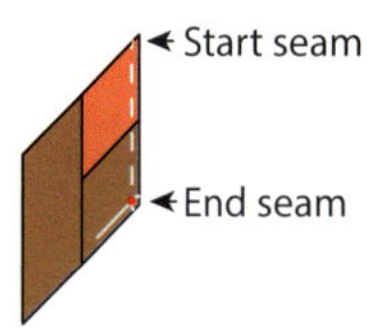

I

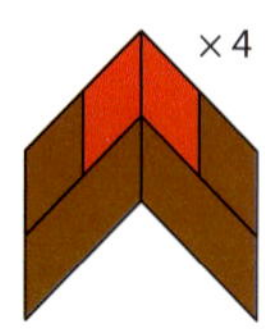

J

QUARTER UNIT ASSEMBLY

Follow Steps 1–6 in Lemoyne Star Quarter Unit Assembly (page 53) to make 4 quarter units. *figs. K–O*

FINAL ASSEMBLY

1. Follow Steps 1–3 in Lemoyne Star, Star Assembly (page 54) to assemble the star. *figs. P–T*

2. Follow Steps 1–6 in Lemoyne Star, Background Square Assembly (page 55) to finish assembling the block. *figs. U–W*

3. Trim the block to 9″ × 9″ (small size) or 14½″ × 14½″ (large size). *fig. X*

> **FINISHED SIZE**
>
> *Be sure there is at least ¼″ from each star point to the edge of the block so the points are not lost when adding the blocks to a quilt or finishing them in another project.*

K

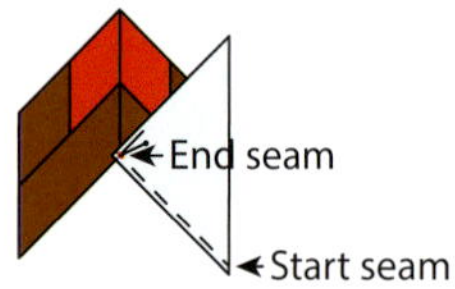

L

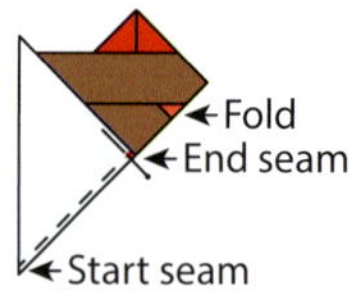

M

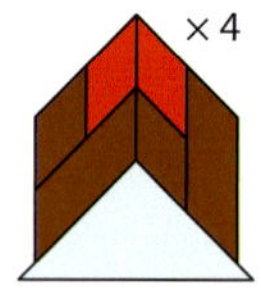

N

O

P

Q

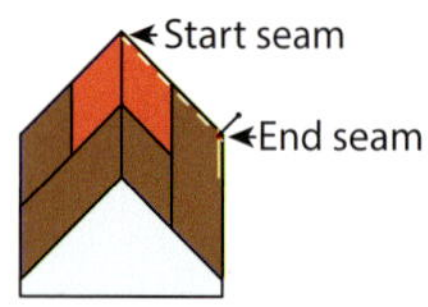

R

S

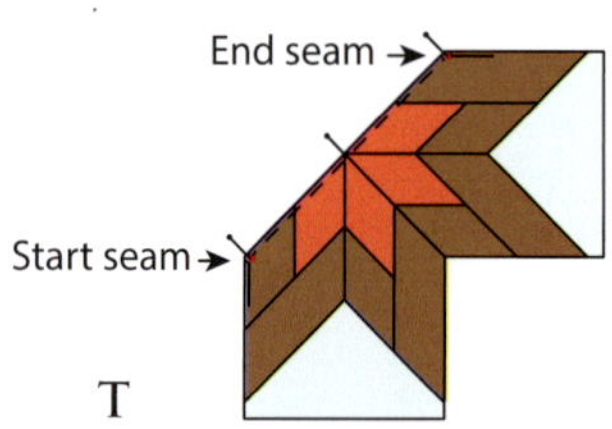

T

U

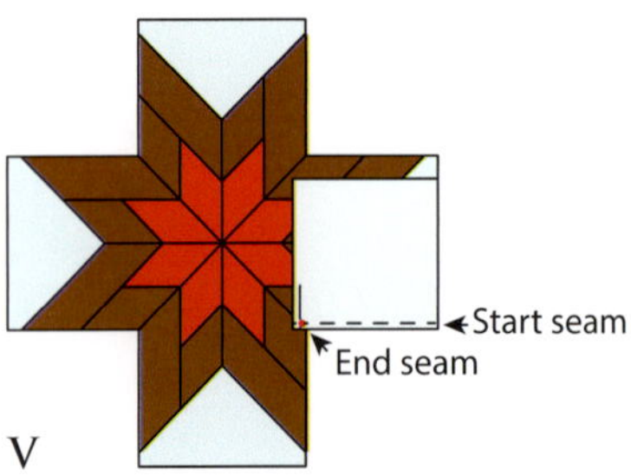

V

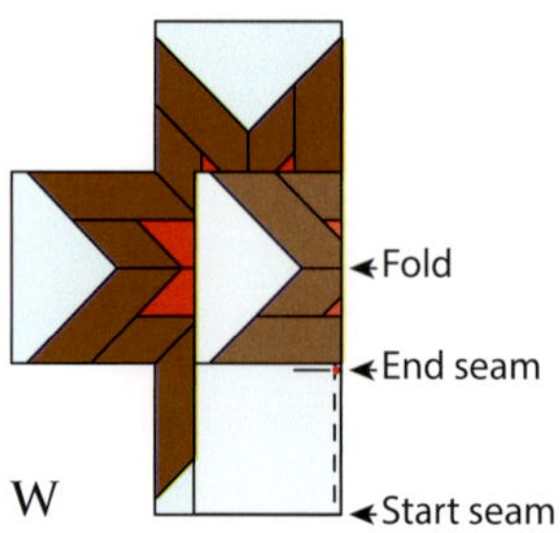

W

X

SINGLE BLOCK PROJECTS

If you've made a pile of star blocks to practice your diamond and Y-seam sewing skills, you might be looking for something to do with them! These cute, simpler, and faster single block projects give you a way to show off your star block skills even before you've tackled a whole quilt.

Tote Bag

FINISHED TOTE SIZE: 11″ wide × 13″ tall × 4″ deep

From trips to the grocery store and the library to carrying your hand sewing projects or traveling—you can never have enough tote bags! Tote bags are also one of my favorite handmade gifts to make. Need a gift for the person who has everything? Well, I bet they could use another tote bag.

The fabric and cutting charts include options for making the tote bag from either size single block and include both quilted and non-quilted options.

MATERIALS

BLOCK SIZE	9″ BLOCK		14½″ BLOCK	
Bag Type	Quilted Bag	Not Quilted Bag	Quilted Bag	Not Quilted Bag
Block	1 block 9″ × 9″	1 block 9″ × 9″	1 block 14½″ × 14½″	1 block 14½″ × 14½″
Background (to match block background)	⅓ yard	¼ yard	¼ yard	⅛ yard
Backing (optional)	2 squares 20″ × 20″	-	2 squares 20″ × 20″	-
Lining	2 squares 16″ × 16″	2 squares 16″ × 16″	2 squares 16″ × 16″	2 squares 16″ × 16″
Tote Back	1 square 20″ × 20″	1 squares 16″ × 16″	1 square 20″ × 20″	1 square 16″ × 16″
Batting	2 squares 24″ × 24″	-	2 squares 24″ × 24″	-
Webbing (1″ wide)	2 pieces 28″ long	2 pieces 28″ long	2 pieces 28″ long	2 pieces 28″ long

CUTTING INSTRUCTIONS

BLOCK SIZE	9″ BLOCK		14½″ BLOCK	
Bag Type	Quilted Bag	Not Quilted Bag	Quilted Bag	Not Quilted Bag
Background	Cut 2 strips 6″ × 9″; Cut 2 strips 6″ × 20″	Cut 2 strips 4″ × 9″; Cut 2 strips 4″ × 16″	Cut 2 strips 3¼″ × 14½″; Cut 2 strips 3¼″ × 20″	Cut 2 strips 1¼″ × 14½″; Cut 2 strips 1¼″ × 16″

Sewing Instructions

PREPARE THE BLOCKS

1. Sew the 2 shorter background fabric strips to opposite sides of the block. Press seams open.

2. Sew the remaining, longer background pieces to the remaining 2 sides of the block. Press seams open.

QUILT (OPTIONAL)

1. Baste both the star block and tote back with a batting piece and backing piece. Quilt as desired (see Finishing the Quilts, page 42). *fig. A*

A

I used a block for each side of the bag instead of the tote back square.

OPTIONAL!

You do not have to quilt with backing fabric because the tote is lined. I used backing fabric because I had my bag pieces longarm quilted, which required the use of a backing.

2. Trim the excess batting and lining fabric, making squares 16″ × 16″. *fig. B*

B

C

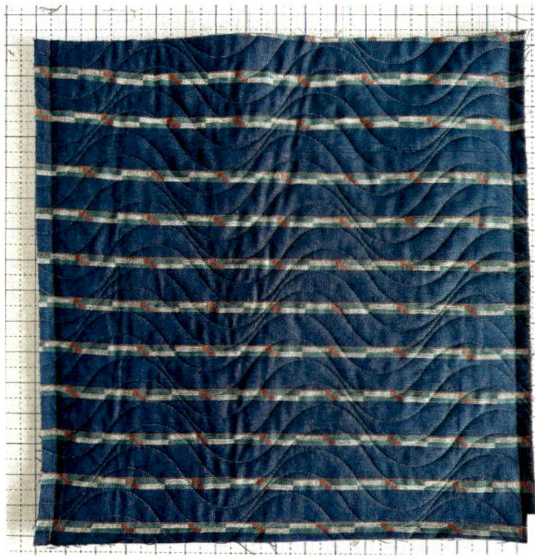
D

E

ASSEMBLY

The assembly instructions show a quilted bag.

1. Lay the block and tote back RST, aligning the raw edges. *fig. C*

2. Pin around the edges and sew around the sides and bottom with a ½″ seam allowance, leaving the top edge open. *fig. D*

3. Lay the lining pieces RST, aligning the raw edges. Pin the edges and sew around the sides and bottom with a ½″ seam, leaving a 6″ opening on the bottom edge. *fig. E*

4. Flatten the corner of the lining so it forms a triangle with the seam in the center. Align the seams in opposite directions on either side of the corner so they nest together. Place a ruler on the seam and adjust so that it measures 4″ from one edge of the triangle to the other. Draw a line. Repeat on the other corner of the lining and both corners of the bag exterior. *figs. F–H*

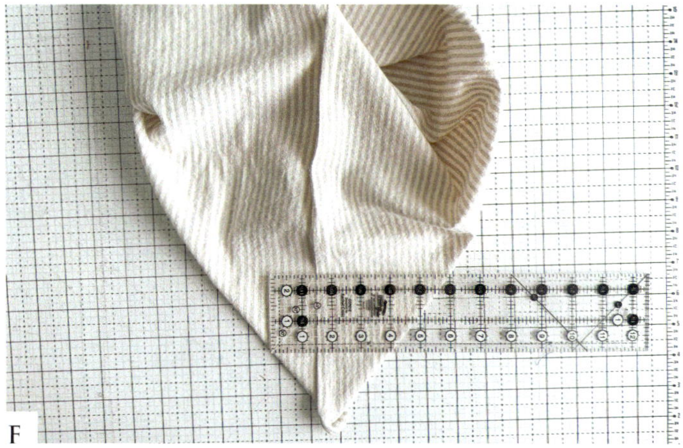
F

G

H

I

J

K

5. Sew along the marked lines, and then cut off the corners, leaving ¼″ seam allowance from the line. *fig. I*

6. Turn the exterior of the bag right side out, and flatten the top of the bag, centering the block. *figs. J–K*

7. Center the webbing on the bag, 3″ from each side fold made in Step 6, with the raw edges of the webbing meeting the raw top edge of the bag. Pin in place. Repeat on the other side of the bag. *figs. L–M*

L

M

N

O

P

8. Sew the straps in place with a ¼″ seam.

9. Insert the exterior of the bag into the lining (lining inside out). Line up the side seams and top edges of the outer and lining. Pin together. *figs. N–P*

10. Sew around the top with a ½″ seam allowance.

11. Pull the outer part of the bag out through the hole left in the bottom of the lining. *fig. Q*

12. Fold the opening under ½″ to match the seam allowance and top stitch ⅛″ from the edge to close the bag. Push the lining down into the bag, pushing out the bottom edges to make sure everything lines up. Press. *fig. R*

13. Top stitch ⅛″ from the edge around the outer top of the bag.

Q

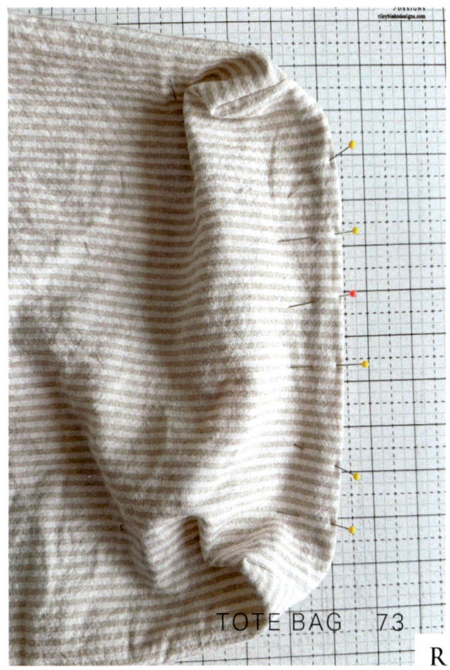

R

PILLOW

FINISHED PILLOW SIZES: 14″ × 14″, 16″ × 16″, or 14″ × 28″

Turning quilt blocks into throw pillows is one of my favorite ways to use blocks (besides quilts). Throw pillows are a quick way to change out your home decor seasonally, add pops of color into your home in a small but impactful way, or simply just add extra coziness to your space. This chapter gives options for 3 different pillow sizes! I'm not someone who has to remove a pile of pillows from my bed before I go to sleep, but I do love the lumbar pillows for adding extra style and comfiness to my bed. Pillows also make a great gift for kids to add to their pile of stuffies or to cuddle up with for movie night.

I prefer using pillow forms versus stuffing because they keep their shape and I can also swap the pillow cover out and reuse the pillow form. But it's up to you! If you have extra pieces of batting or stuffing lying around, feel free to use that to stuff your pillow.

MATERIALS

BLOCK SIZE	9″ BLOCK		14½″ BLOCK		
Pillow Size	14″ Pillow	16″ Pillow	14″ Pillow	16″ Pillow	Lumbar Pillow
Block	1 block 9″ × 9″	1 block 9″ × 9″	1 block 14½″ × 14½″	1 block 14½″ × 14½″	2 blocks 14½″ × 14½″
Background (to match block background)	½ yard	½ yard	¼ yard	⅜ yard	⅝ yard
Backing (for the back of the pillow)	⅜ yard	⅜ yard	⅜ yard	⅜ yard	¾ yard
Lining (for the inside of the pillow)	1 square 18″ × 18″	1 square 20′ × 20″	1 square 18″ × 18″	1 square 20″ × 20″	1 rectangle 22½″ × 36½″
Batting	2 squares 22″ × 22″	2 squares 24″ × 24″	2 squares 22″ × 22″	2 squares 24″ × 24″	2 rectangles 26″ × 40″
Pillow Form	14″ × 14″	16″ × 16″	14″ × 14″	16″ × 16″	14″ × 28″

CUTTING INSTRUCTIONS

BLOCK SIZE	9″ BLOCK		14½″ BLOCK		
Pillow Size	14″ Pillow	16″ Pillow	14″ Pillow	16″ Pillow	Lumbar Pillow
Background	Cut 2 strips 5″ × 9″; Cut 2 strips 5″ × 18″	Cut 2 strips 6″ × 9″; Cut 2 strips 6″ × 20″	-	Cut 2 strips 3¼″ × 14½″; Cut 2 strips 3¼″ × 20″	Cut 2 strips 4½″ × 28½″; Cut 2 strips 4½″ × 22½″
Backing	Cut 2 rectangles 10″ × 14½″	Cut 2 rectangles 12″ × 16½″	Cut 2 rectangles 10″ × 14½″	Cut 2 rectangles 12″ × 16½″	Cut 2 rectangles 14½″ × 18″

Sewing Instructions

PREPARE THE BLOCKS: SQUARE PILLOWS

1. Sew the 2 shorter background fabric strips to opposite sides of the block. Press seams open.

2. Sew the remaining, longer background pieces to the remaining 2 sides of the block. Press seams open.

PREPARE THE BLOCKS: LUMBAR PILLOW

1. Arrange 2 blocks as desired and sew together. Press seams open.

2. Sew the 4½″ × 28″ strips to the top and bottom of blocks. Press seams open.

3. Sew the 4½″ × 22½″ strips to the right and left sides of the blocks. Press seams open.

ASSEMBLY: ALL PILLOWS

Images show a square pillow unless otherwise noted.

1. Baste the pillow front with the batting and lining fabric, and quilt as desired (see Finishing the Quilts, page 42).

2. Trim the sandwich to 14½″ × 14½″ (for the 14″ pillow), 16½″ × 16½″ (for the 16″ pillow), or 14½″ × 28½″ (for the lumbar pillow).

3. For the square pillows, fold and press one long edge of the backing fabric under ½″. Fold and press another ½″. Topstitch the hem with a ¼″ seam to enclose the raw edge of the fabric. Repeat with the remaining backing fabric.

For the lumbar pillow, fold and press one short edge of the backing fabric under ½″. Fold and press another ½″. Topstitch the hem with a ¼″ seam to enclose the raw edge of the fabric. Repeat with the remaining backing fabric. *fig. A*

4. Place the backing pieces RST with the quilted block, arranged as shown. The 2 hemmed edges should overlap in the middle. Pin in place along the outer edges around all sides. *figs. B–D*

5. Sew around the edge of the pillow from Step 4. Turn the pillow cover right side out and insert the pillow form. *fig. E*

A

B

C

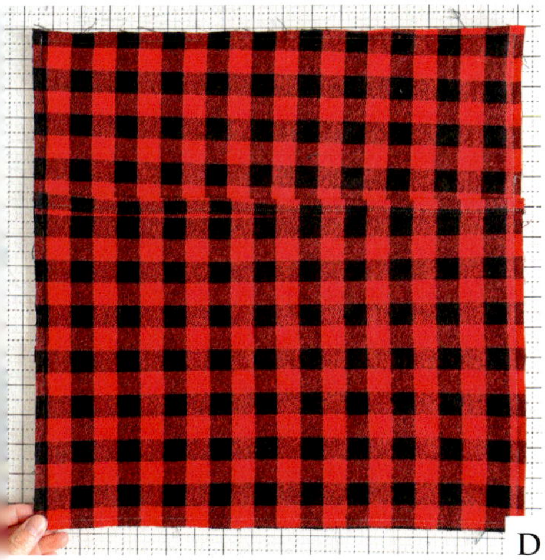

D

E

Wall Hanging

FINISHED SIZES: 9″ × 9″, 14″ × 14″, or 14½″ × 14½″

Quilts and quilt blocks are works of art. Regardless of if you view yourself as an artist or "just a quilter" (which I can relate to!), I firmly believe that quilts should not only be used, but displayed. One of the quickest ways to do this is to turn one of your quilt blocks into a wall hanging using a wooden dowel. In the same way that throw pillows can be changed out seasonally, a wall hanging is a fun way to update your decor and add some texture to your walls. And a bonus—you can also use this wall hanging as table decor when it's not hanging on the wall.

FABRIC REQUIREMENTS

WALL HANGING SIZE	9″ WALL HANGING	14″ WALL HANGING	14½″ WALL HANGING
Block	1 block 9″ × 9″	1 block 9″ × 9″	1 block 14½″ × 14½″
Background	-	2 strips 3″ × 9″ and 2 strips 3″ × 14″	-
Backing	1 square 13″ × 13″	1 square 18″ × 18″	1 square 18″ × 18″
	2 squares 3½″ × 3½″	2 squares 5″ × 5″	2 squares 5″ × 5″
Batting	1 square 13″ × 13″	1 square 18″ × 18″	1 square 18″ × 18″
Binding	1 strip 2½″ × WOF	2 strips 2½″ × WOF	2 strips 2½″ × WOF
Wooden Dowel (¼″–5⁄16″ thick)	7½″	12½″	12½″

Sewing Instructions: 14″ Wall Hanging

1. Sew the 2 shorter background fabric strips to opposite sides of the block. Press the seams open.

2. Sew the remaining, longer background pieces to the remaining 2 sides of the block. Press seams open.

Sewing Instructions: All Sizes

The sewing instructions show a 14″ × 14″ wall hanging.

1. Baste the block with the batting and back fabric, and quilt as desired (see Finishing the Quilts, page 42). Trim the sandwich to 9″ × 9″, 14″ × 14″, or 14½″ × 14½″ for the size you're making.

A

B

C

D

E

2. Fold the small backing squares in half diagonally, wrong sides together, and press. *figs. A–B*

3. Place a folded triangle on each of the 2 top corners of the back side of the wall hanging with the raw edges aligned. Pin in place. *fig. C*

F

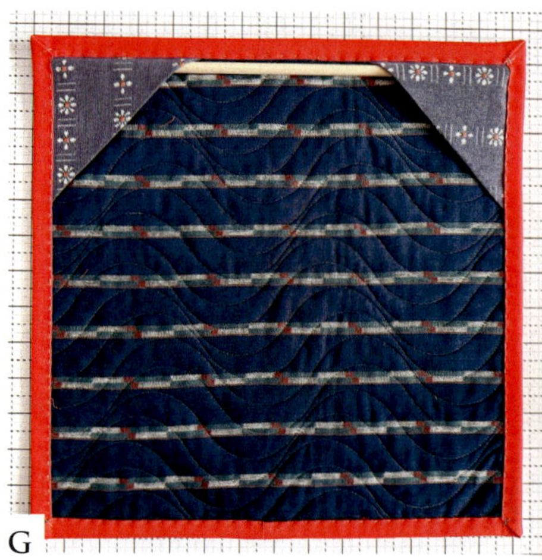

G

4. Stitch the outer edges of the triangles down with a ⅛″ seam. *fig. D*

5. Attach the binding to the front of the wall hanging by following the steps in Preparing & Attaching Binding (page 45). Then, finish binding the wall hanging by hand or machine (See Finishing Binding page 46). *figs. E–F*

6. Insert the wooden dowel into the triangle pockets on the back of the wall hanging and hang as desired. *fig. G*

QUILTS

The quilts in this book are arranged generally from easiest to more challenging. The first quilt, the Steppe Star (page 82) is the only quilt that is not a Broken Star quilt. It would be a good starting point if you are hesitant to jump right into a Broken Star quilt. After the Steppe Star, the next 6 quilt patterns from the Rocky Star (page 94) to Plains Star (page 134) are Broken Star quilt patterns that can be made in either a Crib or Throw size. If you are looking to ease into the Broken Star quilt, I recommend starting with the Rocky Star quilt. The quilt assembly for each is the same; the differences are in the designs. The last two patterns in this book, the Broken Trail Star (page 142) and Broken Steppe Star (page 150) are the most challenging because they are the largest.

STEPPE STAR

CRIB SIZE: 48″ × 48″ • THROW SIZE: 60″ × 70″

A steppe is a large area of unforested grassland. I grew up on the Northern Plains of Montana, where the trees are few and far between, and the grasslands extend to the horizon in all directions. The Steppe Star is a variation of a Lone Star quilt. In it, the two center colors of each diamond are made of longer pieces which resemble steps.

FABRIC REQUIREMENTS

Yardages are based on 42″ wide fabric.

Share what you make!
#steppestarquilt

FABRIC	COLOR NAME	CRIB SIZE	THROW SIZE
Fabric A	Kona Pimento	1/8 yard	1/8 yard
Fabric B	Kona Latte	1/4 yard	1/4 yard
Fabric C	Fableism Canyon Springs Native Nectar in Golden	1/2 yard	1/2 yard
Fabric D	Kona Roasted Pecan	5/8 yard	5/8 yard
Fabric E	Kona Pearl Pink	1/4 yard	1/4 yard
Fabric F	Fableism Canyon Springs in Milkweed	1/4 yard	1/4 yard
Fabric G	Fableism Monarch Grove Track Stripe in Navy	1/8 yard	1/8 yard
Background	Kona Cappuccino	1 1/2 yards	2 3/4 yards
Binding	Fableism Canyon Springs Native Nectar in Golden	1/2 yard	5/8 yards
Backing	Fableism Monarch Grove Track Stripe in Navy	3 1/8 yards	3 7/8 yards
Batting	Warm and White by The Warm Company	56″ × 56″	68″ × 78″

Lemoyne Star (page 52) as background squares

CUTTING INSTRUCTIONS

Fabric A

- Cut 1 strip 2½″ × WOF.

Fabric B

- Cut 2 strips 2½″ × WOF.

Fabric C

- Cut 1 strip 2½″ × WOF.
- Cut 3 strips 4½″ × WOF.

Fabric D

- Cut 1 strip 2½″ × WOF.
- Cut 4 strips 4½″ × WOF.

Fabric E

- Cut 3 strips 2½″ × WOF

Fabric F

- Cut 2 strips 2½″ × WOF.

Fabric G

- Cut 1 strip 2½″ × WOF.

Background (All Sizes)

If you're including interchangeable blocks instead of background squares, see Interchangeable Blocks (page 50) for cutting and piecing instructions.

- Cut 1 strip 21″ × WOF; subcut into 1 square 21″ × 21″.

  Subcut the square into 4 triangles by cutting along each diagonal. If making the throw size, set aside the remainder of the 21″ strip.
- Cut 2 strips 14½″ × WOF; subcut into 4 squares 14½″ × 14½″.

Background (Throw Size)

- Cut 2 strips 11½″ × 42″.
- Cut 1 strip 11½″ × WOF; subcut into 2 pieces 11½″ × 18½″.
- Cut 2 strips 6½″ × 42″.
- From the remaining 21″ strip, subcut 2 rectangles 6½″ × 5½″.

Binding (Crib Size)

- Cut 5 strips 2½″ × WOF.

Binding (Throw Size)

- Cut 7 strips 2½″ × WOF.

BACKING (CRIB SIZE)

Cut and piece the backing fabric as needed to make a backing that equals 56″ × 56″.

BACKING (THROW SIZE)

Cut and piece the backing fabric as needed to make a backing that equals 68″ × 78″.

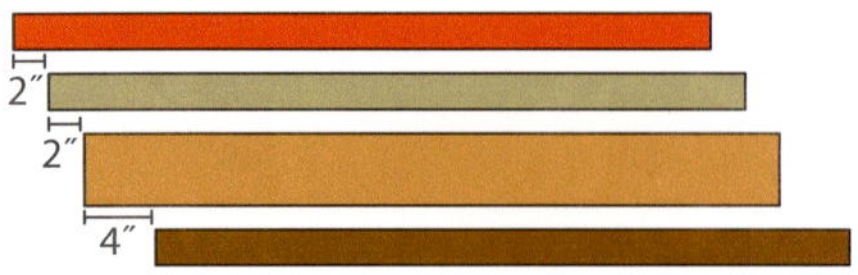

A. Strip Set 1

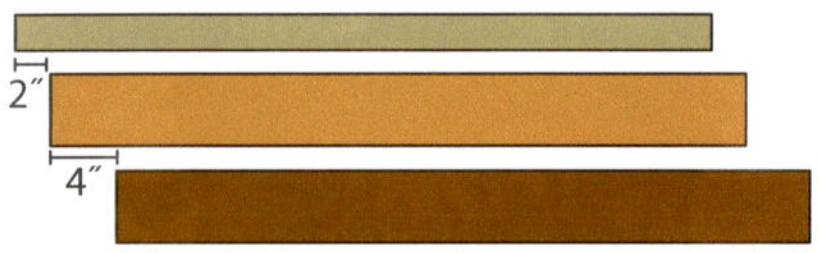

B. Strip Set 2

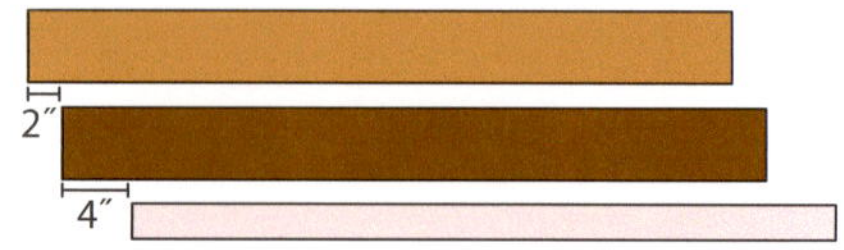

C. Strip Set 3

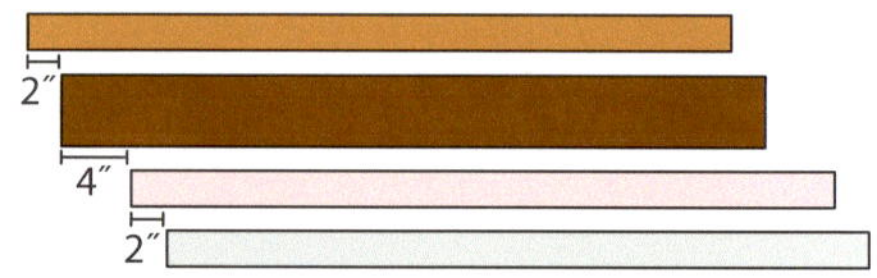

D. Strip Set 4

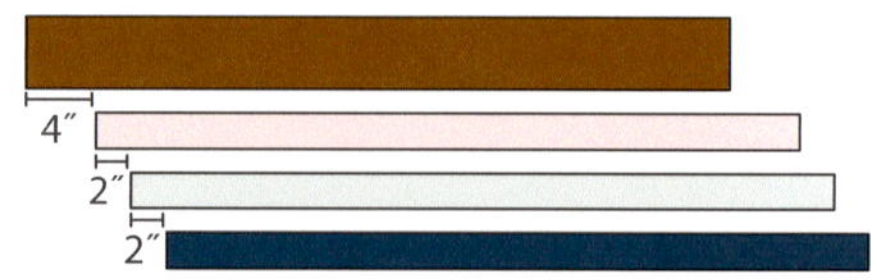

E. Strip Set 5

Sewing Instructions

Seam allowances are ¼″.

STRIP SETS

1. Arrange the strips into strip sets in the order shown in the following chart. Offset the strips by 2″ except when noted by an asterisk (*). When noted by an asterisk, offset those strips by 4″. *figs. A–E*

STRIP SET 1	STRIP SET 2	STRIP SET 3	STRIP SET 4	STRIP SET 5
Fabric A (2½″)	Fabric B (2½″)	Fabric C (4½″)	Fabric C (2½″)	Fabric D (4½″)
Fabric B (2½″)	Fabric C (4½″)	Fabric D (4½″)*	Fabric D (4½″)	Fabric E (2½″)*
Fabric C (4½″)	Fabric D (4½″)*	Fabric E (2½″)*	Fabric E (2½″)*	Fabric F (2½″)*
Fabric D (2½″)*	-	-	Fabric F (2½″)	Fabric G (2½″)*

**Offset strip by 4″*

2. Sew the strips in each set together along the long sides. Press the seams open. *figs. F–J*

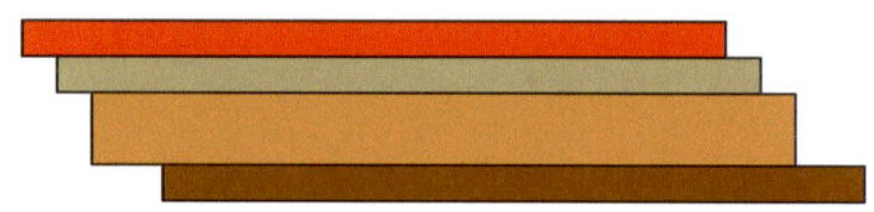
F. Strip Set 1

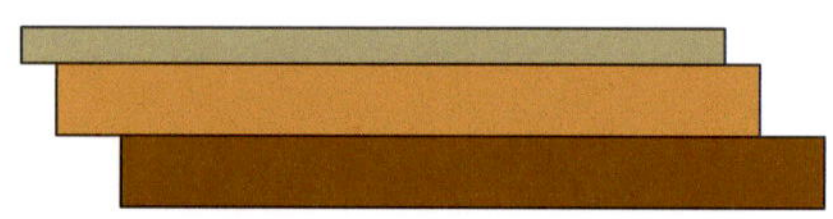
G. Strip Set 2

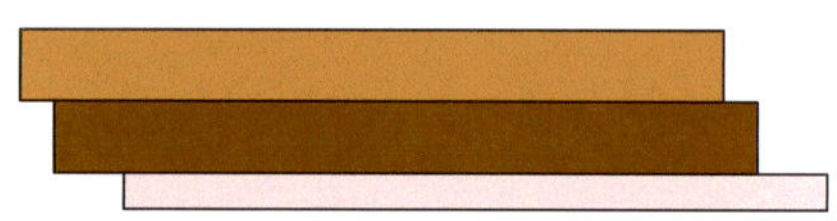
H. Strip Set 3

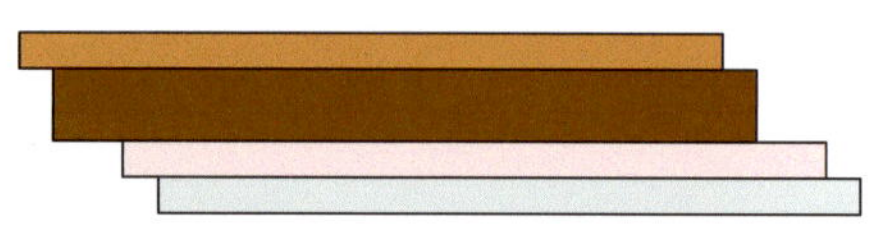
I. Strip Set 4

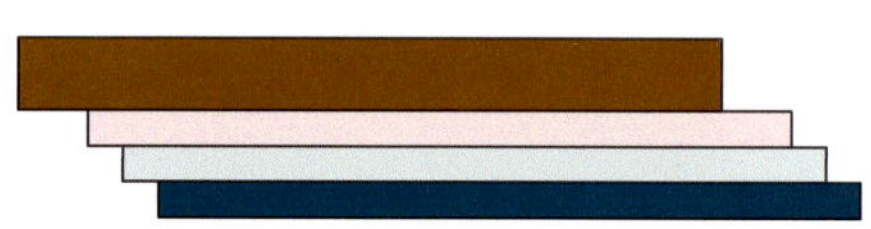
J. Strip Set 5

3. Trim the selvages and cut 8 strip diamonds 2½″ from each strip set. See Cutting and Sewing Diamonds (page 18) for a full tutorial on cutting diamonds. Or, see How to Cut Diamonds (page 53) for a quick reminder. *figs. K–L*

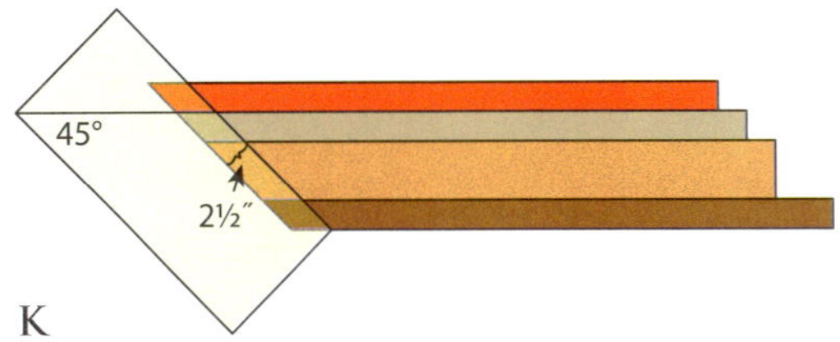

K

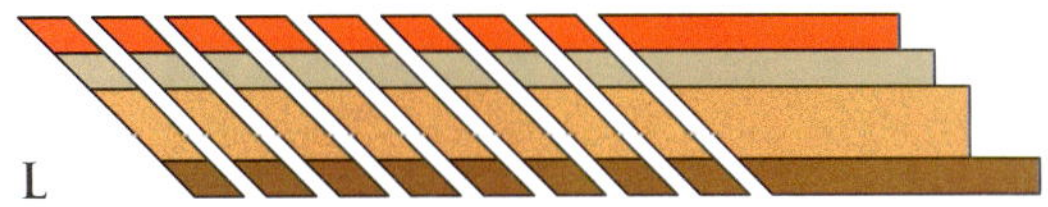

L

IMPORTANT!

Precision on the cuts in Step 3 is vital, so take your time! It's easy for the strip set to get wonky after making a couple of the 2½″ cuts. If the angle does become larger or smaller than 45°, stop, and retrim the strip set correctly to 45° before continuing. If the strips are not cut at the correct angle, the quilt may not sew together properly.

STRIP SET DIAMONDS

1. Select one 2½″ strip from each strip set. Arrange them into a diamond unit, in the order shown. Repeat to arrange all the strips into 8 total strip set diamonds (unsewn). *fig. M*

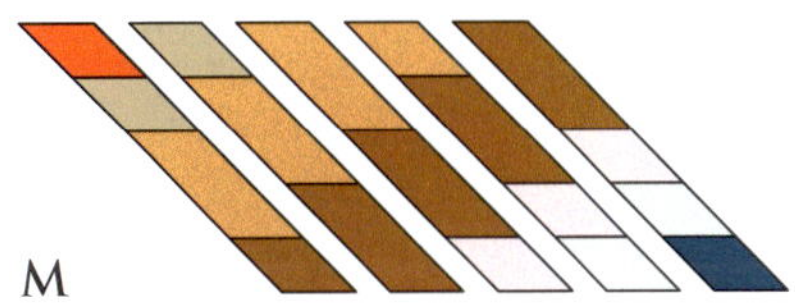

M

2. Begin with the first diamond unit. On the right side of the Strip Set 1 strip, use the ruler and a marking tool to measure and mark ¼″ from the edge of the fabric on the seam where Fabric A and Fabric B meet. Repeat on the wrong side of the Strip Set 2 strip where Fabric B and Fabric C meet. Repeat with the Strip Set 1 and Strip Set 2 strips in all diamond units. *fig. N*

N

3. Starting with the first diamond unit, place the Strip Set 2 strip on top of the Strip Set 1 strip, RST. Place the tip of the top strip approximately ¼″ above the tip of the bottom strip. Insert a pin directly through the seams of both strips, through the marks from Step 2. *fig. O*

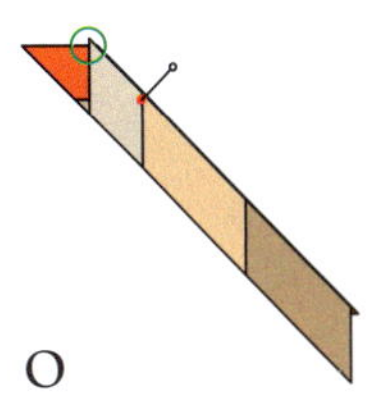

O

IMPORTANT!

Do not skip the marking and pinning in Steps 2–4. Although time consuming, this step is worth the extra effort to ensure the diamond points meet. It'll help you avoid using your seam ripper as much as possible!

4. Repeat Step 3 with each diamond unit, pairing and pinning the strips from Strip Set 1 and Strip Set 2.

5. Sew the pinned strips together into 8 strip pairs. Press the seams open. *fig. P*

6. Begin with the first diamond unit again. On the right side of the Strip Set 3 strip, use the ruler and a marking tool to measure ¼″ from the edge of the fabric on the seam where Fabric D and Fabric E meet. Repeat on the wrong side of the Strip Set 4 strip where Fabric E and Fabric F meet. Repeat with the Strip Set 3 and Strip Set 4 strips in all diamond units. *fig. Q*

7. Repeat Steps 3–5 with the Strip Set 3 and Strip Set 4 strips to make 8 strip pairs. Place the Strip Set 4 strip on top of the Strip Set 3 strip. *figs. R–S*

8. Begin with the first diamond unit again. On the right side of the unit from Step 7, use the ruler and a marking tool to measure ¼″ from the edge of the fabric on the seams where Fabric D and Fabric E and where Fabric E and Fabric F meet. Repeat on the wrong side of the Strip Set 5 strip where Fabric E and Fabric F meet and where Fabric F and G meet. Repeat with the Step 7 unit and Strip Set 5 strips in all diamond units.

9. Repeat Steps 3–5 with the Step 7 unit and Strip Set 5 strips to make 8 strip trios. Place the Strip Set 5 on top of the Step 7 unit. *figs. T–V*

10. Place a unit from Step 5 RST with a unit from Step 9. Place the tip of the top strip approximately ¼″ above the bottom strip. Sew together. Press the seams open. Repeat to make 8 strip set diamonds. *figs. W–Y*

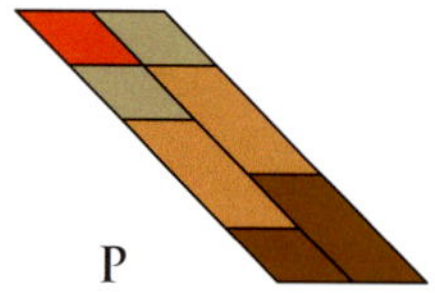
P

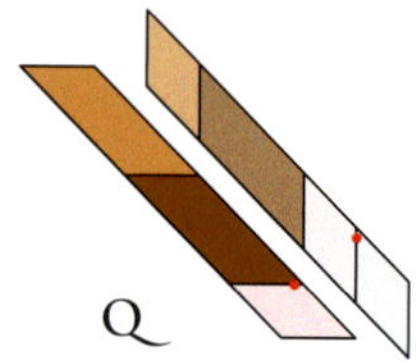
Q

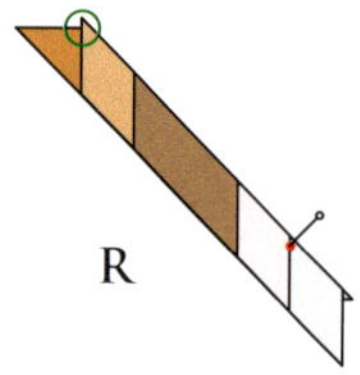
R

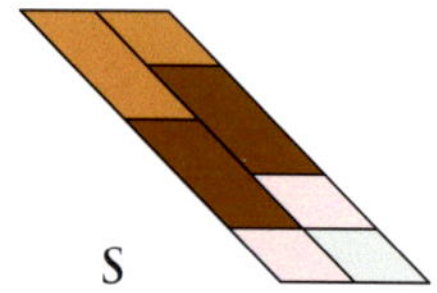
S

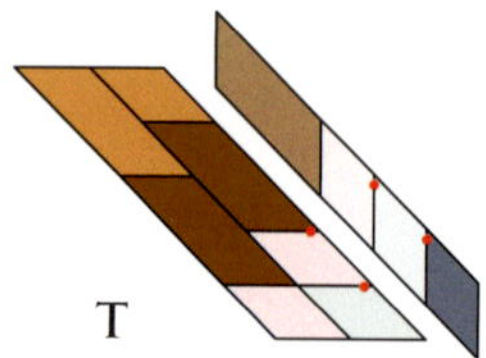
T

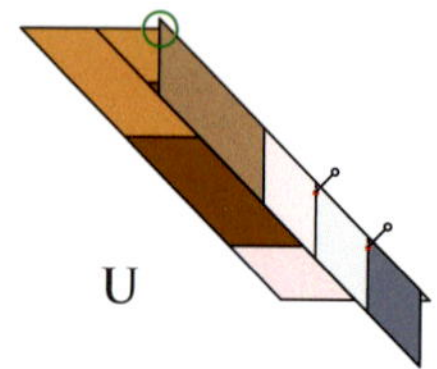
U

V

W

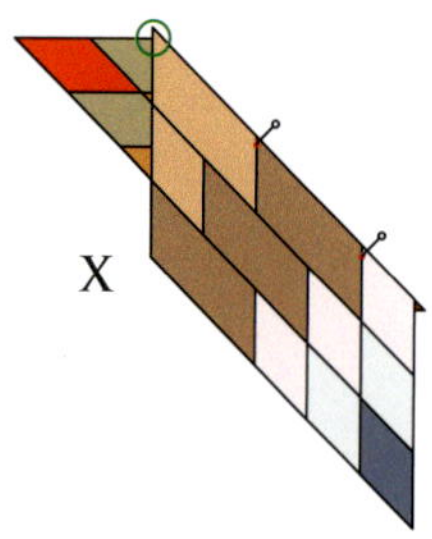
X

Y

Z

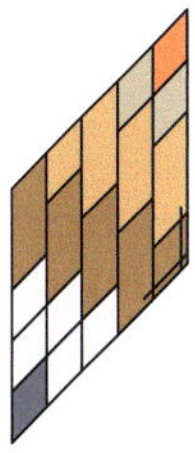

A

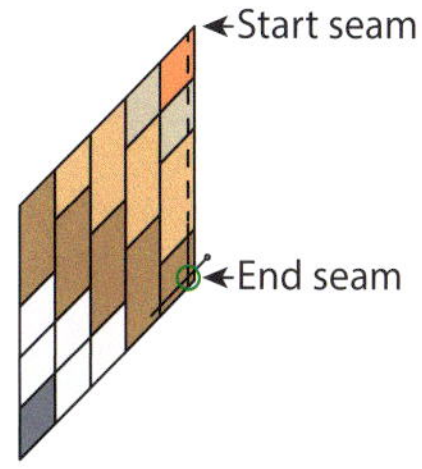

B

C

STAR ASSEMBLY

1. Place 2 diamonds RST. On the wrong side of the top diamond, measure lines ¼″ from two edges that meet at one corner as shown. Make a mark where the lines intersect. Pin through the mark. *figs. Z–A*

2. Start sewing at the top of the diamond and stop sewing (with the needle down) at the mark from Step 1. Backstitch 2–3 stitches. Press the seam to the left. *fig. B*

3. Repeat Steps 1–2 to make 4 total pairs of diamonds. *fig. C*

4. Repeat Steps 1–2 to sew the 4 diamond pairs into 2 half stars. Press the seams to the left. *fig. D*

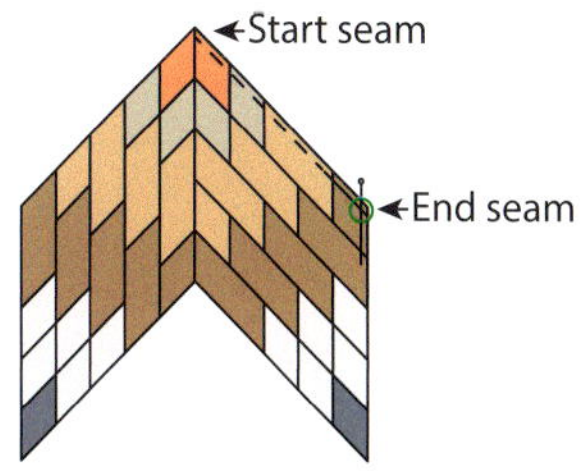

D

5. Place the 2 halves RST. On the wrong side of the top half, measure lines ¼″ from two edges that meet at the top two corners. Make a mark in each corner where the lines intersect. Pin through the marks, and then through the center seam of both units. Pin across the whole remainder of the seam. *fig. E*

E

6. Sew the halves together, starting at one mark and ending on the second mark. Backstitch 2–3 stitches at the beginning and end. Press the seam open. *fig. F*

F

G

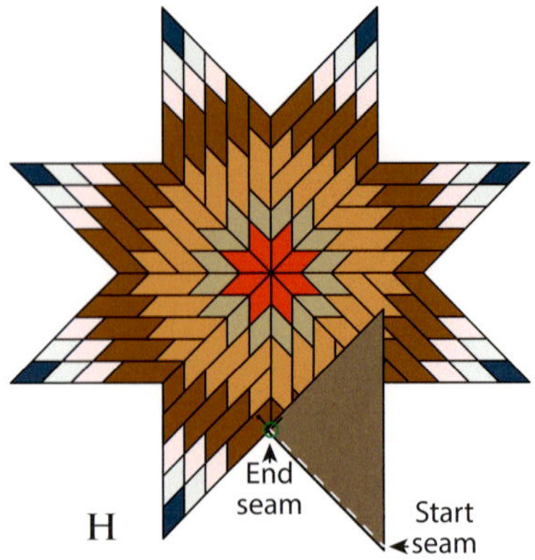

H

QUILT TOP ASSEMBLY

1. On the wrong side of each background triangle, measure lines ¼″ from two edges that meet at the top point as shown. Make a mark where the lines intersect. *fig. G*

2. Place 1 triangle RST with one of the star points. Align the mark from Step 1 with the place the seam ended in the star. Pin through the mark. *fig. H*

3. Start sewing at the outer edge of the block and stop sewing at the pinned mark. Backstitch 2–3 stitches.

4. Flip the background triangle so it is RST with the adjacent star point. Align the mark from Step 1 with the place the seam ended in star. Pin through the mark. Pin along the whole edge. *fig. I*

5. Start sewing at the outer edge of the block and stop sewing at the pinned mark from Step 4. Backstitch 2–3 stitches. Press the seams open. Trim the dog ears. *figs. J–K*

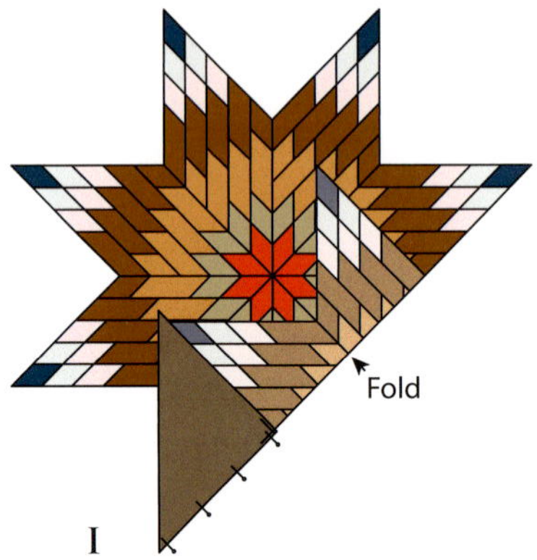

I

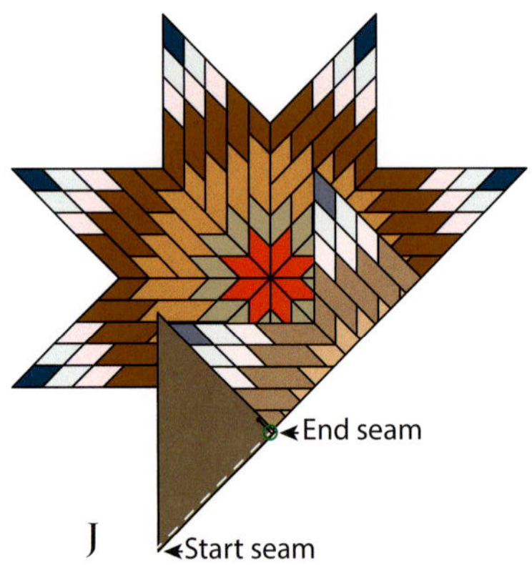

J

K

L

M

6. Repeat Steps 2–5 to attach the remaining three background triangles to the star. *fig. L*

Background Squares

If you're using interchangeable blocks, use them instead of background squares.

1. On the wrong side of each background square, measure lines ¼″ from two edges that meet at one corner. Make a mark where the lines intersect. *fig. M*

2. Place a background square RST with the block as shown. Align the mark from Step 1 with the place where the seam ended in sewing the star together. Pin through the mark. *fig. N*

3. Start sewing at the outer edge of the block and stop sewing at the pinned mark from Step 2. Backstitch 2–3 stitches. *fig. O*

N

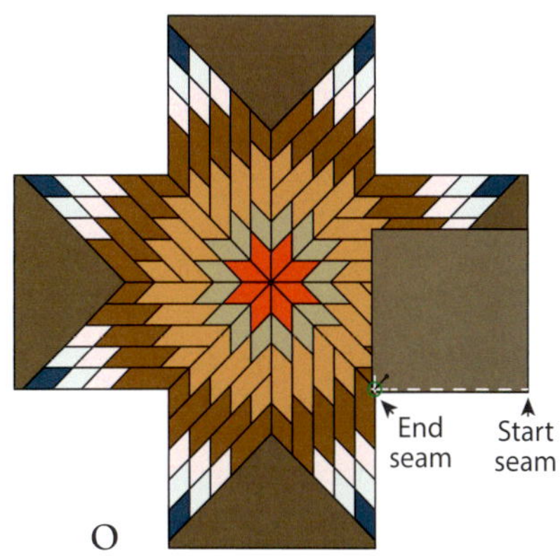

O

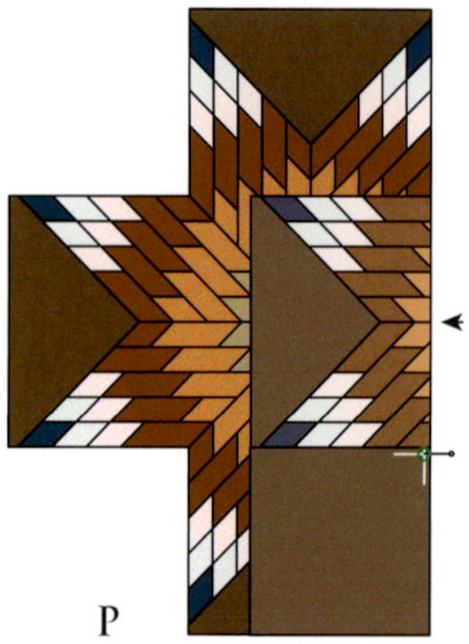

P

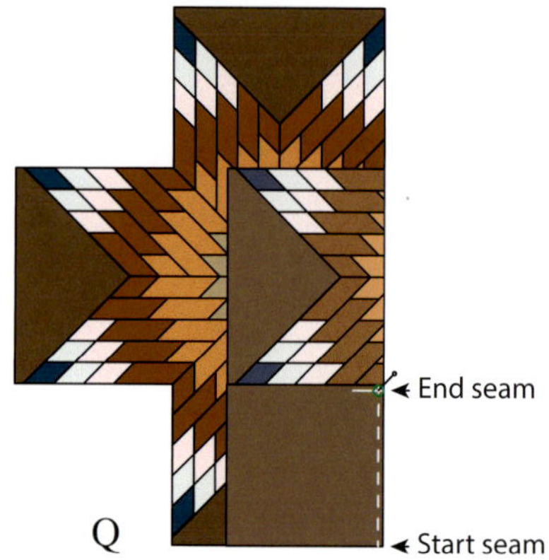

Q

4. Flip the background square so it is RST with the adjacent side of the block's corner. Align the mark from Step 1 with the place the seam ended in Step 3. Pin through the mark. *fig. P*

5. Start sewing at the outer edge of the block and stop sewing at the pinned mark from Step 4. Backstitch 2–3 stitches. Press the seams open. *fig. Q*

6. Repeat Steps 2–5 to attach the remaining 3 squares to the block. If you are making the crib size, the quilt top is complete and measures 48″ × 48″. See Finishing the Quilts (page 42) to quilt and bind. *fig. R*

R

Finished crib size quilt top

Throw Size Quilt Top

1. Sew a 6½″ × 5½″ rectangle to a 6½″ × 42″ strip. Press the seam open. *fig. S*

2. Repeat Step 1 for the remaining 6½″ × 5½″ rectangle and 6½″ × 42″ strip. *fig. S*

3. Sew an 11½″ × 42″ strip to a 11½″ × 18½″ strip along the 11½″ sides. Press the seam open. *fig. S*

4. Repeat Step 3 for the remaining 11½″ × 42″ and 11½″ × 18½″ strips. *fig. S*

S

5. Sew the 6½″ × 48″ strips to the left and right sides of the quilt top. Press seams as desired.

6. Sew the 11½″ × 60″ strips to the top and bottom sides of the quilt. Press seams as desired. The quilt top is complete and measures 60″ × 70″. See Finishing the Quilts (page 42) to quilt and bind. *fig. T*

T

Throw Size Quilt

Longarm quilting by Ashlee Doyle, Crinkly Quilts

Quilting pantograph: Drift designed by Barbie Mills, The Quilting Mill

Rocky Star

SMALL THROW SIZE: 61½″ × 65½″ • LARGE THROW SIZE: 75½″ × 75½″

The Rocky Star Quilt is the perfect introduction to the Broken Star quilt design. Once the diamonds and background are cut, you are ready for quilt top assembly—no need to make blocks first. In this pattern, there is one fabric used for the center star and one fabric used for the outer ring. However, this quilt can easily be made "scrappy" with multiple fabrics in your stash, made with the same fabric for both the center star and outer ring, or any other fabric plan you can envision. The quilt is made up of 32 diamonds 6½″ that can be cut from as few or as many fabrics as desired.

FABRIC REQUIREMENTS

Yardages are based on 43″ wide fabric.

Share what you make! #rockystarquilt

FABRIC	COLOR NAME	SMALL THROW SIZE	LARGE THROW SIZE
Fabric A	Kona Flame	½ yard	½ yard
Fabric B	Kona Roasted Pecan	1¼ yard	1¼ yard
Background	Robert Kaufman Essex Sparkle in Chambray	2⅜ yards	3⅝ yards
Binding	Kona Black	⅝ yard	⅝ yard
Backing	Robert Kaufman Mammoth Flannel	4 yards	4¾ yards
Batting	Warm & Natural by The Warm Company	69″ × 73″	83″ × 83″

Scrappy Version using a variety of blues and whites from my fabric stash.

Longarm quilting by Ashlee Doyle, Crinkly Quilts

Quilting pantograph: Partial Eclipse designed by Barbie Mills, The Quilting Mill

CUTTING INSTRUCTIONS

For a full tutorial on cutting diamonds, see Cutting and Sewing Diamonds (page 18). Or, for a quick reminder on cutting diamonds, see How to Cut Diamonds (page 53).

Note: For the 6½″ diamonds, if the usable width of your fabric is less than 43″, do not trim off the selvages before cutting the diamonds. Trim the diamond point after sewing together if needed.

Fabric A

- Cut 2 strips 6½″ × WOF; subcut into 8 diamonds 6½″ (4 from each strip).

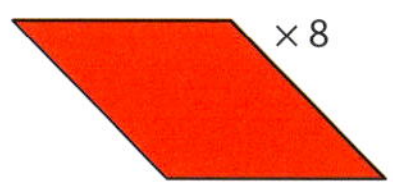

Fabric B

- Cut 6 strips 6½″ × WOF; subcut into 24 diamonds 6½″ (4 from each strip).

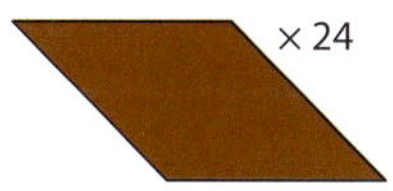

Background (All Sizes)

If you're including interchangeable blocks instead of background squares, see Interchangeable Blocks (page 50) for cutting and piecing instructions.

- Cut 1 strip 13½″ × WOF; subcut into 2 squares 13½″ × 13½″.

  Subcut each 13½″ square into 4 triangles by cutting along each diagonal.

- Cut 5 strips 9″ × WOF; subcut into 20 squares 9″ × 9″.

Background (Small Throw Size)

- Cut 4 strips 2″ × WOF; subcut into:

  2 strips 2″ × 42″.

  2 strips 2″ × 24″

- Cut 3 strips 4″ × WOF; subcut into:

  2 strips 4″ × 42″

  2 strips 4″ × 17″

Background (Large Throw Size)

- Cut 7 strips 9″ × WOF; subcut into:

  4 strips 9″ × 42″

  2 strips 9″ × 34″

  2 strips 9″ × 17″

Binding (Small Throw Size)

- Cut 7 strips 2½″ × WOF.

Binding (Large Throw Size)

- Cut 8 strips 2½″ × WOF.

Backing (Small Throw Size)

Cut and piece the backing fabric as needed to make a backing that equals 69″ × 73″.

Backing (Large Throw Size)

Cut and piece the backing fabric as needed to make a backing that equals 83″ × 83″.

Quilt Top Assembly

Broken Star Quilt assembly is the same for every Broken Star quilt. To assemble this quilt, follow the instructions in Broken Star Quilt Assembly (page 30).

Reference the following to create Unit 1 (page 30), Unit 2 (page 32), Unit 3 (page 34), and Unit 4 (page 35):

1. Make 4 Unit 1s in Fabric A. Make 12 Unit 1s in Fabric B. *figs. A–B*

2. Make 4 Unit 2s with Fabric B Unit 1s and Background fabric. *fig. C*

3. Make 4 Unit 3s with Fabric B Unit 1s and Background fabric. *fig. D*

4. Make 4 Unit 4s with Fabric A Unit 1s and the Unit 3s. *fig. E*

5. Using Units 1, 2, 3, and 4 and the remaining background squares, continue making Units 5–10 by following the instructions in Broken Star Quilt Assembly (page 30) to finish the quilt top.

6. After Step 5 is completed, refer to the following instructions for making your quilt either a Small Throw or Large Throw size quilt.

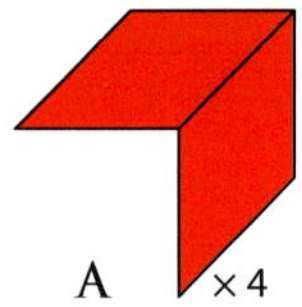

A ×4

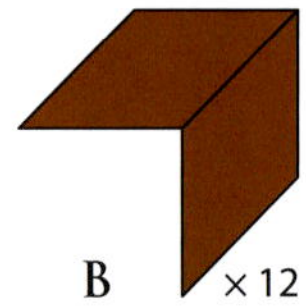

B ×12

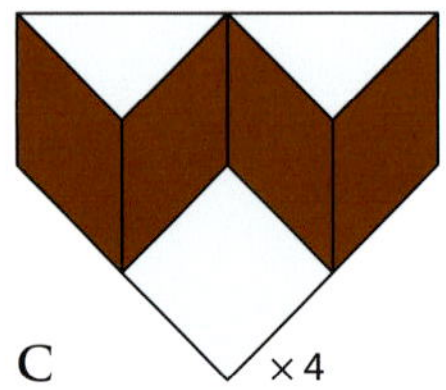

C ×4

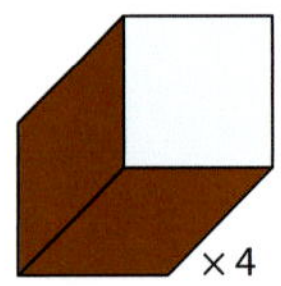

D ×4

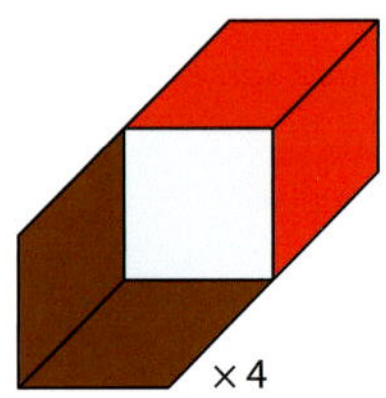

E ×4

SMALL THROW SIZE QUILT TOP

1. Sew a 2″ × 42″ strip to a 2″ × 24″ strip along the 2″ sides. Press the seam open.

2. Repeat Step 1 for the remaining 2″ × 42″ and 2″ × 24″ strips.

3. Sew an 4″ × 42″ strip to a 4″ × 17″ strip along the 4″ sides. Press the seam open.

4. Repeat Step 3 for the remaining 4″ × 42″ and 4″ × 17″ strips.

5. Sew the 4″ × 58½″ strips to the top and bottom sides of the quilt top. Press seams as desired.

6. Sew the 2″ × 65½″ strips to the left and right sides of the quilt. Press seams as desired.

The quilt top is complete and measures 61½″ × 65½″. See Finishing the Quilts (page 42) to quilt and bind.

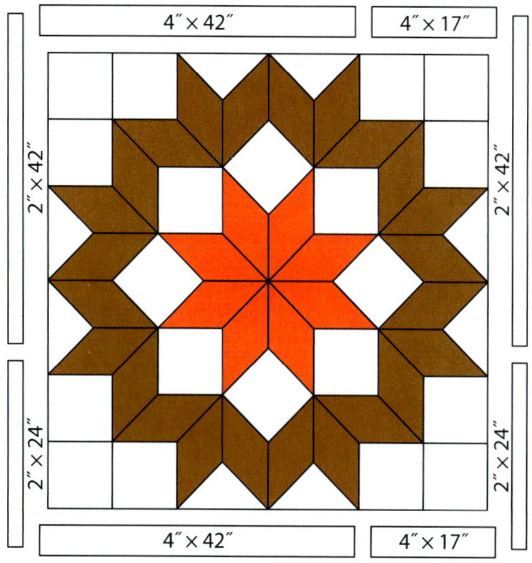

LARGE THROW SIZE QUILT TOP

1. Sew a 9″ × 42″ strip to a 9″ × 17″ strip along the 9″ sides. Press the seam open.

2. Repeat Step 1 with another 9″ × 42″ strip and the remaining 9″ × 17″ strip.

3. Sew a 9″ × 42″ strip to a 9″ × 34″ strip along the 9″ sides. Press the seam open.

4. Repeat Step 3 for the remaining 9″ × 42″ and 9″ × 34″ strips.

5. Sew the 9″ × 58½″ strips to the top and bottom of the quilt top. Press seams as desired.

6. Sew the 9″ × 75½″ strips to the left and right sides of the quilt. Press seams as desired.

The quilt top is complete and measures 75½″ × 75½″. See Finishing the Quilts (page 42) to quilt and bind.

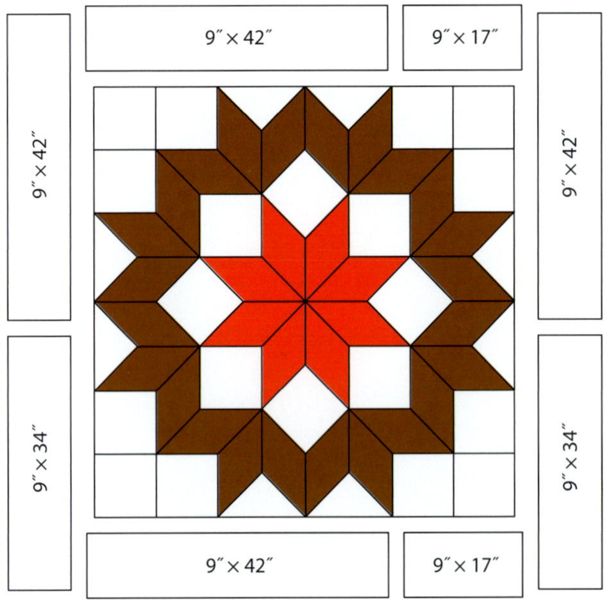

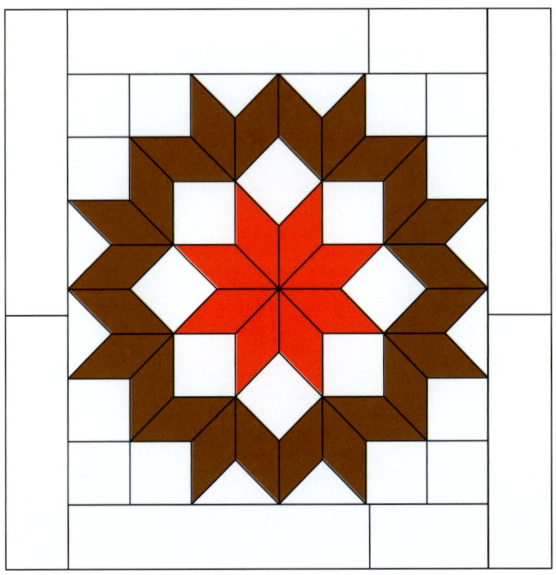

Longarm quilting by Ashlee Doyle, Crinkly Quilts

Quilting pantograph: Bubble Glitter designed by Melissa Kelley

Horizon Star

SMALL THROW SIZE: 61½″ × 65½″ • LARGE THROW SIZE: 75½″ × 75½″

Montana is often referred to as Big Sky Country. This might be hard to picture if you've never been to Montana, but the sky truly does feel big. *Much bigger than other states I've visited. So, the horizon is often miles in the distance. The strips in the outer ring of this quilt reminded me of the horizon lines in eastern Montana, the area where I grew up.*

FABRIC REQUIREMENTS

Yardages are based on 43″ wide fabric.

Share what you make!
#horizonstarquilt

FABRIC	COLOR NAME	SMALL THROW SIZE	LARGE THROW SIZE
Fabric A	Kona Pimento	½ yard	½ yard
Fabric B	Carolyn Friedlander CF Collection in Spice	½ yard	½ yard
Fabric C	Fableism Forest Forage Daisies in Denim	½ yard	½ yard
Fabric D	Neon Neppy in Royal	½ yard	½ yard
Background	Robert Kaufman Essex Speckle Yarn Dye in Speckle Mauve	2⅜ yards	3⅝ yards
Binding	Neon Neppy in Royal	⅝ yard	⅝ yard
Backing	Peppered Cotton in Rust	4 yards	4¾ yards
Batting	Warm & Natural by The Warm Company	69″ × 73″	83″ × 83″

Lemoyne Star (page 52) blocks as background squares.

CUTTING INSTRUCTIONS

For a full tutorial on cutting diamonds, see Cutting and Sewing Diamonds (page 18). Or, for a quick reminder on cutting diamonds, see How to Cut Diamonds (page 53).

Note: For the 6½″ diamonds, if the usable width of your fabric is less than 43″, do not trim off the selvages before cutting the diamonds. Trim the diamond point after sewing together if needed.

Fabric A

- Cut 2 strips 6½″ × WOF; subcut into 8 diamonds 6½″ (4 per strip).

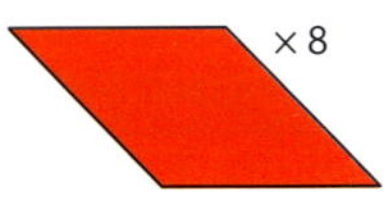

- Cut 1 strip 13½″ × WOF; subcut into 2 squares 13½″ × 13½″.

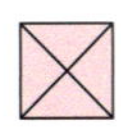

Subcut each 13½″ square along each diagonal into 4 triangles.

- Cut 5 strips 9″ × WOF; subcut into 20 squares 9″ × 9″.

Fabric B

- Cut 6 strips 2½″ × WOF.

Fabric C

- Cut 6 strips 2½″ × WOF.

Fabric D

- Cut 6 strips 2½″ × WOF.

Background (All Sizes)

If you're including interchangeable blocks instead of background squares, see Interchangeable Blocks (page 50) for cutting and piecing instructions.

Background (Small Throw Size)

- Cut 4 strips 2″ × WOF; subcut into:

  2 strips 2″ × 42″

  2 strips 2″ × 24″

- Cut 3 strips 4″ × WOF; subcut into:

  2 strips 4″ × 42″

  2 strips 4″ × 17″

Background (Large Throw Size)

- Cut 7 strips 9″ × WOF; subcut into:

  4 strips 9″ × 42″

  2 strips 9″ × 34″

  2 strips 9″ × 17″

Binding (Small Throw Size)

- Cut 7 strips 2½″ × WOF.

Binding (Large Throw Size)

- Cut 8 strips 2½″ × WOF.

Backing (Small Throw Size)

Cut and piece the backing fabric as needed to make a backing that equals 69″ × 73″.

Backing (Large Throw Size)

Cut and piece the backing fabric as needed to make a backing that equals 83″ × 83″.

Sewing Instructions

STRIP DIAMONDS

1. Arrange 1 of each Fabric B, C, and D in groups as shown, and offset the strips by 2″. Place the B and C strips RST, and sew together along one long side. Place the B/C pair and the D strip RST, and sew together along one long side. Press the seams open. *figs. A–D*

2. Repeat Step 1 to create 3 total strip sets.

3. Arrange 1 of each Fabric D, C, and B strips in groups as shown, and offset the strips by 2″. Repeat Step 1 to sew the 3 strips together. *figs. E–F*

4. Repeat Step 3 to create 3 total strip sets.

5. Trim the selvages and cut 12 diamonds 6½″ from the Step 2 (B/C/D) strip sets and 12 diamonds from the Step 4 (D/C/B) strip sets (4 diamonds per strip set). See Cutting and Sewing Diamonds (page 18) for a full tutorial on cutting diamonds. Or see How to Cut Diamonds (page 53) for a quick reminder. *figs. G–H*

QUILT TOP ASSEMBLY

Broken Star Quilt assembly is the same for every Broken Star quilt. To assemble this quilt, follow the instructions in Broken Star Quilt Assembly (page 30).

Reference the following to create Unit 1 (page 30), Unit 2 (page 32), Unit 3 (page 34), and Unit 4 (page 35):

1. Make 4 Unit 1s in Fabric A. *fig. I*

2. Make 8 Unit 1s from 8 B/C/D strip set diamonds and 8 D/C/B strip set diamonds. *fig. J*

3. Make 4 Unit 1s from 4 B/C/D strip set diamonds and 4 D/C/B strip set diamonds. *fig. K*

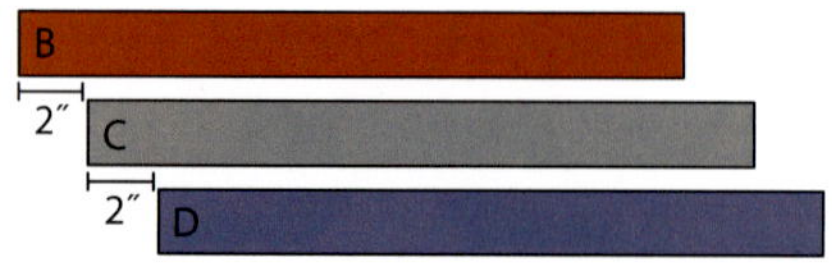

A

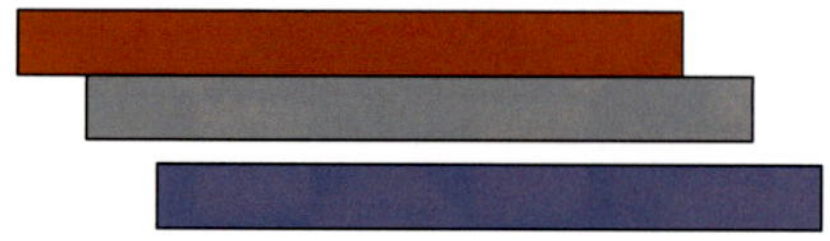
B

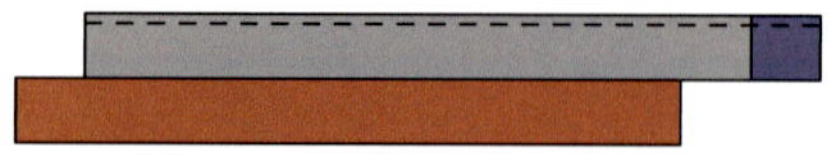
C

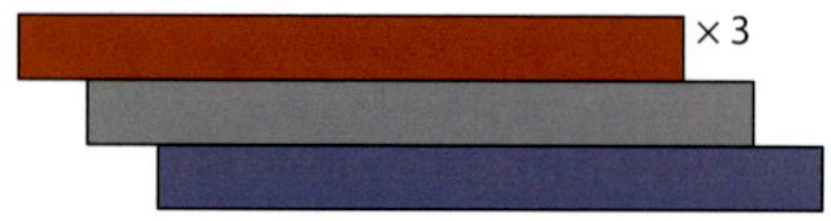

D

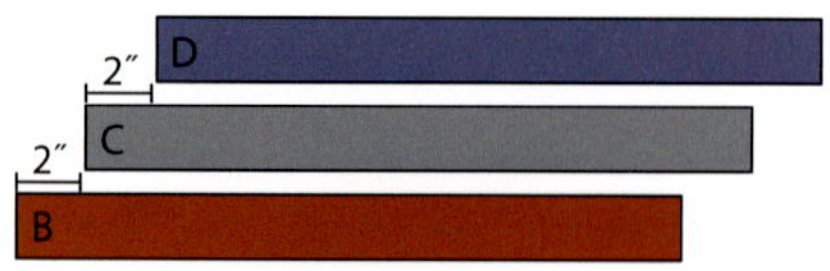

E

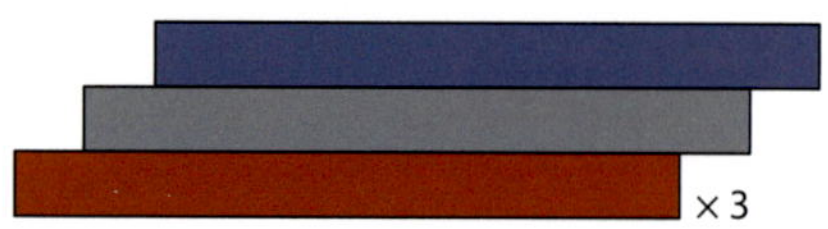

F

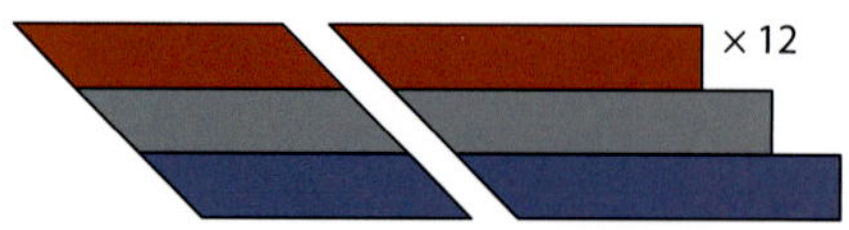

G

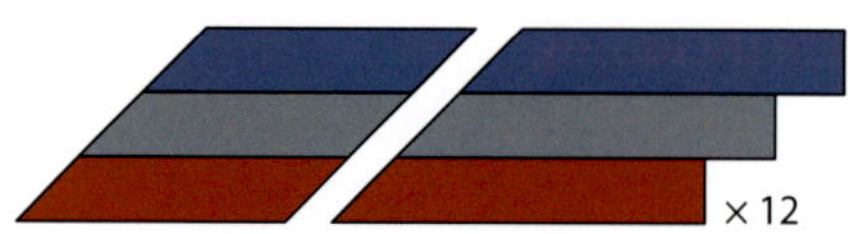

H

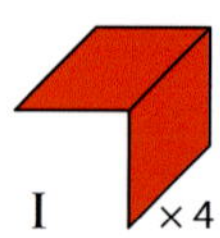

I

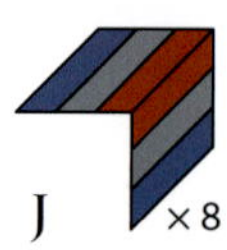

J

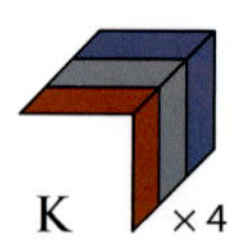

K

4. Make 4 Unit 2s from the Unit 1s with Fabric B at the center and background fabric. *fig. L*

5. Make 4 Unit 3s from the Unit 1s with Fabric D at the outer sides and background fabric. *fig. M*

6. Make 4 Unit 4s from Fabric A Unit 1s and the Unit 3s. *fig. N*

7. Using Units 1, 2, 3, and 4 and the remaining background squares, continue making Units 5–10 by following the instructions in Broken Star Quilt Assembly (page 30) to finish the quilt top.

8. After Step 7 is completed, refer to the following instructions for making your quilt either a Small Throw or Large Throw size quilt.

Small Throw Size Quilt Top

1. Sew a 2″ × 42″ strip to a 2″ × 24″ strip along the 2″ sides. Press the seam open. *figs. O–P*

2. Repeat Step 1 for the remaining 2″ × 42″ and 2″ × 24″ strips. *figs. O–P*

3. Sew an 4″ × 42″ strip to a 4″ × 17″ strip along the 4″ sides. Press the seam open.*figs. O–P*

4. Repeat Step 3 for the remaining 4″ × 42″ and 4″ × 17″ strips. *figs. O–P*

5. Sew the 4″ × 58½″ strips to the top and bottom sides of the quilt top. Press seams as desired. *figs. O–P*

6. Sew the 2″ × 65½″ strips to the left and right sides of the quilt. Press seams as desired. *figs. O–P*

The quilt top is complete and measures 61½″ × 65½″. See Finishing the Quilts (page 42) to quilt and bind.

L

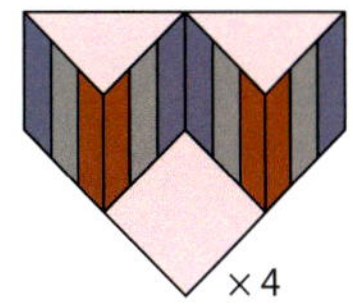

M

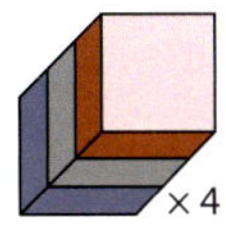

N

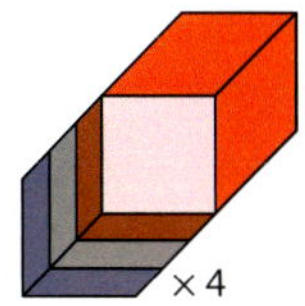

O

P

Large Throw Size Quilt Top

1. Sew a 9″ × 42″ strip to a 9″ × 17″ strip along the 9″ sides. Press the seam open.

2. Repeat Step 1 with another 9″ × 42″ strip and the remaining 9″ × 17″ strip.

3. Sew a 9″ × 42″ strip to a 9″ × 34″ strip along the 9″ sides. Press the seam open.

4. Repeat Step 3 for the remaining 9″ × 42″ and 9″ × 34″ strips.

5. Sew the 9″ × 58½″ strips to the top and bottom sides of the quilt top. Press seams as desired.

6. Sew the 9″ × 75½″ strips to the left and right sides of the quilt. Press seams as desired.

The quilt top is complete and measures 75½″ × 75½″. See Finishing the Quilts (page 42) to quilt and bind.

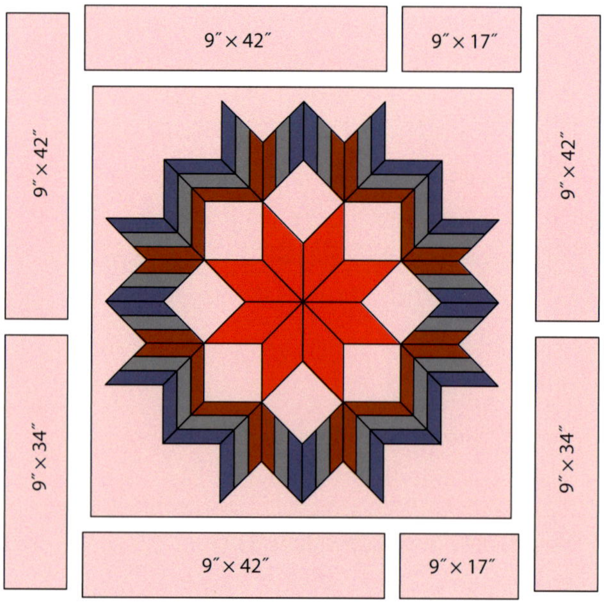

Longarm quilting by Ashlee Doyle, Crinkly Quilts

Quilting pantograph: Crystal Ball designed by Karlee Porter

Backcountry Star

SMALL THROW SIZE: 61½″ × 65½″ • LARGE THROW SIZE: 75½″ × 75½″

There is a stretch of highway that I often drive with a sign calling the road a Backcountry Byway. I love that name, and it is totally fitting—seeing only 1 or 2 other vehicles on the 40-plus mile stretch is not uncommon. Exiting the interstate to this Backcountry Byway means I'm getting closer to home. This Broken Star pattern is made up of a classic Lone Star at the center of the quilt and large diamonds that form the outer ring of the star. The outer star can be one of the same fabrics as the center star or a different fabric.

FABRIC REQUIREMENTS

Yardages are based on 43″ wide fabric.

Share what you make!
#backcountrystarquilt

FABRIC	COLOR NAME	SMALL THROW SIZE	LARGE THROW SIZE
Fabric A	Fableism Forest Forage Daisies in Prairie	⅛ yard	⅛ yard
Fabric B	Kona Yarrow	¼ yard	¼ yard
Fabric C	Kona Black	¼ yard	¼ yard
Fabric D	Kona Evergreen	¼ yard	¼ yard
Fabric E	Kona Pimento	⅛ yard	⅛ yard
Fabric F	Fableism Forest Forage Daisies in Denim	1⅜ yards	1⅜ yards
Background	Kona Latte	2⅜ yards	3⅝ yards
Binding	Kona Evergreen	⅝ yard	⅝ yard
Backing	Robert Kaufman Mammoth Flannel	4 yards	4¾ yards
Batting	Warm & Natural by The Warm Company	69″ × 73″	83″ × 83″

A Backcountry Star with Lone Star blocks (page 60).

CUTTING INSTRUCTIONS

For a full tutorial on cutting diamonds, see Cutting and Sewing Diamonds (page 18). Or, for a quick reminder on cutting diamonds, see How to Cut Diamonds (page 53).

Note: For the 6½″ diamonds, if the usable width of your fabric is less than 43″, do not trim off the selvages before cutting the diamonds. Trim the diamond point after sewing together if needed.

Fabric A

- Cut 1 strip 2½″ × WOF.

Fabric B

- Cut 2 strips 2½″ × WOF.

Fabric C

- Cut 3 strips 2½″ × WOF.

Fabric D

- Cut 2 strips 2½″ × WOF.

Fabric E

- Cut 1 strip 2½″ × WOF.

Fabric F

- Cut 6 strips 6½″ × WOF; subcut into 24 diamonds 6½″.

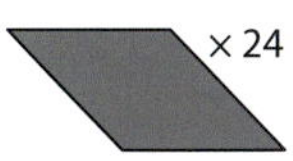

Background (All Sizes)

If you're including interchangeable blocks instead of background squares, see Interchangeable Blocks (page 50) for cutting and piecing instructions.

- Cut 1 strip 13½″ × WOF; subcut into 2 squares 13½″ × 13½″.

  Subcut each 13½″ square along each diagonal into 4 triangles.

- Cut 5 strips 9″ × WOF; subcut into 20 squares 9″ × 9″.

Background (Small Throw Size)

- Cut 4 strips 2″ × WOF; subcut into:

  2 strips 2″ × 42″

  2 strips 2″ × 24″
- Cut 3 strips 4″ × WOF; subcut into:

  2 strips 4″ × 42″

  2 strips 4″ × 17″

Background (Large Throw Size)

- Cut 7 strips 9″ × WOF; subcut into:

  4 strips 9″ × 42″

  2 strips 9″ × 34″

  2 strips 9″ × 17″

Binding (Small Throw Size)

- Cut 7 strips 2½″ × WOF.

Binding (Large Throw Size)

- Cut 8 strips 2½″ × WOF.

Backing (Small Throw Size)

Cut and piece the backing fabric as needed to make a backing that equals 69″ × 73″.

BACKING (LARGE THROW SIZE)

Cut and piece the backing fabric as needed to make a backing that equals 83″ × 83″.

Sewing Instructions

STRIP SETS

1. Group the strips, offset by 2″, into the following combinations, using one strip per color in each group: A/B/C, B/C/D, and C/D/E. *figs. A–C*

2. Place the first 2 strips in each group RST and sew together along one long side (A/B, B/C, C/D). Then, add the third strip to each pair, and sew together along one long side. Press the seams open. *figs. D–F*

3. Trim the selvages and cut 8 diamond strips 2½″ from each strip set. See Cutting and Sewing Diamonds (page 18) for a full tutorial on cutting diamonds. Or, see How to Cut Diamonds (page 53) for a quick reminder. *fig. G*

STRIP SET DIAMONDS

1. Select a 2½″ strip from each strip set. Arrange them into a diamond unit, in the order shown. Repeat to arrange all the strips into 8 total strip set diamonds (unsewn). *fig. H*

2. Begin with the first diamond unit. On the right side of the A/B/C diamond strip, use the ruler and a marking tool to measure and mark ¼″ from the edge of the fabric on each seam. Repeat on the wrong side of the B/C/D diamond strip. *fig. I*

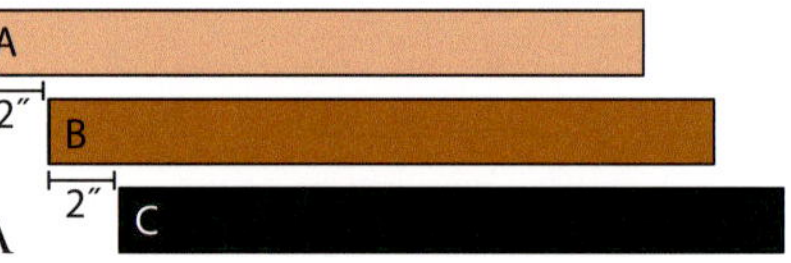

A

B

C

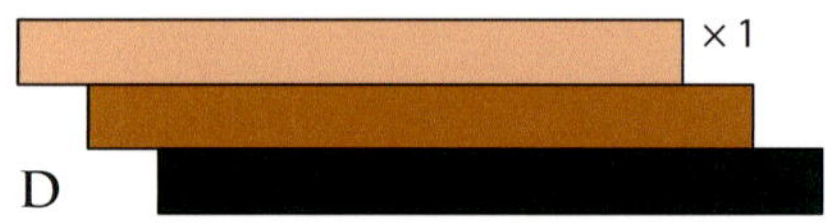

D

E

F

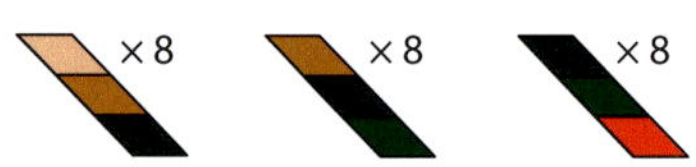

G

H

I

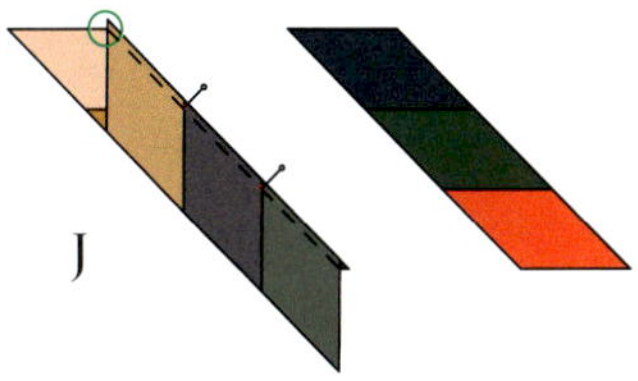
J

K

L

3. Place the B/C/D strip on top of the A/B/C strip, RST. Place the tip of the top strip approximately ¼″ above the tip of the bottom strip. Insert a pin directly through the seams of both strips, through the marks from Step 2. *fig. J*

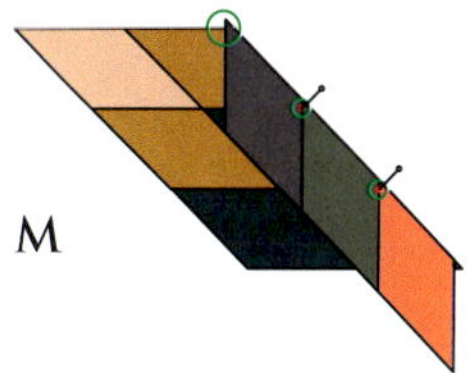
M

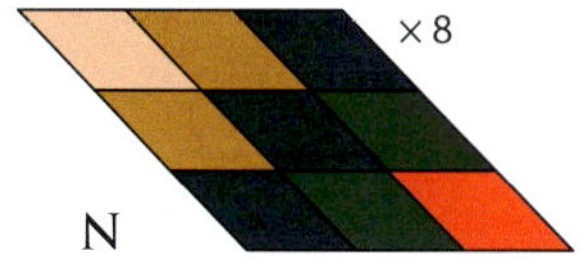

N

4. Sew the diamond strips together and press the seam open. *fig. K*

5. Repeat Steps 2–4 with the Step 4 unit and the remaining C/D/E strip. *figs. L–M*

6. Repeat Steps 2–5 with all of the strips to create 8 strip set diamonds. *fig. N*

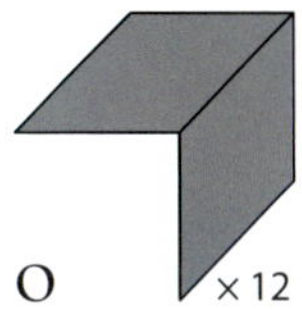

O

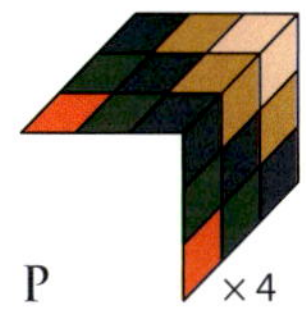

P

QUILT TOP ASSEMBLY

Broken Star Quilt assembly is the same for every Broken Star quilt. To assemble this quilt, follow the instructions in Broken Star Quilt Assembly (page 30).

Reference the following to create Unit 1 (page 30), Unit 2 (page 32), Unit 3 (page 34), and Unit 4 (page 35):

1. Make 12 Unit 1s in Fabric F. *fig. O*

2. Make 4 Unit 1s from strip set diamonds. *fig. P*

3. Make 4 Unit 2s from Fabric F Unit 1s and background fabric. *fig. Q*

Make 4 Unit 3s from Fabric F Unit 1s and background fabric. *fig. R*

Make 4 Unit 4s from the strip set diamonds and Unit 3s. *fig. S*

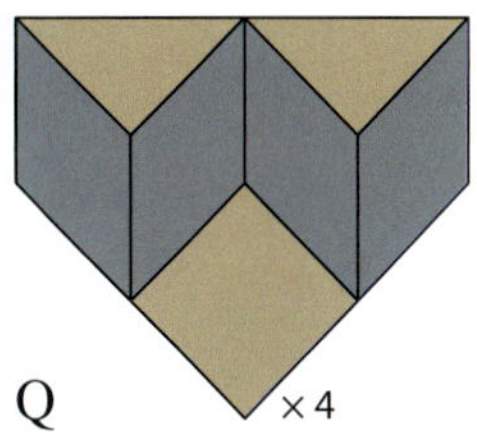

Q

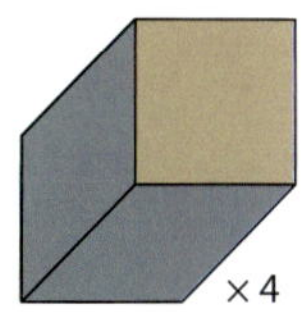

R

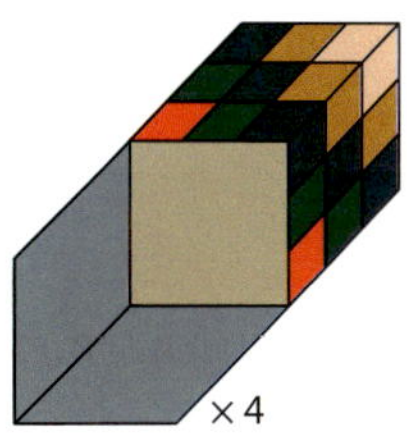

S

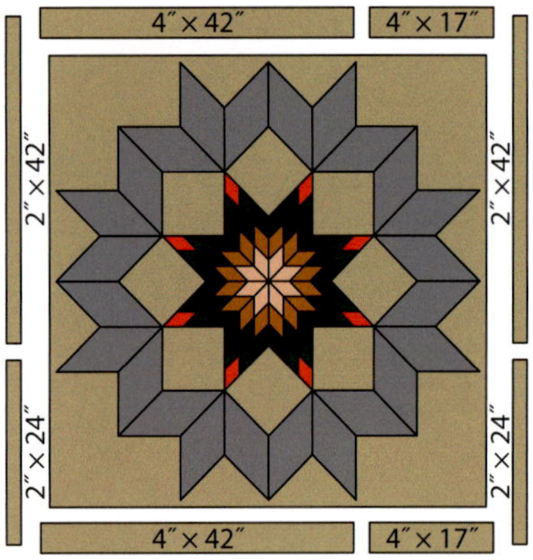

T

U

6. Using Units 1, 2, 3, and 4 and the remaining background squares, continue making Units 5–10 by following the instructions in Broken Star Quilt Assembly (page 30) to finish the quilt top.

7. After Step 6 is completed, refer to the following instructions for making your quilt either a Small Throw or Large Throw size quilt.

V

Small Throw Size Quilt Top

1. Sew a 2″ × 42″ strip to a 2″ × 24″ strip along the 2″ sides. Press the seam open. *figs. T–U*

2. Repeat Step 1 for the remaining 2″ × 42″ and 2″ × 24″ strips. *figs. T–U*

3. Sew an 4″ × 42″ strip to a 4″ × 17″ strip along the 4″ sides. Press the seam open. *figs. T–U*

4. Repeat Step 3 for the remaining 4″ × 42″ and 4″ × 17″ strips. *figs. T–U*

5. Sew the 4″ × 58½″ strips to the top and bottom sides of the quilt top. Press seams as desired. *figs. T–U*

6. Sew the 2″ × 65½″ strips to the left and right sides of the quilt. Press seams as desired. *figs. T–U*

The quilt top is complete and measures 61½″ × 6½″. See Finishing the Quilts (page 42) to quilt and bind.

W

Large Throw Size Quilt Top

1. Sew a 9″ × 42″ strip to a 9″ × 17″ strip along the 9″ sides. Press the seam open. *figs.* V–W

2. Repeat Step 1 with another 9″ × 42″ strip and the remaining 9″ × 17″ strip. *figs.* V–W

3. Sew a 9″ × 42″ strip to a 9″ × 34″ strip along the 9″ sides. Press the seam open. *figs.* V–W

4. Repeat Step 3 for the remaining 9″ × 42″ and 9″ × 34″ strips. *figs.* V–W

5. Sew the 9″ × 58½″ strips to the top and bottom sides of the quilt top. Press seams as desired. *figs.* V–W

6. Sew the 9″ × 75½″ strips to the left and right sides of the quilt. Press seams as desired. *figs.* V–W

The quilt top is complete and measures 75½″ × 75½″. See Finishing the Quilts (page 42) to quilt and bind.

Longarm quilting by Ashlee Doyle, Crinkly Quilts

Quilting pantograph: City of Fountains designed by Julie Hirt

BACKWOODS STAR

SMALL THROW SIZE: 61½″ × 65½″ • LARGE THROW SIZE: 75½″ × 75½″

Montana is the fourth largest state and also one of the least populated, so there are a lot of remote and unsettled (aka backwoods) areas to explore. This Broken Star is made up of large diamonds for the center star and pieced diamonds for the outer ring. I used the same color for the center star diamonds as one of the fabrics in the outer ring. Just as there are vast areas to explore in the backwoods, there are many options when it comes to making this quilt your own.

FABRIC REQUIREMENTS

Yardages are based on 43″ wide fabric.

Share what you make!
#backwoodsstarquilt

FABRIC	COLOR NAME	SMALL THROW SIZE	LARGE THROW SIZE
Fabric A	Kona Spice	½ yard	½ yard
Fabric B	Kona Gumdrop	¼ yard	¼ yard
Fabric C	Kona Spice	½ yard	½ yard
Fabric D	Kona Black	¾ yard	¾ yard
Fabric E	Kona Latte	½ yard	½ yard
Fabric F	Kona Yarrow	¼ yard	¼ yard
Background	Kona Natural	2⅜ yards	3⅝ yards
Binding	Kona Yarrow	⅝ yard	⅝ yard
Backing	Fableism Everyday Chambray in Cinnabar	4 yards	4¾ yards
Batting	Warm & Natural by The Warm Company	69″ × 73″	83″ × 83″

A Backwoods Star with Window Star blocks (page 64).

CUTTING INSTRUCTIONS

For a full tutorial on cutting diamonds, see Cutting and Sewing Diamonds (page 18). Or, for a quick reminder on cutting diamonds, see How to Cut Diamonds (page 53).

Note: For the 6½″ diamonds, if the usable width of your fabric is less than 43″, do not trim off the selvages before cutting the diamonds. Trim the diamond point after sewing together if needed.

Fabric A

- Cut 2 strips 6½″ × WOF; subcut into 8 diamonds 6½″.

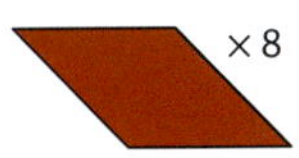

Fabric B

- Cut 3 strips 2½″ × WOF.

Fabric C

- Cut 6 strips 2½″ × WOF.

Fabric D

- Cut 9 strips 2½″ × WOF.

Fabric E

- Cut 6 strips 2½″ × WOF.

Fabric F

- Cut 3 strips 2½″ × WOF.

Background (All Sizes)

If you're including interchangeable blocks instead of background squares, see Interchangeable Blocks (page 50) for cutting and piecing instructions.

- Cut 1 strip 13½″ × WOF; subcut into 2 squares 13½″ × 13½″.

  Subcut each 13½″ square along each diagonal into 4 triangles.

- Cut 5 strips 9″ × WOF; subcut into 20 squares 9″ × 9″.

Background (Small Throw Size)

- Cut 4 strips 2″ × WOF; subcut into:

  2 strips 2″ × 42″

  2 strips 2″ × 24″

- Cut 3 strips 4″ × WOF; subcut into:

  2 strips 4″ × 42″

  2 strips 4″ × 17″

Background (Large Throw Size)

- Cut 7 strips 9″ × WOF; subcut into:

  4 strips 9″ × 42″

  2 strips 9″ × 34″

  2 strips 9″ × 17″

Binding (Small Throw Size)

- Cut 7 strips 2½″ × WOF.

Binding (Large Throw Size)

- Cut 8 strips 2½″ × WOF.

Backing (Small Throw Size)

Cut and piece the backing fabric as needed to make a backing that equals 69″ × 73″.

Backing (Large Throw Size)

Cut and piece the backing fabric as needed to make a backing that equals 83″ × 83″.

Sewing Instructions

STRIP SETS

1. Group the strips, offset by 2″, into the following combinations, using one strip per color in each group: B/C/D, C/D/E, and D/E/F. *figs. A–C*

2. Place the first 2 strips in each group RST and sew together along one long side (B/C, C/D, D/E). Then, add the third strip to each pair, and sew together along one long side. Press the seams open. Repeat Steps 1–2 to make 3 of each strip set. *figs. D–F*

3. Trim the selvages and cut 24 diamond strips 2½″ in each color (8 from each individual strip set). See Cutting and Sewing Diamonds (page 18) for a full tutorial on cutting diamonds. Or see How to Cut Diamonds (page 53) for a quick reminder. *fig. G*

> KEEP THOSE EXTRA DIAMOND STRIPS
>
> *You should be able to cut 10 or 11 diamond strips 2½″ from each strip set which is more than is needed for this pattern. Set aside the extra diamond strips to use in a Plains Star quilt on page 134.*

STRIP SET DIAMONDS

1. Select a 2½″ strip from each strip set. Arrange them into a diamond unit, in the order shown. Repeat to arrange all the strips into 24 total strip set diamonds (unsewn). *fig. H*

2. Begin with the first diamond unit. On the right side of the B/C/D diamond strip, use the ruler and a marking tool to measure and mark ¼″ from the edge of the fabric on each seam. Repeat on the wrong side of the C/D/E diamond strip. *fig. I*

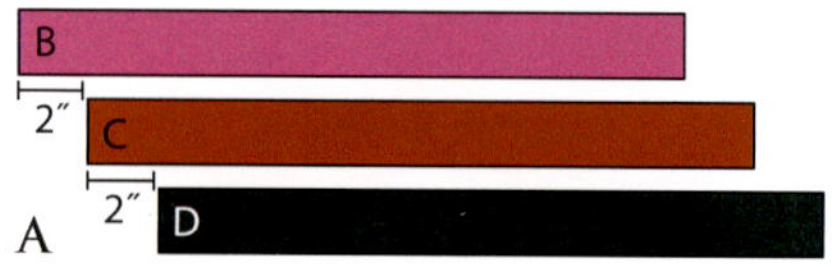

A

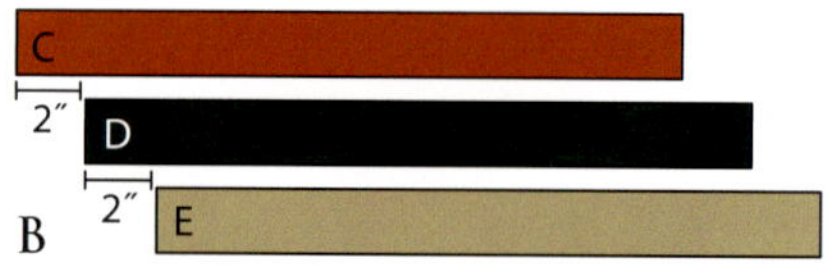

B

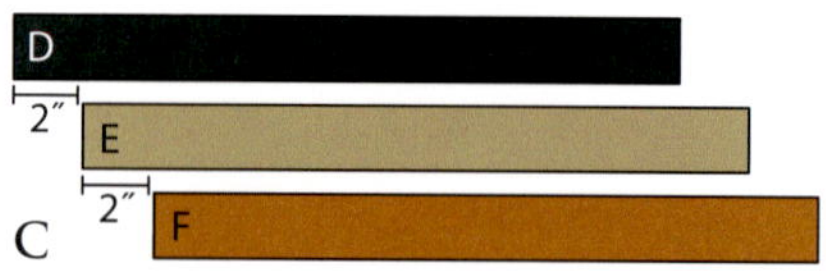

C

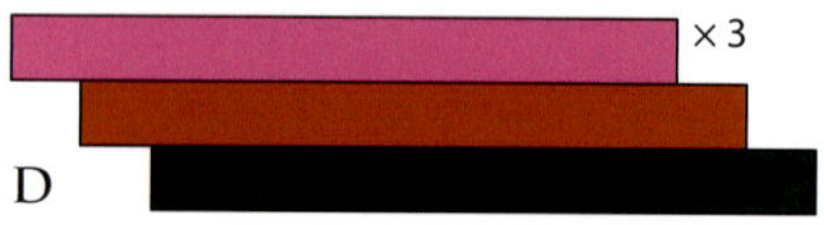

D

E

F

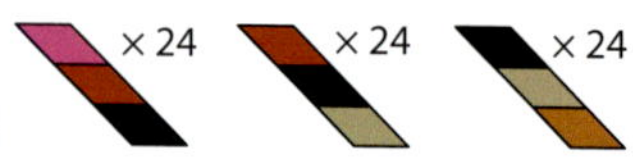

G

H

I

3. Place the C/D/E strip on top of the B/C/D strip, RST. Place the tip of the top strip approximately ¼″ above the tip of the bottom strip. Insert a pin directly through the seams of both strips, through the marks from Step 2. *fig. J*

4. Sew the strip sets together and press the seam open. *fig. K*

5. Repeat Steps 2–4 with the Step 4 unit and the remaining D/E/F strip. *figs. L–M*

6. Repeat Steps 2–5 with all of the strips to create 24 strip set diamonds. *fig. N*

QUILT TOP ASSEMBLY

Broken Star Quilt assembly is the same for every Broken Star quilt. To assemble this quilt, follow the instructions in Broken Star Quilt Assembly (page 30).

Reference the following to create Unit 1 (page 30), Unit 2 (page 32), Unit 3 (page 34), and Unit 4 (page 35):

1. Make 4 Unit 1s in Fabric A. *fig. O*

2. Make 8 Unit 1s from strip set diamonds as arranged to the right. *fig. P*

3. Make 4 Unit 1s from strip set diamonds as arranged to the right. *fig. Q*

4. Make 4 Unit 2s from View A Unit 1s and background fabric. *fig. R*

5. Make 4 Unit 3s from View B Unit 1s and background fabric. *fig. S*

6. Make 4 Unit 4s from Fabric A diamonds and the Unit 3s. *fig. T*

J
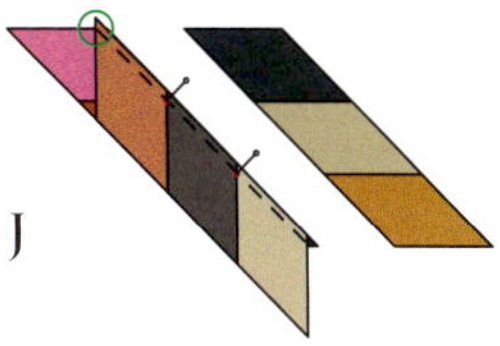

K
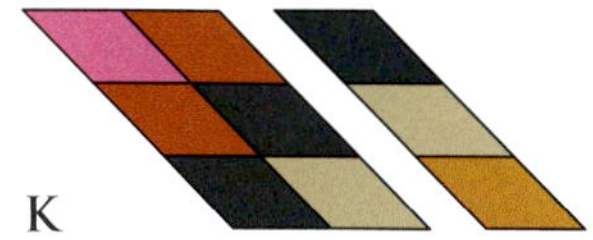

L

M
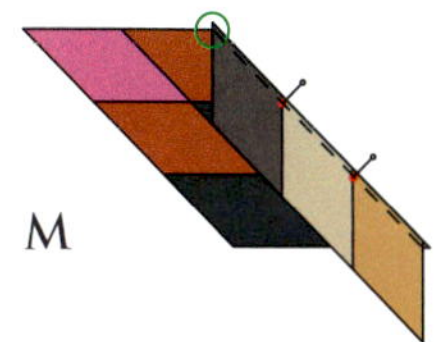

N
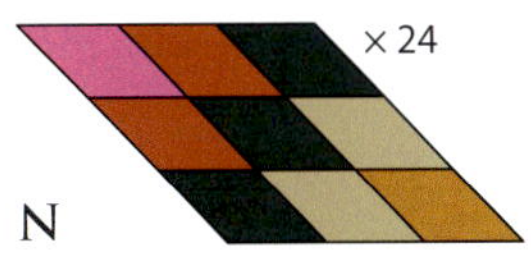

O
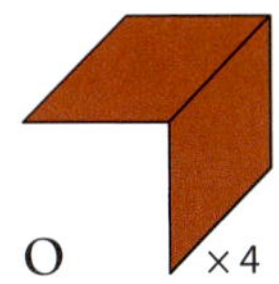

P
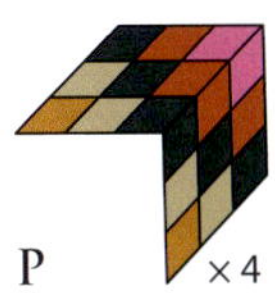

Q

R
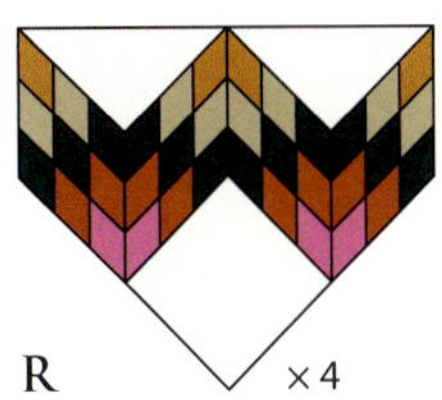

S

T
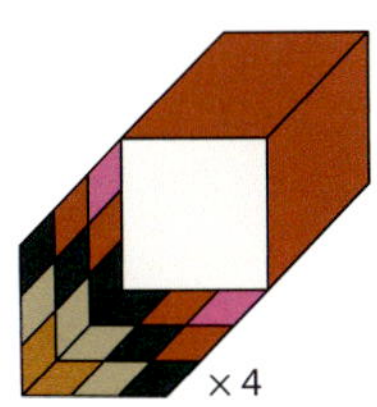

U

V

7. Using Units 1, 2, 3, and 4 and the remaining background squares, continue making Units 5–10 by following the instructions in Broken Star Quilt Assembly (page 30) to finish the quilt top.

8. After Step 7 is completed, refer to the following instructions for making your quilt either a Small Throw or Large Throw size quilt.

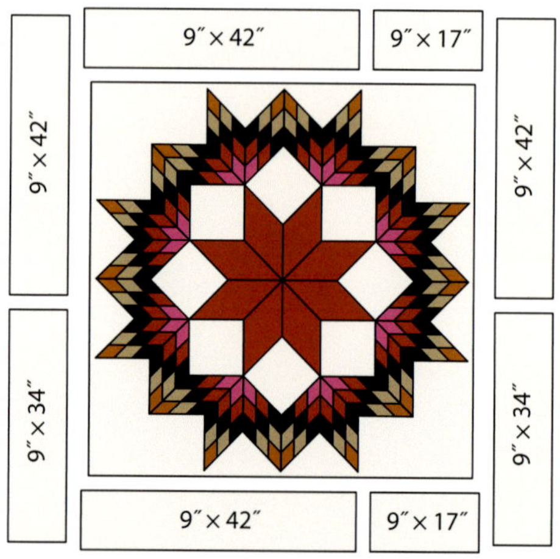

W

Small Throw Size Quilt Top

1. Sew a 2″ × 42″ strip to a 2″ × 24″ strip along the 2″ sides. Press the seam open. *figs. U–V*

2. Repeat Step 1 for the remaining 2″ × 42″ and 2″ × 24″ strips. *figs. U–V*

3. Sew an 4″ × 42″ strip to a 4″ × 17″ strip along the 4″ sides. Press the seam open. *figs. U–V*

4. Repeat Step 3 for the remaining 4″ × 42″ and 4″ × 17″ strips. *figs. U–V*

5. Sew the 4″ × 58½″ strips to the top and bottom sides of the quilt top. Press seams as desired. *figs. U–V*

6. Sew the 2″ × 65½″ strips to the left and right sides of the quilt. Press seams as desired. *figs. U–V*

The quilt top is complete and measures 61½″ × 65½″. See Finishing the Quilts (page 42) to quilt and bind.

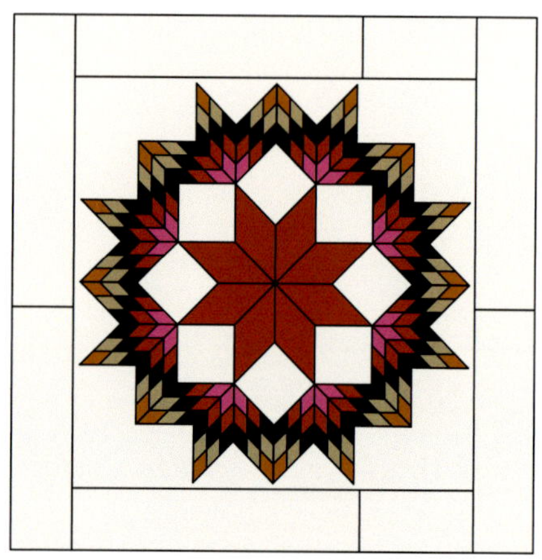
X

Large Throw Size Quilt Top

1. Sew a 9″ × 42″ strip to a 9″ × 17″ strip along the 9″ sides. Press the seam open. *figs. W–X*

2. Repeat Step 1 with another 9″ × 42″ strip and the remaining 9″ × 17″ strip. *figs. W–X*

3. Sew a 9″ × 42″ strip to a 9″ × 34″ strip along the 9″ sides. Press the seam open. *figs. W–X*

4. Repeat Step 3 for the remaining 9″ × 42″ and 9″ × 34″ strips. *figs. W–X*

5. Sew the 9″ × 58½″ strips to the top and bottom sides of the quilt top. Press seams as desired. *figs. W–X*

6. Sew the 9″ × 75½″ strips to the left and right sides of the quilt. Press seams as desired. *figs. W–X*

The quilt top is complete and measures 75½″ × 75½″. See Finishing the Quilts (page 42) to quilt and bind.

Longarm quilting by Ashlee Doyle, Crinkly Quilts

Quilting pantograph: Bubble Clams designed by Melissa Kelley

MAJESTIC STAR

SMALL THROW SIZE: 61½″ × 65½″ • LARGE THROW SIZE: 75½″ × 75½″

There is a line in the song America the Beautiful that describes the Rockies as "purple mountains majesties". Whenever the sun is shining on the mountains just right to give them that purple hue I think of this song. The Majestic Star quilt pattern is a good one once you have become familiar with the skills in this book and are ready for a challenge (you are ready!). This version uses five fabrics in the diamonds. The Broken Trail Star (page 142) is a bed size version of this pattern if you're looking for something even bigger.

FABRIC REQUIREMENTS

Yardages are based on 42″ wide fabric.

Share what you make! #majesticstarquilt

FABRIC	COLOR NAME	SMALL THROW SIZE	LARGE THROW SIZE
Fabric A	Kona Coral	¼ yard	¼ yard
Fabric B	Fableism Native Nectar in Pink Sky	½ yard	½ yard
Fabric C	Kona Gumdrop	¾ yard	¾ yard
Fabric D	Kona Spice	½ yard	½ yard
Fabric E	Neon Neppy in Chambray	¼ yard	¼ yard
Background	Neon Neppy in Denim	2⅜ yards	3⅝ yards
Binding	Kona Spice	⅝ yard	⅝ yard
Backing	Fableism Native Nectar in Pink Sky	4 yards	4¾ yards
Batting	Warm & White by The Warm Company	69″ × 73″	83″ × 83″

A Majestic Star quilt with Fish Tails blocks (page 56).

CUTTING INSTRUCTIONS

For a full tutorial on cutting diamonds, see Cutting and Sewing Diamonds (page 18). Or, for a quick reminder on cutting diamonds, see How to Cut Diamonds (page 53).

Fabric A

- Cut 3 strips 2½″ × WOF.

Fabric B

- Cut 6 strips 2½″ × WOF.

Fabric C

- Cut 9 strips 2½″ × WOF.

Fabric D

- Cut 6 strips 2½″ × WOF.

Fabric E

- Cut 3 strips 2½″ × WOF.

Background (All Sizes)

If you're including interchangeable blocks instead of background squares, see Interchangeable Blocks (page 50) for cutting and piecing instructions.

- Cut 1 strip 13½″ × WOF; subcut into 2 squares 13½″ × 13½″.

  Subcut each 13½″ square along each diagonal into 4 triangles.

- Cut 5 strips 9″ × WOF; subcut into 20 squares 9″ × 9″.

Background (Small Throw Size)

- Cut 4 strips 2″ × WOF; subcut into:

  2 strips 2″ × 42″

  2 strips 2″ × 24″

- Cut 3 strips 4″ × WOF; subcut into:

  2 strips 4″ × 42″

  2 strips 4″ × 17″

Background (Large Throw Size)

- Cut 7 strips 9″ × WOF; subcut into:

  4 strips 9″ × 42″

  2 strips 9″ × 34″

  2 strips 9″ × 17″

Binding (Small Throw Size)

- Cut 7 strips 2½″ × WOF.

Binding (Large Throw Size)

- Cut 9 strips 2½″ × WOF.

Backing (Small Throw Size)

Cut and piece the backing fabric as needed to make a backing that equals 69″ × 73″.

BACKING (LARGE THROW SIZE)

Cut and piece the backing fabric as needed to make a backing that equals 83″ × 83″.

Sewing Instructions

STRIP SETS

1. Group the strips, offset by 2″, into the following combinations, using one strip per color in each group: A/B/C, B/C/D, and C/D/E. *figs. A–C*

2. Place the first 2 strips in each group RST and sew together along one long side (A/B, B/C, C/D). Then, add the third strip to each pair, and sew together along one long side. Press the seams open. Repeat Steps 1–2 to make 3 of each strip set. *figs. D–F*

3. Trim the selvages and cut 32 diamond strips 2½″ in each color (11 from two strip sets and 10 from the third strip set). See Cutting and Sewing Diamonds (page 18) for a full tutorial on cutting diamonds. Or, see How to Cut Diamonds (page 53) for a quick reminder. *fig. G*

STRIP SET DIAMONDS

1. Select a 2½″ strip from each strip set. Arrange them into a diamond unit, in the order shown. Repeat to arrange all the strips into 8 total strip set diamonds (unsewn). *fig. H*

2. Begin with the first diamond unit. On the right side of the A/B/C diamond strip, use the ruler and a marking tool to measure and mark ¼″ from the edge of the fabric on each seam. Repeat on the wrong side of the B/C/D diamond strip. *fig. I*

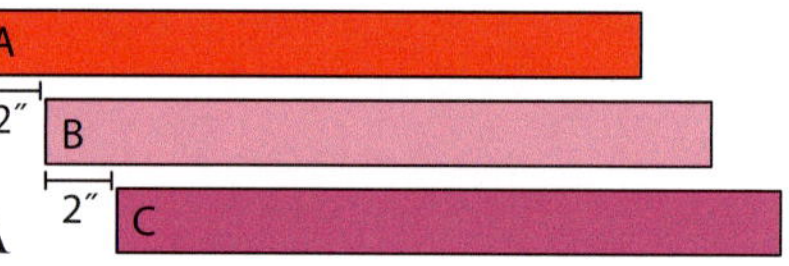

A

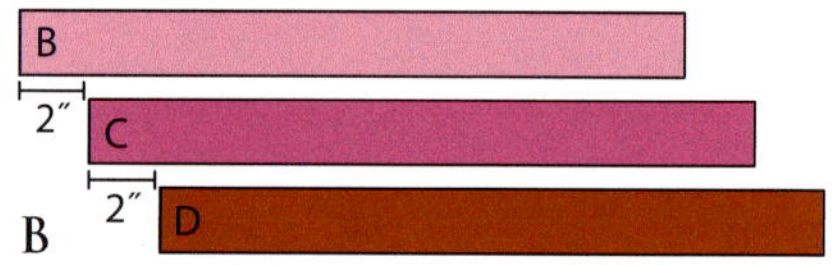

B

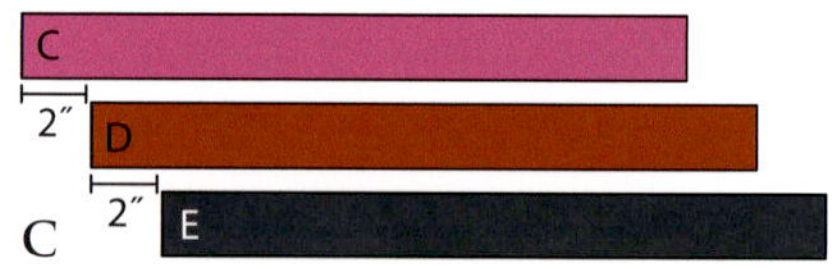

C

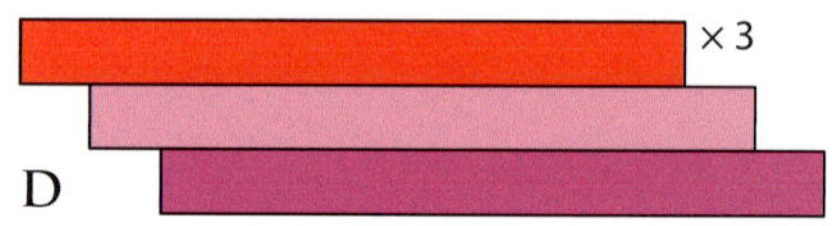

D

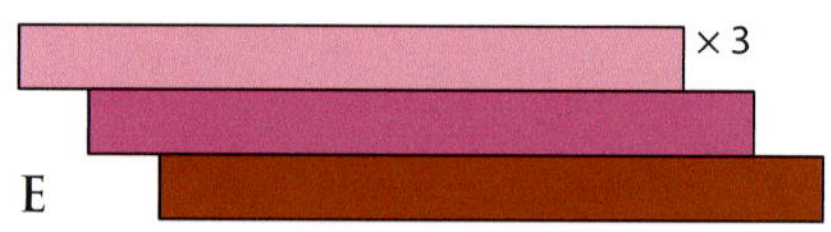

E

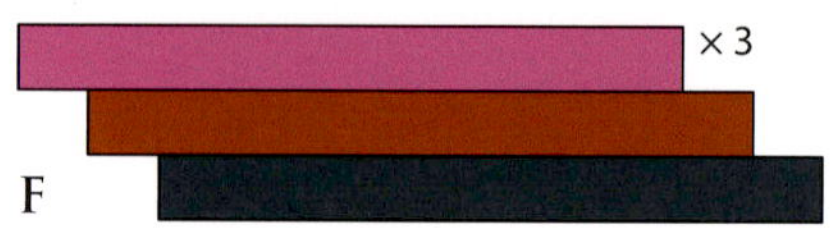

F

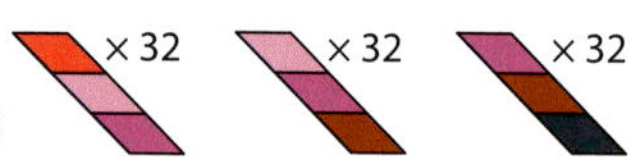

G

H

I

3. Place the B/C/D strip on top of the A/B/C strip, RST. Place the tip of the top strip approximately ¼″ above the tip of the bottom strip. Insert a pin directly through the seams of both strips, through the marks from Step 2. *fig. J*

4. Sew the diamond strips together and press the seam open. *fig. K*

5. Repeat Steps 2–4 with the Step 4 unit and the remaining C/D/E strip. *figs. L–M*

6. Repeat Steps 2–5 with all of the strips to create 32 strip set diamonds. *fig. N*

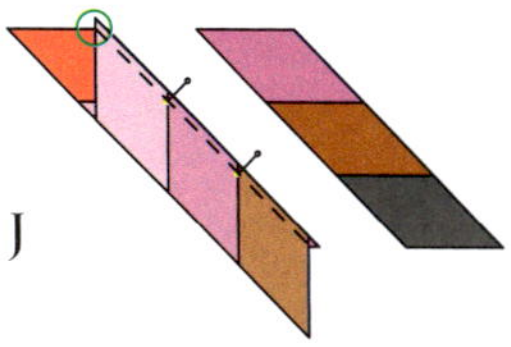
J

K

L

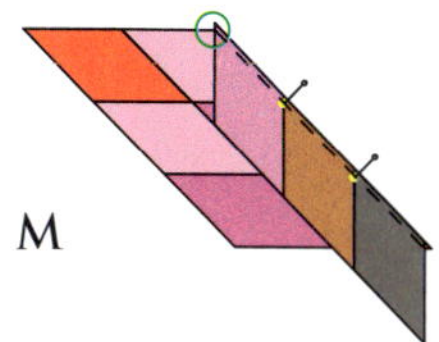
M

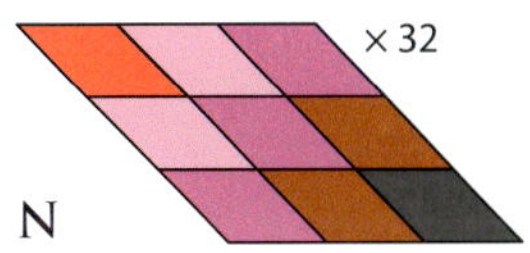

N

QUILT TOP ASSEMBLY

Broken Star Quilt assembly is the same for every Broken Star quilt. To assemble this quilt, follow the instructions in Broken Star Quilt Assembly (page 30).

Reference the following to create Unit 1 (page 30), Unit 2 (page 32), Unit 3 (page 34), and Unit 4 (page 35):

1. Make 8 Unit 1s from strip set diamonds as arranged to the right. *fig. O*

2. Make 8 Unit 1s from strip set diamonds as arranged to the right. *fig. P*

3. Make 4 Unit 2s from View B Unit 1s and background fabric. *fig. Q*

4. Make 4 Unit 3s from View A Unit 1s and background fabric. *fig. R*

5. Make 4 Unit 4s from View A Unit 1s and the Unit 3s. *fig. S*

6. Using Units 1, 2, 3, and 4 and the remaining background squares, continue making Units 5–10 by following the instructions in Broken Star Quilt Assembly (page 30) to finish the quilt top.

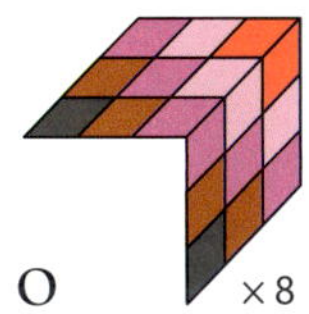

O

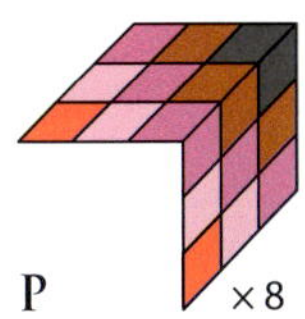

P

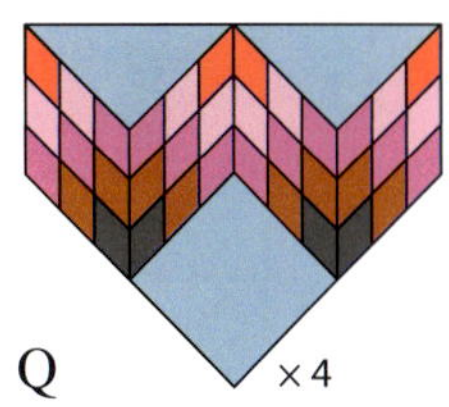

Q

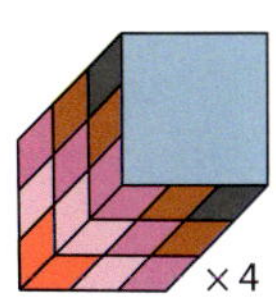

R

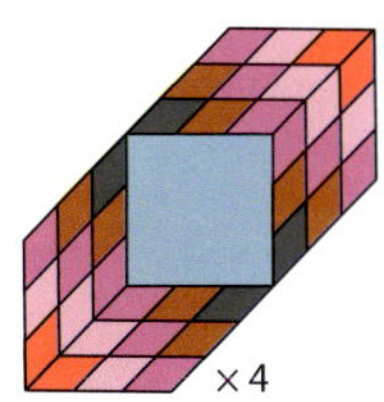

S

T

U

7. After Step 6 is completed, refer to the following instructions for making your quilt either a Small Throw or Large Throw size quilt.

Small Throw Size Quilt Top

1. Sew a 2″ × 42″ strip to a 2″ × 24″ strip along the 2″ sides. Press the seam open. *figs. T–U*

2. Repeat Step 1 for the remaining 2″ × 42″ and 2″ × 24″ strips. *figs. T–U*

3. Sew an 4″ × 42″ strip to a 4″ × 17″ strip along the 4″ sides. Press the seam open. *figs. T–U*

4. Repeat Step 3 for the remaining 4″ × 42″ and 4″ × 17″ strips. *figs. T–U*

5. Sew the 4″ × 58½″ strips to the top and bottom sides of the quilt top. Press seams as desired. *figs. T–U*

6. Sew the 2″ × 65½″ strips to the left and right sides of the quilt. Press seams as desired. *figs. T–U*

The quilt top is complete and measures 61½″ × 65½″. See Finishing the Quilts (page 42) to quilt and bind.

V

W

Large Throw Size Quilt Top

1. Sew a 9″ × 42″ strip to a 9″ × 17″ strip along the 9″ sides. Press the seam open. *figs. V–W*

2. Repeat Step 1 with another 9″ × 42″ strip and the remaining 9″ × 17″ strip. *figs. V–W*

3. Sew a 9″ × 42″ strip to a 9″ × 34″ strip along the 9″ sides. Press the seam open. *figs. V–W*

4. Repeat Step 3 for the remaining 9″ × 42″ and 9″ × 34″ strips. *figs. V–W*

5. Sew the 9″ × 58½″ strips to the top and bottom sides of the quilt top. Press seams as desired. *figs. V–W*

6. Sew the 9″ × 75½″ strips to the left and right sides of the quilt. Press seams as desired. *figs. V–W*

The quilt top is complete and measures 75½″ × 75½″. See Finishing the Quilts (page 42) to quilt and bind.

Longarm quilting by Ashlee Doyle, Crinkly Quilts

Quilting pantograph: Vortex designed by Barbie Mills, The Quilting Mill

Plains Star

SMALL THROW SIZE: 61½″ × 65½″ • LARGE THROW SIZE: 75½″ × 75½″

The Plains Star is designed to use the extra diamond strips that are leftover from the Backwoods Star (page 118). You may also have extra strips set aside from other projects in this book, and they can also be used here. The Plains Star has 3 different design options, and within them, the layout variations are endless. Get creative to use those extra strips!

FABRIC REQUIREMENTS

Yardages are based on 43″ wide fabric.

Share what you make!
#plainsstarquilt

FABRIC	COLOR NAME	OPTION 1	OPTION 2	OPTION 3	SMALL THROW	LARGE THROW
Diamond strips 2½″	From the Backwoods Star (page 118) strip sets (or other leftover strip sets)	24	3	12	-	-
Fabric A	Kona Spice	1⅜ yards	1⅜ yards	1⅜ yards	-	-
Fabric B	Kona Yarrow	-	⅝ yard	⅜ yard	-	-
Background	Fableism Forest Forage Daisies in Denim	-	-	-	2¼ yards	3½ yards
Binding	-	-	-	-	⅝ yard	⅝ yard
Backing	-	-	-	-	4 yards	4¾ yards
Batting	-	-	-	-	69″ × 73″	83″ × 83″

Option 1

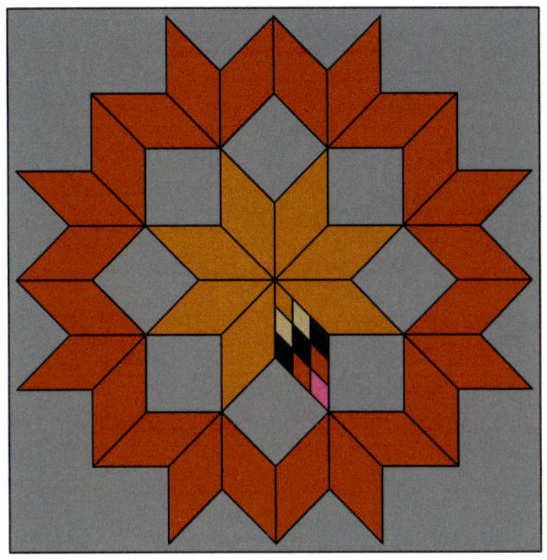

Option 2

Option 3

CUTTING INSTRUCTIONS

For a full tutorial on cutting diamonds, see Cutting and Sewing Diamonds (page 18). Or, for a quick reminder on cutting diamonds, see How to Cut Diamonds (page 53).

Note: For the 6½″ diamonds, if the usable width of your fabric is less than 43″, do not trim off the selvages before cutting the diamonds. Trim the diamond point after sewing together if needed.

Option 1

FABRIC A

- Cut 6 strips 6½″ × WOF; subcut into 24 diamonds 6½″.

Option 2

FABRIC A

- Cut 6 strips 6½″ × WOF; subcut into 24 diamonds 6½″.

FABRIC B

- Cut 2 strips 6½″ × WOF; subcut into 7 diamonds 6½″.

Option 3

FABRIC A

- Cut 6 strips 6½″ × WOF; subcut into 24 diamonds 6½″.

FABRIC B

- Cut 1 strip 6½″ × WOF; subcut into 4 diamonds 6½″.

Background (All Sizes)

If you're including interchangeable blocks instead of background squares, see Interchangeable Blocks (page 50) for cutting and piecing instructions.

- Cut 1 strip 13½″ × WOF; subcut into 2 squares 13½″ × 13½″.

  Subcut each 13½″ square along each diagonal into 4 triangles.

- Cut 5 strips 9″ × WOF; subcut into 20 squares 9″ × 9″.

BACKGROUND (SMALL THROW SIZE)

- Cut 4 strips 2″ × WOF; subcut into:

  2 strips 2″ × 42″

  2 strips 2″ × 24″

- Cut 3 strips 4″ × WOF; subcut into:

  2 strips 4″ × 42″

  2 strips 4″ × 17″

BACKGROUND (LARGE THROW SIZE)

- Cut 7 strips 9″ × WOF; subcut into:

  4 strips 9″ × 42″

  2 strips 9″ × 34″

  2 strips 9″ × 17″

Binding (Small Throw Size)

- Cut 7 strips 2½″ × WOF.

Binding (Large Throw Size)

- Cut 8 strips 2½″ × WOF.

Backing (Small Throw Size)

Cut and piece the backing fabric as needed to make a backing that equals 69″ × 73″.

Backing (Large Throw Size)

Cut and piece the backing fabric as needed to make a backing that equals 83″ × 83″.

Sewing Instructions

Broken Star Quilt assembly is the same for every Broken Star quilt. To assemble this quilt, follow the instructions in Broken Star Quilt Assembly (page 30).

OPTION 1

1. Reference the following to create Unit 1 (page 30), Unit 2 (page 32), Unit 3 (page 34), and Unit 4 (page 35): *figs. A–E*

2. Using Units 1, 2, 3, and 4 and the remaining background squares, continue making Units 5–10 by following the instructions in Broken Star Quilt Assembly (page 30) to finish the quilt top.

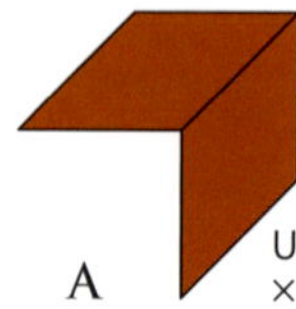

A Unit 1 × 12

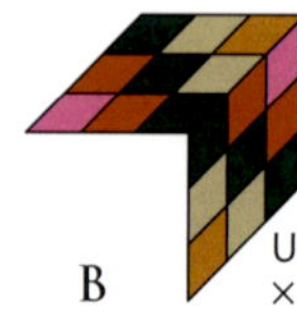

B Unit 1 × 4

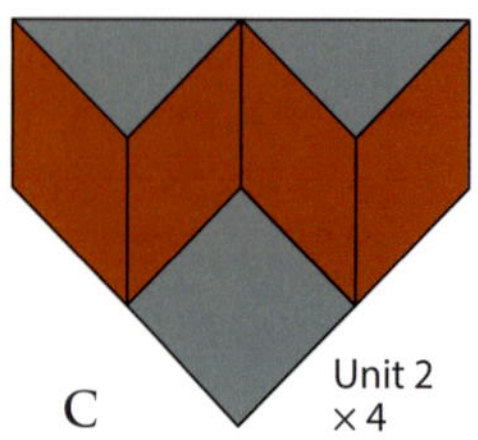

C Unit 2 × 4

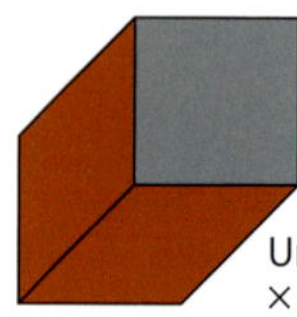

D Unit 3 × 4

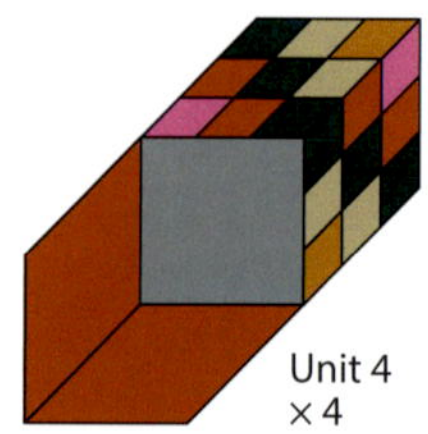

E Unit 4 × 4

OPTION 2

1. Reference the following to create Unit 1 (page 30), Unit 2 (page 32), Unit 3 (page 34), and Unit 4 (page 35): *figs. F–L*

2. Using Units 1, 2, 3, and 4 and the remaining background squares, continue making Units 5–10 by following the instructions in Broken Star Quilt Assembly (page 30) to finish the quilt top.

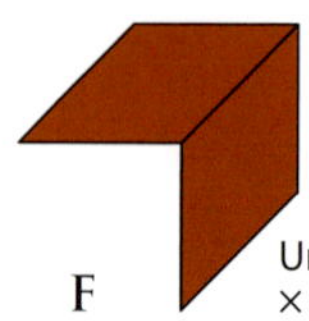

F Unit 1 × 12

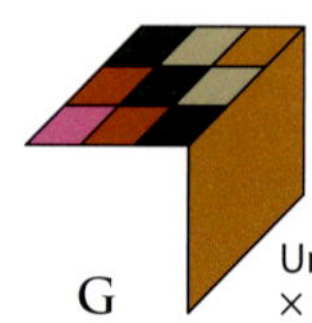

G Unit 1 × 1

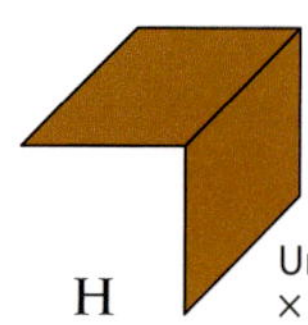

H Unit 1 × 3

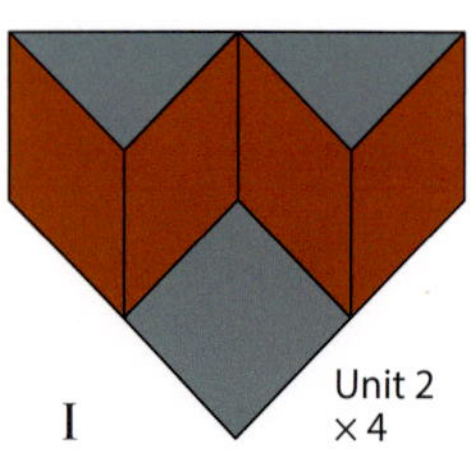

I Unit 2 × 4

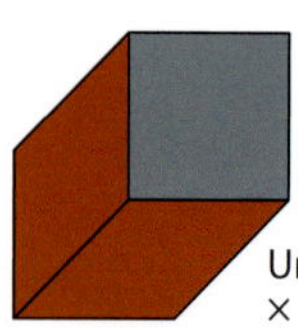

J Unit 3 × 4

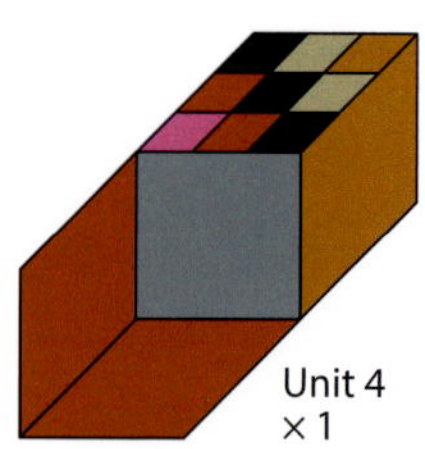

K Unit 4 × 1

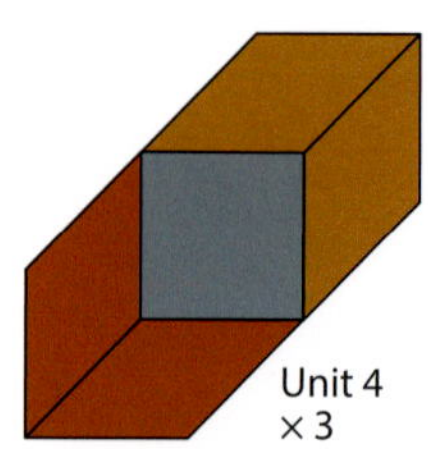

L Unit 4 × 3

OPTION 3

1. Reference the following to create Unit 1 (page 30), Unit 2 (page 32), Unit 3 (page 34), and Unit 4 (page 35): *figs. M–V*

2. Using Units 1, 2, 3, and 4 and the remaining background squares, continue making Units 5–10 by following the instructions in Broken Star Quilt Assembly (page 30) to finish the quilt top.

M

Unit 1 × 1

N

Unit 1 × 1

O
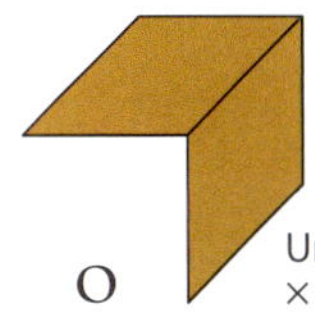
Unit 1 × 1

P
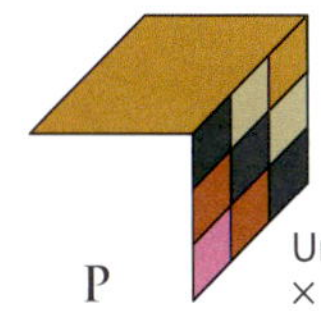
Unit 1 × 1

Q
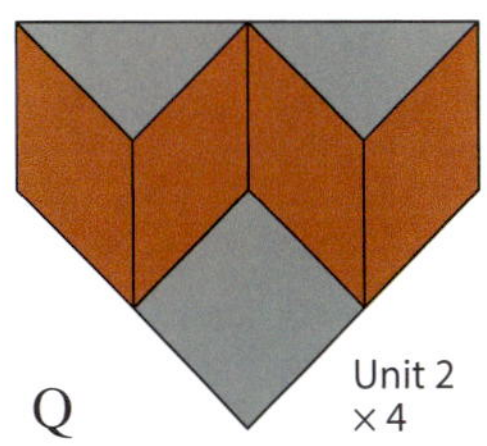
Unit 2 × 4

R
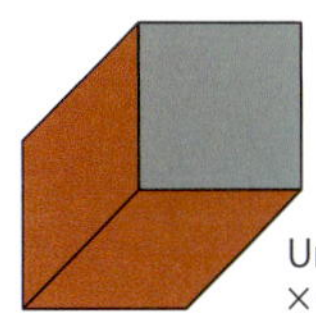
Unit 3 × 4

S

Unit 4 × 1

T
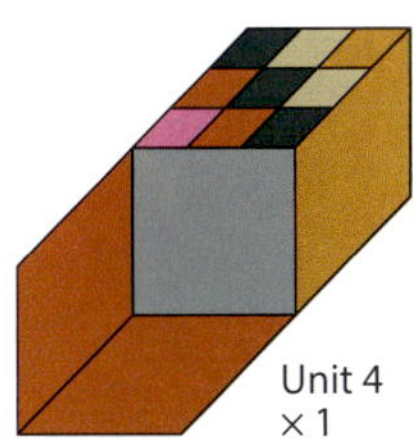
Unit 4 × 1

U
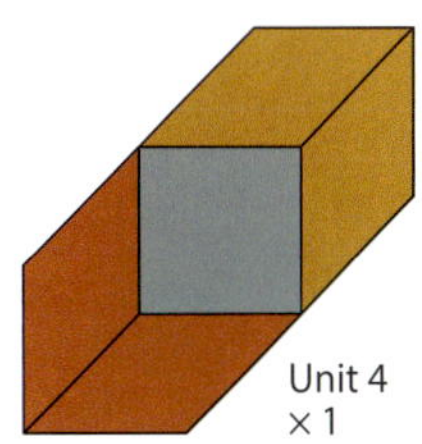
Unit 4 × 1

V
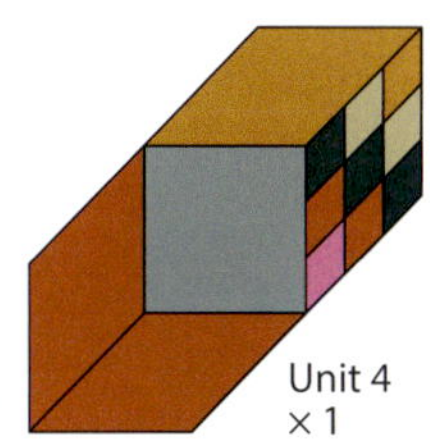
Unit 4 × 1

W

X

ALL OPTIONS

After Step 2 is completed, refer to the following instructions for making your quilt either a Small Throw or Large Throw size quilt.

Small Throw Size Quilt Top

1. Sew a 2″ × 42″ strip to a 2″ × 24″ strip along the 2″ sides. Press the seam open. *figs. W–X*

2. Repeat Step 1 for the remaining 2″ × 42″ and 2″ × 24″ strips. *figs. W–X*

3. Sew an 4″ × 42″ strip to a 4″ × 17″ strip along the 4″ sides. Press the seam open. *figs. W–X*

4. Repeat Step 3 for the remaining 4″ × 42″ and 4″ × 17″ strips. *figs. W–X*

5. Sew the 4″ × 58½″ strips to the top and bottom sides of the quilt top. Press seams as desired. *figs. W–X*

6. Sew the 2″ × 65½″ strips to the left and right sides of the quilt. Press seams as desired. *figs. W–X*

The quilt top is complete and measures 61½″ × 65½″. See Finishing the Quilts (page 42) to quilt and bind.

Y

Z

Large Throw Size Quilt Top

1. Sew a 9″ × 42″ strip to a 9″ × 17″ strip along the 9″ sides. Press the seam open. *figs. Y–Z*

2. Repeat Step 1 with another 9″ × 42″ strip and the remaining 9″ × 17″ strip. *figs. Y–Z*

3. Sew an 9″ × 42″ strip to a 9″ × 34″ strip along the 9″ sides. Press the seam open. *figs. Y–Z*

4. Repeat Step 3 for the remaining 9″ × 42″ and 9″ × 34″ strips. *figs. Y–Z*

5. Sew the 9″ × 58½″ strips to the top and bottom sides of the quilt top. Press seams as desired. *figs. Y–Z*

6. Sew the 9″ × 75½″ strips to the left and right sides of the quilt. Press seams as desired. *figs. Y–Z*

The quilt top is complete and measures 75½″ × 75½″. See Finishing the Quilts (page 42) to quilt and bind.

Longarm quilting by Ashlee Doyle, Crinkly Quilts

Quilting pantograph: Funky Fans designed by Lisa H. Calle

Broken Trail Star

FINISHED QUILT SIZE: 96½″ × 96½″

The Broken Trail Star is a bed size version of the classic Broken Star quilt with stars made completely from strip sets—it uses 9 different fabrics! This is the quilt pattern to make once you are comfortable with cutting and sewing on a bias, matching diamond points, sewing Y-seams, and Broken Star quilt assembly. This is the most time consuming quilt in this book, but it also has the biggest payoff. This quilt is a showstopper and is destined to be a treasured heirloom.

FABRIC REQUIREMENTS

Yardages are based on 42″ wide fabric.

Share what you make!
#brokentrailstarquilt

FABRIC	COLOR NAME	BED SIZE
Fabric A	Kona Natural	¼ yard
Fabric B	Kona Sky	½ yard
Fabric C	Kona Latte	¾ yard
Fabric D	Warp and Weft Stitch in Cayenne by Alexia Abegg	⅞ yard
Fabric E	Fableism Everyday Chambray in Cinnabar	1⅛ yard
Fabric F	Kona Earth	⅞ yard
Fabric G	Kona Yarrow	¾ yard
Fabric H	Kona Primrose	½ yards
Fabric I	Kona Thistle	¼ yard
Background	Neon Neppy in Royal	5½ yards
Binding	Fableism Everyday Chambray in Cinnabar	⅞ yard
Backing	Mammoth Flannel in Denim	8¾ yards
Batting	Warm & Natural by The Warm Company	104″ × 104″

CUTTING INSTRUCTIONS

For a full tutorial on cutting diamonds, see Cutting and Sewing Diamonds (page 18). Or, for a quick reminder on cutting diamonds, see How to Cut Diamonds (page 53).

Fabric A

- Cut 3 strips 2½″ × WOF.

Fabric B

- Cut 6 strips 2½″ × WOF.

Fabric C

- Cut 9 strips 2½″ × WOF.

Fabric D

- Cut 12 strips 2½″ × WOF.

Fabric E

- Cut 15 strips 2½″ × WOF.

Fabric F

- Cut 12 strips 2½″ × WOF.

Fabric G

- Cut 9 strips 2½″ × WOF.

Fabric H

- Cut 6 strips 2½″ × WOF.

Fabric I

- Cut 3 strips 2½″ × WOF.

Background

If you're including interchangeable blocks instead of background squares, see Interchangeable Blocks (page 50) for cutting and piecing instructions.

- Cut 2 strips 22″ × WOF; subcut into 2 squares 22″ × 22″.

  Subcut each 22″ square along each diagonal into 4 triangles.

- Cut 10 strips 14½″ × WOF; subcut into 20 squares 14½″ × 14½″.

Binding

- Cut 10 strips 2½″ × WOF.

Backing

Cut and piece the backing fabric as needed to make a backing that equals 104″ × 104″.

Sewing Instructions

STRIP SETS

1. Arrange the strips into strip sets in the order shown in the following chart. Offset the strips by 2″. Arrange 3 of each strip set. *figs. A–E*

2. Sew the strips in each set together along the long sides. Press the seams open. *figs. F–J*

STRIP SET 1	STRIP SET 2	STRIP SET 3	STRIP SET 4	STRIP SET 5
Fabric A	Fabric B	Fabric C	Fabric D	Fabric E
Fabric B	Fabric C	Fabric D	Fabric E	Fabric F
Fabric C	Fabric D	Fabric E	Fabric F	Fabric G
Fabric D	Fabric E	Fabric F	Fabric G	Fabric H
Fabric E	Fabric F	Fabric G	Fabric H	Fabric I

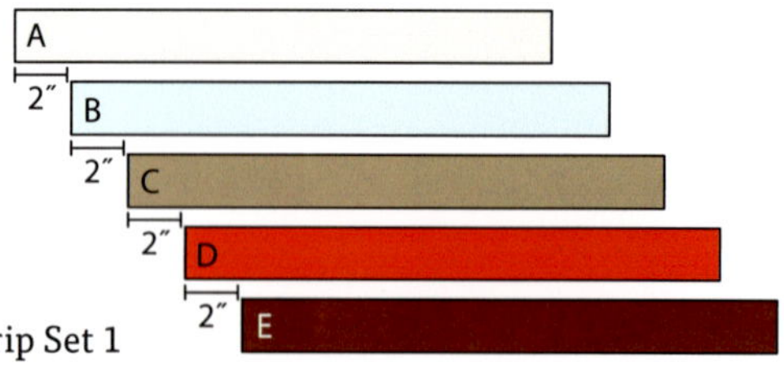

A. Strip Set 1

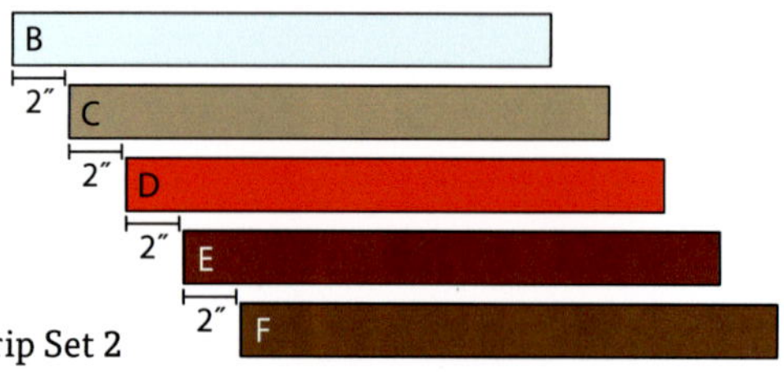

B. Strip Set 2

C. Strip Set 3

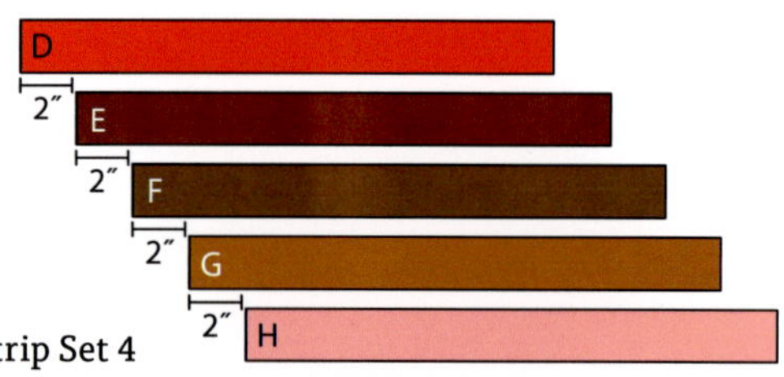

D. Strip Set 4

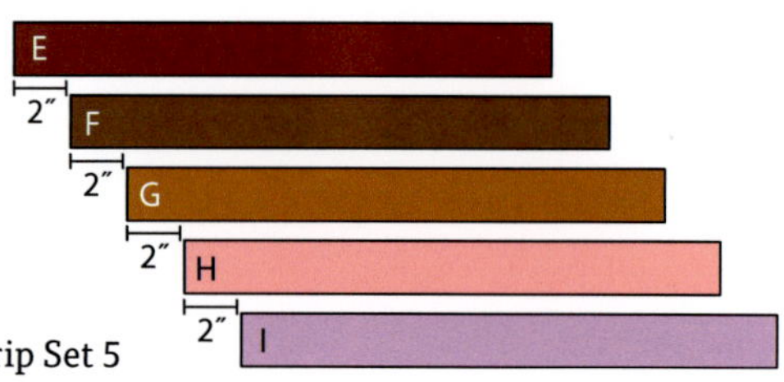

E. Strip Set 5

F

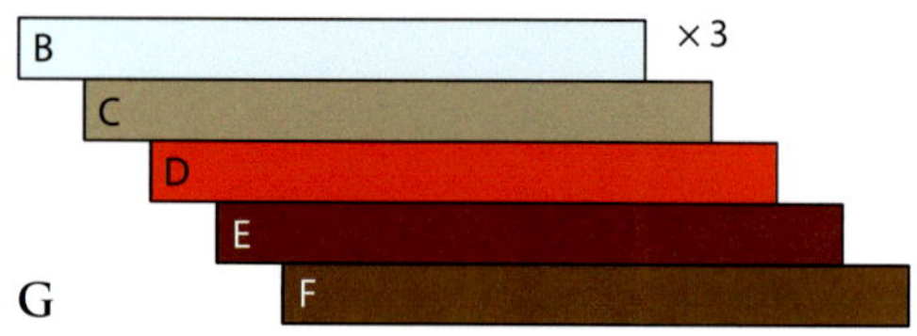

G

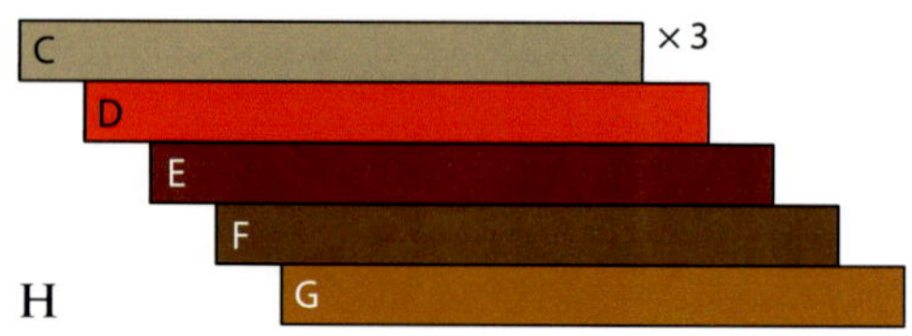

H

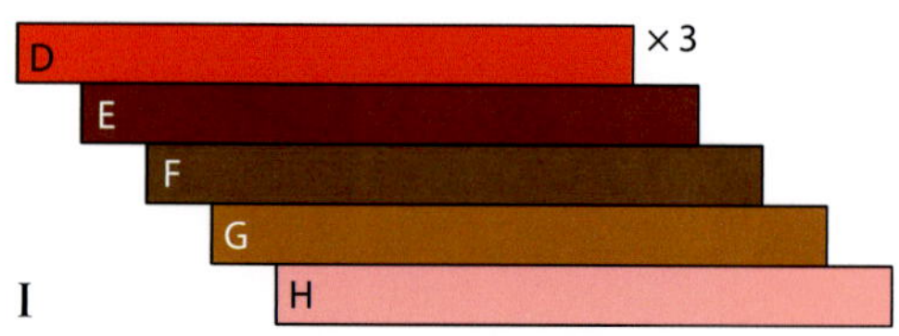

I

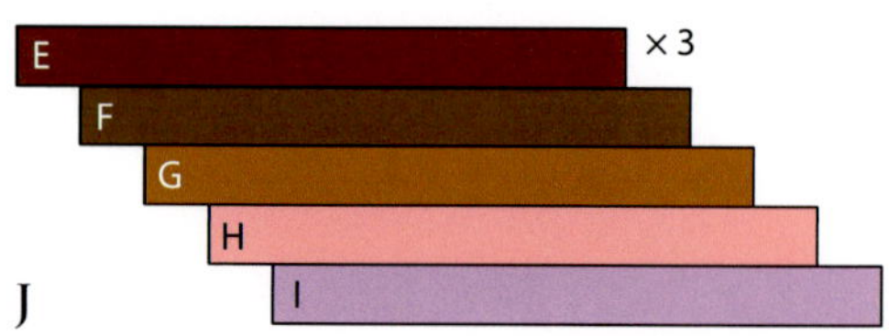

J

3. Trim the selvages and cut 32 strip diamonds 2½″ from each color of strip sets (cut 11 from 2 strip sets and 10 from the third strip set). See Cutting and Sewing Diamonds (page 18) for a full tutorial on cutting diamonds. Or see How to Cut Diamonds (page 53) for a quick reminder. *fig. K*

K

STRIP SET DIAMONDS

1. Select a 2½″ strip from each strip set. Arrange them into a diamond unit, in the order shown. Repeat to arrange all the strips into 32 total strip set diamonds (unsewn). *fig. L*

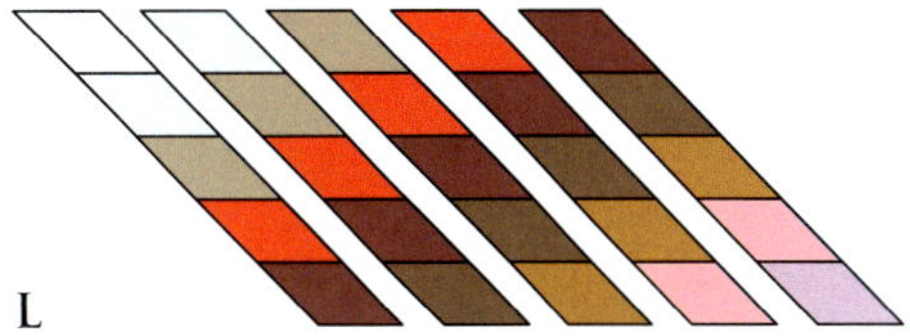
L

2. Begin with the first diamond unit. On the right side of the Strip Set 1 strip, use the ruler and a marking tool to measure and mark ¼″ from the edge of the fabric on each seam. Repeat on the wrong side of the Strip Set 2. Repeat with the Strip Set 1 and Strip Set 2 strips in all diamond units. *fig. M*

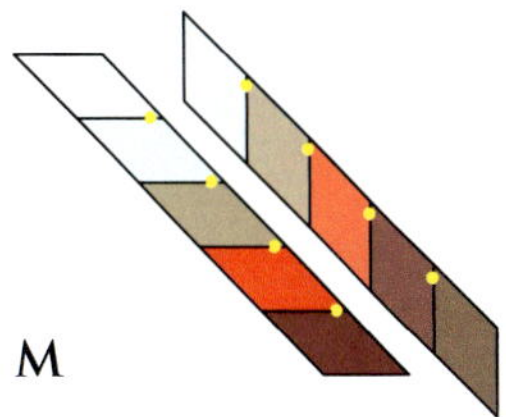
M

3. Starting with the first diamond unit, place the Strip Set 2 strip on top of the Strip Set 1 strip, RST. Place the tip of the top strip approximately ¼″ above the tip of the bottom strip. Insert a pin directly through the seams of both strips, through the marks from Step 2. Repeat with each diamond unit, pairing and pinning the strips from Strip Set 1 and Strip Set 2.

4. Sew the pinned strips together into 32 strip pairs. Press the seams open. *fig. N*

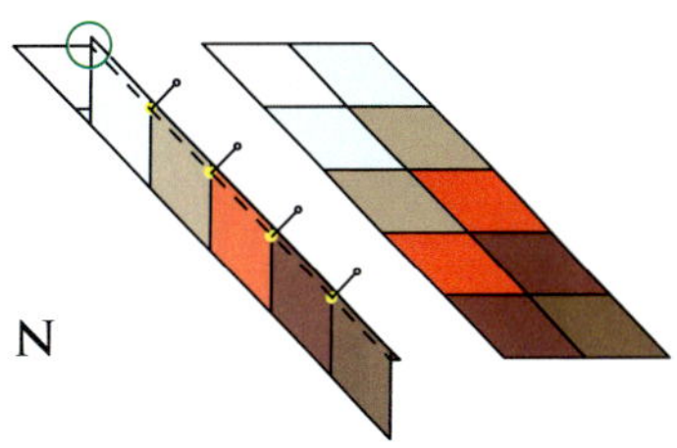
N

5. Begin with the first diamond unit again. On the right side of the Strip Set 3 strip, use the ruler and a marking tool to measure ¼″ from the edge of the fabric on each seam. Repeat on the wrong side of Strip Set 4. Repeat with the Strip Set 3 and Strip Set 4 strips in all diamond units. *fig. O*

O

6. Repeat Steps 3–4 with the Strip Set 3 and Strip Set 4 strips to make 32 strip pairs. Place the Strip Set 4 strip on top of the Strip Set 3 strip. *fig. P*

7. Begin with the first diamond unit again. On the right side of the unit from Step 6, use the ruler and a marking tool to measure ¼″ from the edge of the fabric on each seam. Repeat on the wrong side of the Strip Set 5 strip on each seam. Repeat with the Step 6 unit and Strip Set 5 strips in all diamond units. *fig. Q*

8. Repeat Steps 2–4 with the Step 6 unit and Strip Set 5 strips to make 32 strip set trios. Place the Strip Set 5 on top of the Step 6 unit. *fig. R*

9. Place a unit from Step 4 RST with a unit from Step 8. Repeat Steps 2–4 to make 32 strip set diamonds. Press the seams open. *figs. S–T*

Quilt Top Assembly

Broken Star Quilt assembly is the same for every Broken Star quilt. To assemble this quilt, follow the instructions in Broken Star Quilt Assembly (page 30).

Reference the following to create Unit 1 (page 30), Unit 2 (page 32), Unit 3 (page 34), and Unit 4 (page 35):

1. Make 8 View A Unit 1s from the strip set diamonds arranged as shown. *fig. U*

2. Make 8 View B Unit 1s from the strip set diamonds arranged as shown. *fig. V*

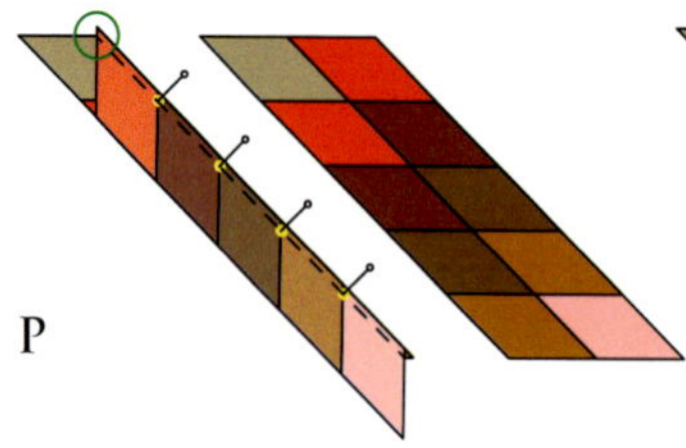
P

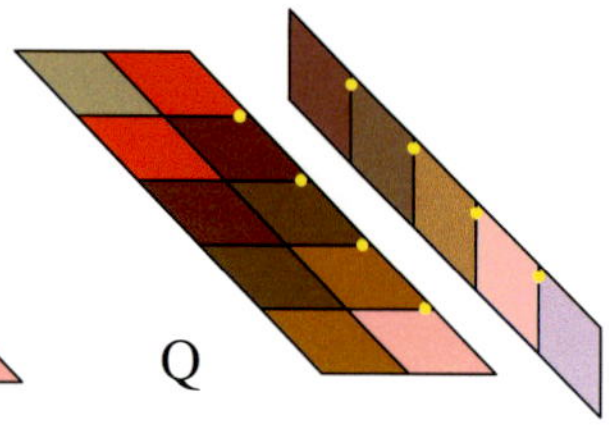
Q

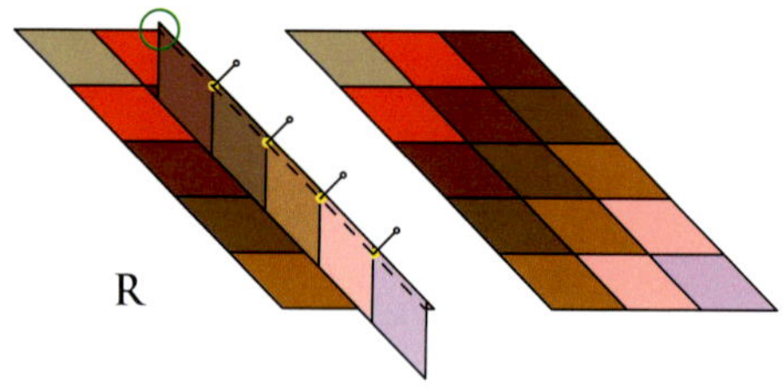
R

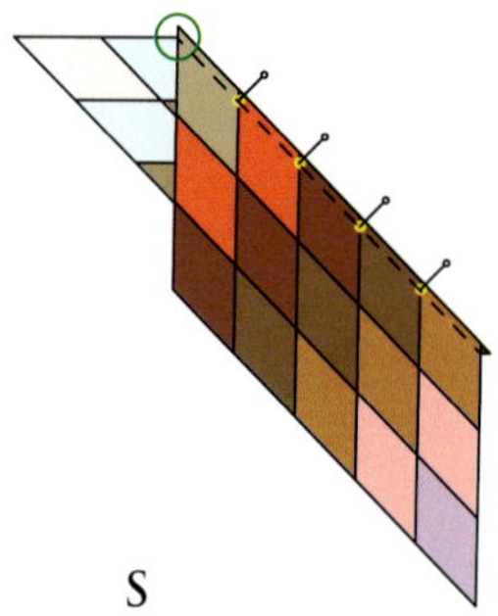
S

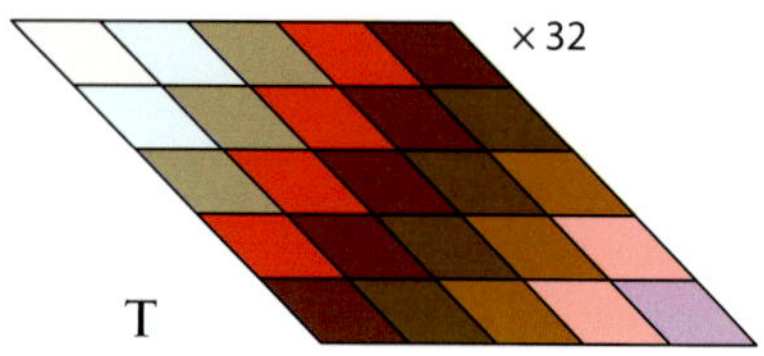

T

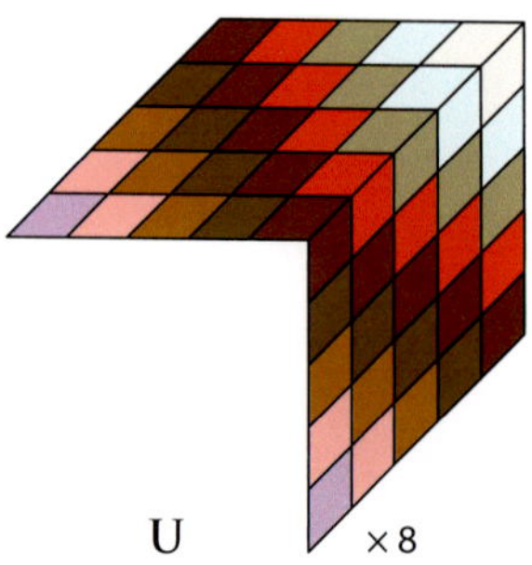

U

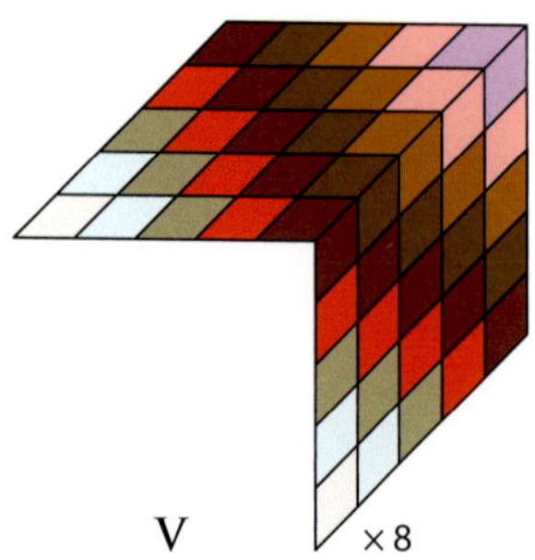

V

3. Make 4 Unit 2s from View B Unit 1s and background fabric. *fig. W*

4. Make 4 Unit 3s from View A Unit 1s and background fabric. *fig. X*

5. Make 4 Unit 4s from View B strip set diamonds and the Unit 3s. *fig. Y*

6. Using Units 1, 2, 3, and 4 and the remaining background squares, continue making Units 5–10 by following the instructions in Broken Star Quilt Assembly (page 30) to finish the quilt top.

The quilt top is complete and measures 96½″ × 96½″. See Finishing the Quilts (page 42) to quilt and bind.

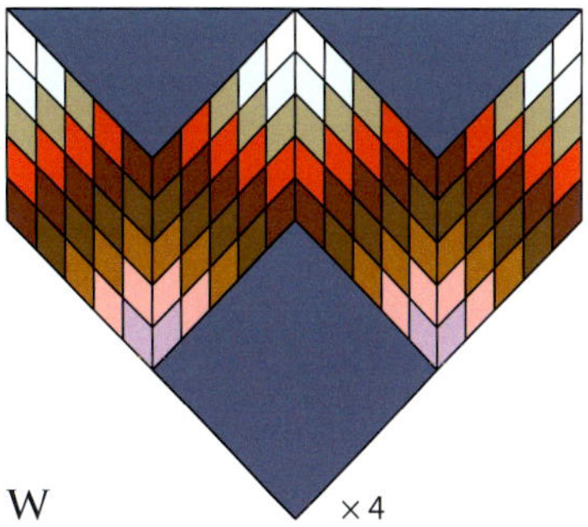

W

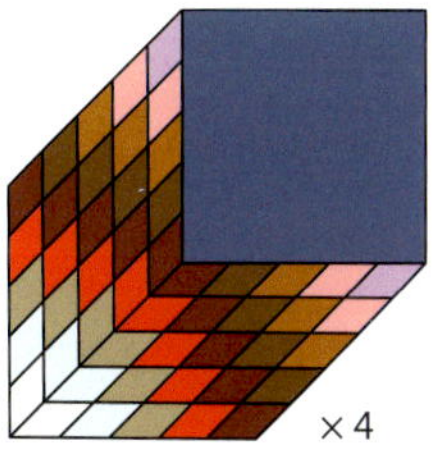

X

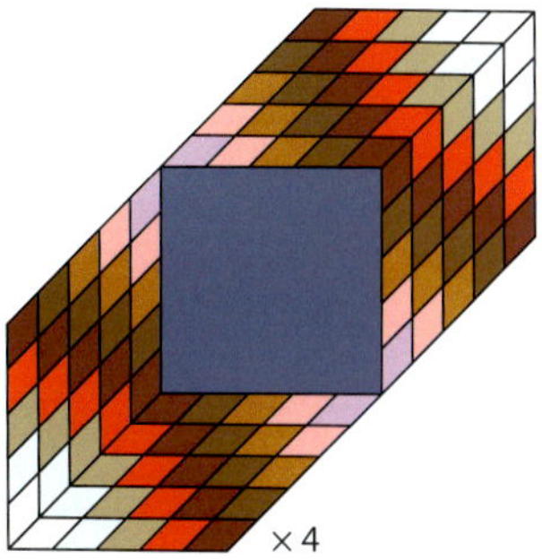

Y

Longarm quilting by Ashlee Doyle, Crinkly Quilts

Quilting pantograph: Modern Curves designed by Anita Shackelford

BROKEN STEPPE STAR

FINISHED QUILT SIZE: 96½″ × 96½″

The Broken Steppe Star is the Broken Star version of the first quilt pattern in this book—the Steppe Star (page 82). It is just as impressive as the Broken Trail Star (page 142), and it's the same size, but it's a bit less time consuming because there are fewer fabrics and fewer diamond points to match. Pay close attention to the cutting instructions for this star because some fabrics use 2½″ strips and some use 4½″ strips.

FABRIC REQUIREMENTS

Yardages are based on 42″ wide fabric.

Share what you make! #brokensteppestarquilt

FABRIC	COLOR NAME	BED SIZE
Fabric A	Fableism Native Nectar in Pink Sky	¼ yard
Fabric B	Fableism Skinny Stripe in Foxglove	½ yard
Fabric C	Fableism Arcade Woven in Acorn	1½ yards
Fabric D	Neon Neppy in Charcoal	1⅞ yards
Fabric E	Fableism Forest Forage Daisies in Homestead	¾ yard
Fabric F	Fableism Everyday Chambray in Cinnabar	½ yard
Fabric G	Warp and Weft Wovens Cross Weave in Persimmon	¼ yard
Background	Kona Natural	5½ yards
Binding	Neon Neppy in Charcoal	⅞ yard
Backing	Peppered Cotton Yarn Dye in Fog	8¾ yards
Batting	Warm & Natural by The Warm Company	104″ × 104″

CUTTING INSTRUCTIONS

For a full tutorial on cutting diamonds, see Cutting and Sewing Diamonds (page 18). Or, for a quick reminder on cutting diamonds, see How to Cut Diamonds (page 53).

Fabric A

- Cut 3 strips 2½″ × WOF.

Fabric B

- Cut 6 strips 2½″ × WOF.

Fabric C

- Cut 3 strips 2½″ × WOF.
- Cut 9 strips 4½″ × WOF.

Fabric D

- Cut 3 strips 2½″ × WOF.
- Cut 12 strips 4½″ × WOF.

Fabric E

- Cut 9 strips 2½″ × WOF.

Fabric F

- Cut 6 strips 2½″ × WOF.

Fabric G

- Cut 3 strips 2½″ × WOF.

Background

If you're including interchangeable blocks instead of background squares, see Interchangeable Blocks (page 50) for cutting and piecing instructions.

- Cut 2 strips 22″ × WOF; subcut into 2 squares 22″ × 22″. 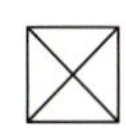

  Subcut each 22″ square along each diagonal into 4 triangles. 
- Cut 10 strips 14½″ × WOF; subcut into 20 squares 14½″ × 14½″.

Binding

- Cut 10 strips 2½″ × WOF.

Backing

Cut and piece the backing fabric as needed to make a backing that equals 105″ × 105″.

Sewing Instructions

STRIP SETS

1. Arrange the strips into strip sets in the order shown in the following chart. Offset the strips by 2″ except when noted by an asterisk (*). When noted by an asterisk, offset those strips by 4″. Arrange 3 of each strip set. *figs. A–E*

2. Sew the strips in each set together along the long sides. Press the seams open. *figs. F–J*

STRIP SET 1	STRIP SET 2	STRIP SET 3	STRIP SET 4	STRIP SET 5
Fabric A (2½″)	Fabric B (2½″)	Fabric C (4½″)	Fabric C (2½″)	Fabric D (4½″)
Fabric B (2½″)	Fabric C (4½″)	Fabric D* (4½″)	Fabric D (4½″)	Fabric E* (2½″)
Fabric C (4½″)	Fabric D* (4½″)	Fabric E* (2½″)	Fabric E* (2½″)	Fabric F (2½″)
Fabric D* (2½″)	-	-	Fabric F (2½″)	Fabric G (2½″)

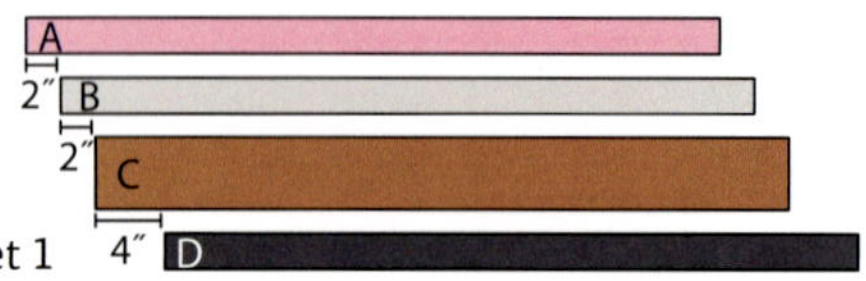

A. Strip Set 1

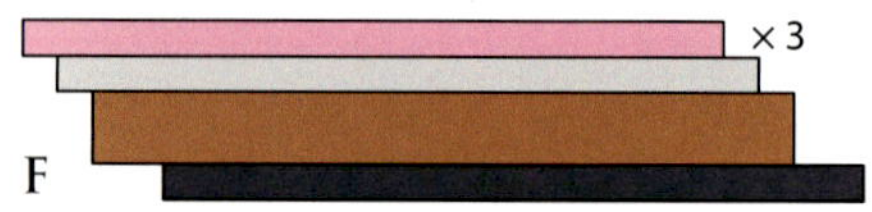

F

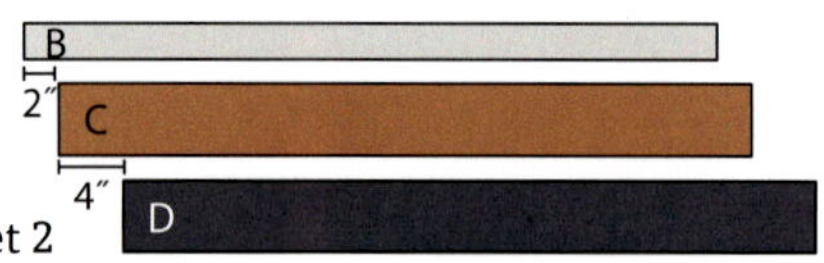

B. Strip Set 2

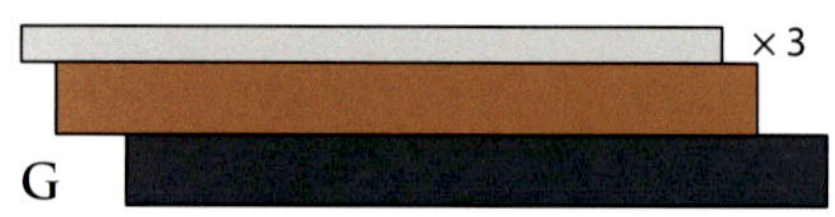

G

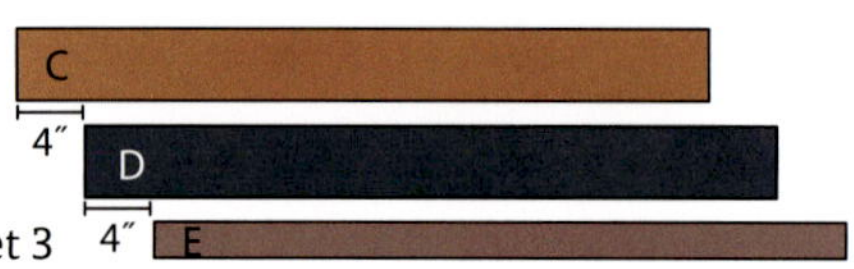

C. Strip Set 3

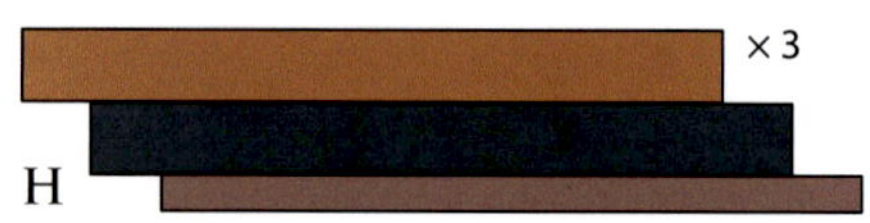

H

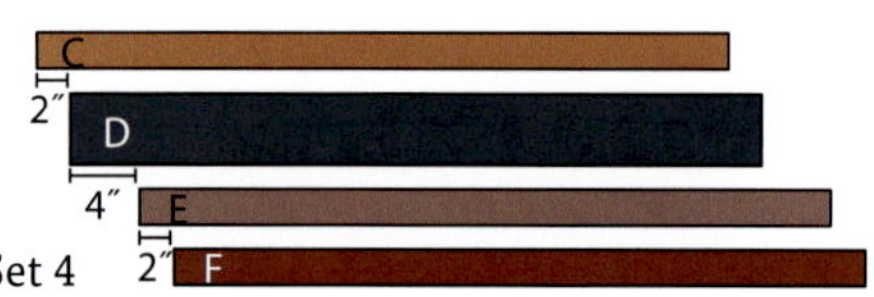

D. Strip Set 4

I

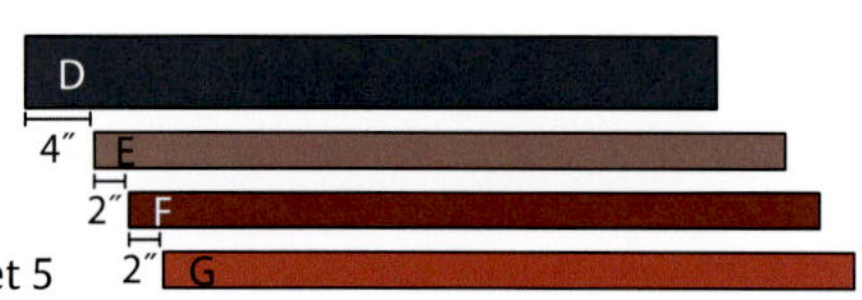

E. Strip Set 5

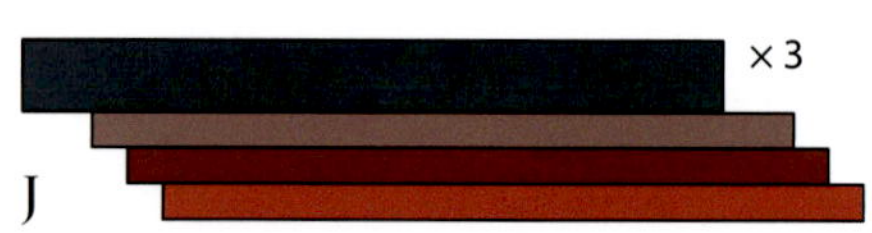

J

3. Trim the selvages and cut 32 strip diamonds 2½″ from each color of strip sets (cut 11 from 2 strip sets and 10 from the third strip set). See Cutting and Sewing Diamonds (page 18) for a full tutorial on cutting diamonds. Or see How to Cut Diamonds (page 53) for a quick reminder. *fig. K*

K

STRIP SET DIAMONDS

1. Select a strip from each strip set. Arrange them into a diamond unit, in the order shown. Repeat to arrange all the strips into 32 total strip set diamonds (unsewn). *fig. L*

L

2. Begin with the first diamond unit. On the right side of the Strip Set 1 strip, use the ruler and a marking tool to measure and mark ¼″ from the edge of the fabric on the seam where Fabric A and Fabric B meet. Repeat on the wrong side of the Strip Set 2 strip where Fabric B and Fabric C meet. Repeat with the Strip Set 1 and Strip Set 2 strips in all diamond units. *fig. M*

M

3. Starting with the first diamond unit, place the Strip Set 2 strip on top of the Strip Set 1 strip, RST. Place the tip of the top strip approximately ¼″ above the tip of the bottom strip. Insert a pin directly through the seams of both strips, through the marks from Step 2. Repeat with all pairs. *fig. N*

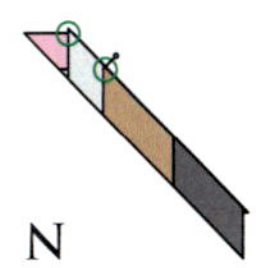
N

4. Sew the pinned strips together into 32 strip pairs. Press the seams open. *fig. O*

O

5. Begin with the first diamond unit again. On the right side of the Strip Set 3 strip, use the ruler and a marking tool to measure ¼″ from the edge of the fabric on each seam. Repeat on the wrong side of Strip Set 4. Repeat with the Strip Set 3 and Strip Set 4 strips in all diamond units. *fig. P*

P

6. Begin with the first diamond unit again. On the right side of the Strip Set 3 strip, use the ruler and a marking tool to measure ¼″ from the edge of the fabric on the seam where Fabric D and Fabric E meet. Repeat on the wrong side of the Strip Set 4 strip where Fabric E and Fabric F meet. Repeat with the Strip Set 3 and Strip Set 4 strips in all diamond units. *fig. Q*

7. Repeat Steps 3–4 with the Strip Set 3 and Strip Set 4 strips to make 32 strip pairs. Place the Strip Set 4 strip on top of the Strip Set 3 strip. *fig. R*

8. Begin with the first diamond unit again. On the right side of the unit from Step 7, use the ruler and a marking tool to measure ¼″ from the edge of the fabric on the seams where Fabric D and Fabric E and where Fabric E and Fabric F meet. Repeat on the wrong side of the Strip Set 5 strip where Fabric E and Fabric F meet and where Fabric F and G meet. Repeat with the Step 7 unit and Strip Set 5 strips in all diamond units. *fig. S*

9. Repeat Steps 3–4 with the Step 7 unit and Strip Set 5 strips to make 32 strip trios. Place the Strip Set 5 on top of the Step 7 unit. *figs. T–U*

10. Place a unit from Step 4 RST with a unit from Step 9. Place the tip of the top strip approximately ¼″ above the bottom strip. Sew together. Press the seams open. Repeat to make 32 strip set diamonds. *figs.V–W*

QUILT TOP ASSEMBLY

Broken Star Quilt assembly is the same for every Broken Star quilt. To assemble this quilt, follow the instructions in Broken Star Quilt Assembly (page 30).

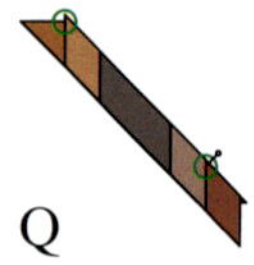
Q

R

S

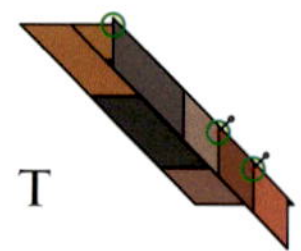
T

U

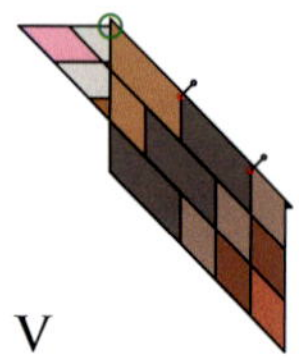
V

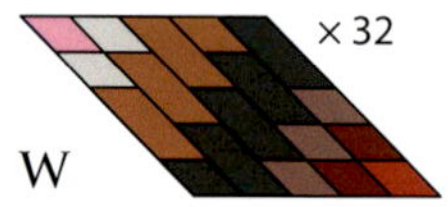
W ×32

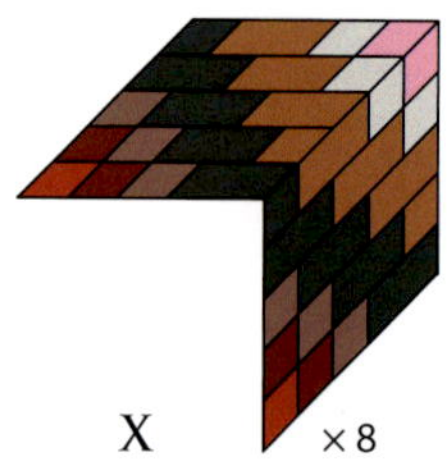
X ×8

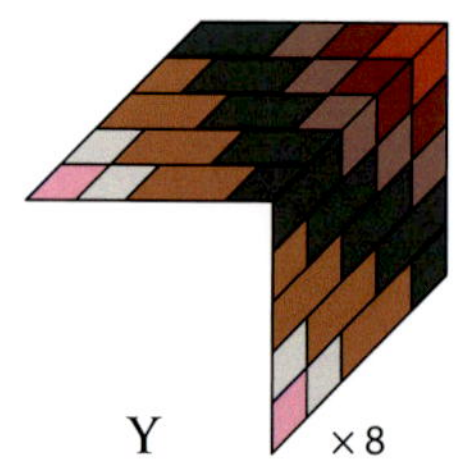
Y ×8

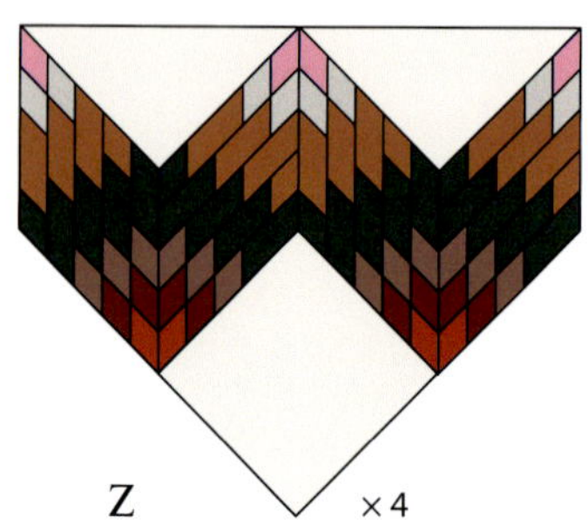
Z ×4

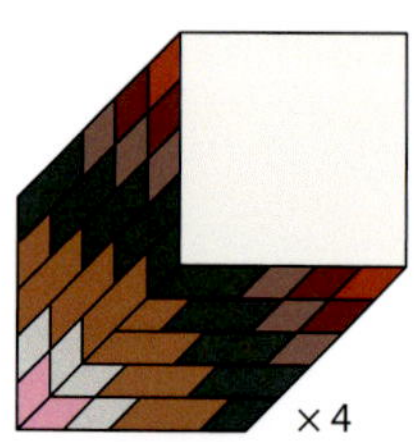
A ×4

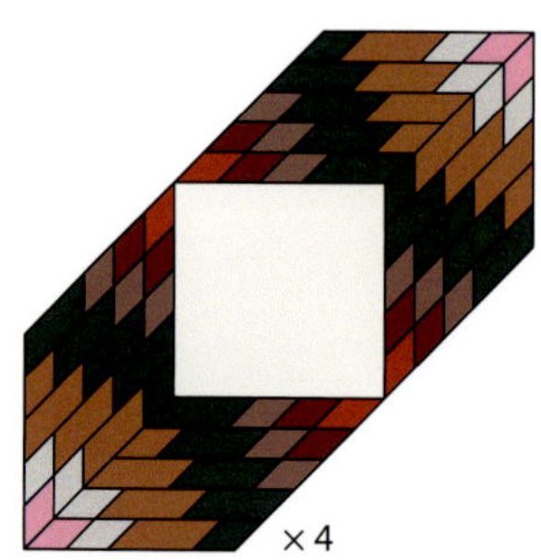
B ×4

Reference the following to create Unit 1 (page 30), Unit 2 (page 32), Unit 3 (page 34), and Unit 4 (page 35):

1. Make 8 View A Unit 1s from strip set diamonds arranged as shown. *fig. X*

2. Make 8 View B Unit 1s from strip set diamonds arranged as shown. *fig. Y*

3. Make 4 Unit 2s from View B Unit 1s and background fabric. *fig. Z*

4. Make 4 Unit 3s from View A Unit 1s and background fabric. *fig. A*

5. Make 4 Unit 4s from View A Unit 1s and the Unit 3s. *fig. B*

6. Using Units 1, 2, 3, and 4 and the remaining background squares, continue making Units 5–10 by following the instructions in Broken Star Quilt Assembly (page 30) to finish the quilt top.

The quilt top is complete and measures 96½″ × 96½″. See Finishing the Quilts (page 42) to quilt and bind.

Longarm quilting by Ashlee Doyle, Crinkly Quilts

Quilting pantograph: Behold designed by Jess Zeigler

Coloring Pages

Steppe Star

Rocky Star

Horizon Star

Backroad Star

To access the quilt design coloring pages at a larger size in a downloadable PDF, scan the QR code or go to **tinyurl.com/11612-patterns-download**

Backwoods Star

Majestic Star

Broken Trail Star (Bed)

Broken Steppe Star (Bed)

About the Author

In college, Lindlee Smith enlisted her mom's help to make her first quilt. She was drawn to the Lone Star design early on, and it continues to be her favorite quilt to make.

Lindlee started designing quilt patterns in 2020 and has taught several online workshops, assisting others in creating their own heirloom quilts. Her favorite thing is taking a quilt pattern that seems intimidating or complex and making it accessible and enjoyable.

Lindlee lives in Bozeman, Montana with her husband, two kids, and dog. She enjoys reading, baking, eating baked goods, and getting outside to walk, run, or garden.

Visit Lindlee online and follow on social media!
Website: plainsandpine.com
Facebook: /plainsandpine
Instagram: @plainsandpine
Pinterest: /plainsandpine

About the Photographer

Hayley Heser Pawlowski

Hayley Heser Pawlowski is a wife, mother, and photographer from rural Montana. Hayley has been capturing weddings, couples, and families, and commercial work for the past in eleven years in Montana's beautiful landscapes. **HayleyHeser.com**

About the Longarm Quilter

Ashlee Doyle

Ashlee Doyle is a longarm quilter and quilt pattern designer from Manhattan, Montana. She started her business, Crinkly Quilts, in 2020 after falling in love with longarm quilting two years prior. She loves how quilting designs add texture, charm, and dimension to the quilts she works on. Ashlee loves to help people take their quilts to the next level by choosing designings that enhance and accentuate the quilt pattern and fabric used, creating cherished heirlooms to be handed down and loved for generations. Ashlee is often inspired by traditional quilts and modern fabrics that blend into a perfect mix of past meets present.